D1352632

Items should be returned on or before the last date shown below. Items not already requested by other borrowers may be renewed in person, in writing or by telephone. To renew, please quote the number on the barcode label. To renew online a PIN is required. This can be requested at your local library.
Renew online @ **www.dublincitypubliclibraries.ie**
Fines charged for overdue items will include postage incurred in recovery. Damage to or loss of items will be charged to the borrower.

Leabharlanna Poiblí Chathair Bhaile Átha Cliath
Dublin City Public Libraries

Baile Átha Cliath
Dublin City

Brainse Fhionnglaise   Finglas Library
T: (01) 834 4906 E: finglaslibrary@dublincity.ie

Date Due	Date Due	Date Due
	10 JUL 2018	
	1 5 APR 2019	

ISBN-13 978-1481898508

ISBN-10 1481898507

BROKEN GROUND

AN EXPLOSIVE ACCOUNT OF THE HAITI EARTHQUAKE.

Written by Patrick Doyle

TABLE OF CONTENTS

MAP

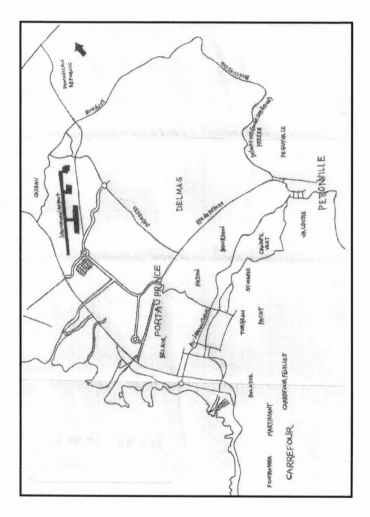

Map of Port au Prince

ACKNOWLEDGEMENTS

I had originally thought about writing this book as a short story. So one winter's night, as the rain belted against my bedroom window, I sat in front of a desk, pulled out a pen and a notepad, and began to write. I wrote specifically about the earthquake and what I had witnessed in that time. It took me three months to recollect every memory (painful or otherwise) that I could. When I eventually looked at the pages on my kitchen table one morning in March 2012, I didn't feel, nor did the story look, complete. I felt that if I was going to write about the end of my time in Haiti, then surely I should tell the story from what I considered to be the beginning.

I wish to thank my editor Dara. When I met you for a coffee and a chat on a cloudy August afternoon in Galway, with several hundred pages of gibberish under my arm, you took them away, read them and told me there was a story in there, somewhere. Best of all though, you taught me to stop listening to the voice of the man from 'The Wonder Years' and concentrate on my own. For all the long days, late nights and the advice that you gave to me, I thank you Dara. You are a fantastic teacher and a true friend.

I consider this book and myself particularly indebted to Stephen O' Connor of WebMarket.ie. Without Steve I would not have been able to bring this project to where it is. For a man who was only supposed to take care of the book's website, you have continued to amaze me with your guidance, dedicated hard work and generosity. Your words of encouragement and continual support throughout will never be forgotten Steve. You are a great friend and a fantastic web designer. Thank you!!

I know that it's a little cliché, however I must mention my family. My mother and father, Pat and Maryann, my sister Karen, her husband Shea and the two most wonderful nephews I could ever wish for, Jack and Harry. The love and support that you constantly show me keeps the sadness away each time I have to leave you. I carry you all in my heart no matter where I am in this world. You always believe in me and that belief has kept me scribbling into many late hours of countless nights. You are my life and I am forever yours.

I wish I could thank many of my former security colleagues in Haiti by name. You deserve to be recognized. Most of you boys are still in the private security sector, so I'm not going to do that. I hope that this book is something you can all enjoy.

I do wish to thank all the clients in Digicel who offered us their friendship, respect and understanding during our time in country. You know who you are and I am pretty certain that I speak on behalf of my brothers when I say thank you.

I'd like to mention Ambroise Pinchinat, Julio Reischoffer, Bryan Gonzales, Frantzy, Sophia Stransky and Dominique Francinque for sharing their incredibly brave stories. These accounts of January 2010 show the strength and tenacity that lies within so many of those who remained on in Haiti. Your words are inspiring and an honor to share. Thank you.

A very special thank you also to Josefa Gauthier and Rachel Pamela Pierre of the Digicel Foundation in Haiti. Without your hard work and assistance, I would not have been able to bring this book the final lap. Thank you so much ladies. You are incredible in what you do in your work. Mesi Anpil!!

I am extremely grateful to Craig and Kane Fay of Bright Harbour Productions for their donation of so many incredible pictures to the website (www.brokenground.ie). They show the beauty of Haiti and its people and also portray the undeserved suffering of a nation. I am honored to be able to share your talented work with the world. Thanks so much guys.

I am especially indebted to those who didn't make it home. Their stories are a part of their legacy. If you are looking down on me now, please know that I treated each story very carefully and did my very best to describe them with the respect they deserved. It was a privilege to put your characters to paper, and perhaps in some way, also help to honor your memories..

The words grateful or beholden do not even come close when I try to thank my Haitian friends and acquaintances. It took a long time for my eyes to open up and to really begin to understand and appreciate your nation. I know that I don't just speak for myself when I say that Haiti, your places and your people, are always in the hearts of those of us who have long since left your shores. My time was cut short with you. In the end, I was the right man, in the right place, with the wrong job. This book would not exist without you and I know that my passport will be stamped with the Haitian seal many times before I leave this world. I will see you again.

A very special thank you to Mr Denis O' Brien. Your state of the art eleven story building in Turgeau saved the lives of hundreds of people on that Tuesday evening. Furthermore, the wheels that you set in motion in the immediate aftermath of the quake, gave every Digicel employee, contractor and tenant (like myself) the strength to believe that we were not alone and that help was coming. Though I did not know it at the time, you had ordered that the Digicel building in Turgeau be built to withstand earthquakes. I, like so many others, am here today because of you. Due to the hard work and tough decisions of your people, Digicel ensured that millions of people around the world could eventually communicate with family and friends in Haiti in the days and weeks to follow. I'd even heard stories of survivors being found because their phones had become their lifeline. Dare I say in no short part to the relentless work carried out by management and technicians whom I saw work around the clock to make it happen. To write about the support that you have given Haiti since your arrival is a book in its own right. Thank you once again.

A grateful thank you to Terry Clune from taxback.com, for all his mentorship and support both before the earthquake and after. I learned a lot about myself, which I would never have known had I not met you Terry. I thank you for that and the support that you offered me in the days and weeks that followed. You had my back when I didn't even know it. Thank you.

To the men and women of the five branches of the US Armed Forces and other international forces who came to Haiti's aid when she truly believed that nobody cared for her. To doctors, nurses, paramedics and rescue volunteers worldwide. Seeing you arrive on the tarmac was awe-inspiring. Also, the healthcare and medical professionals who were already living and working in Haiti and who reacted so swiftly, with little or no tools at hand. I'm not a big fan of the word 'heroes', but you are exactly that. Thank you.

A special note to the MINUSTAH mission. Your response to the disaster was made so much more difficult due to the loss of so many of your people in the Christopher Hotel. However, you were still there, effortlessly working to help the people of Haiti.

Thank you to nannie Doyle, for watching over me through those dark days after January 12th.

To my nannie Burke who sadly passed away earlier this year. You are deeply missed and will be forever loved.

Finally, to Breda. Whatever stroke of luck I pulled to have you come into my life, I know that I am blessed and a great adventure lies ahead with you by my side.

AUTHOR'S NOTE

Over the years, I've come to realize through talking with others, that I am blessed (or possibly cursed) with a reasonably sharp memory for events that have occurred during the course of my life. This book is written almost completely from such memories of events which unfolded during my time spent in Haiti. There have been moments, over the years, when I have wondered if writing this book was a good idea. Was it worth the late nights, sitting in front of a laptop screen or scribbling notes onto a writing pad? Would it evoke too many painful memories for people and was I the right person, worthy to tell such a tale? Some of these I have answered while others still remain unknown. What I do know is that most of the characters in this book, though many of their names have been changed, have had a substantial impact on my life to date. It is because of their tenacity, strength and good humor that I found myself compelled to keep on writing into the early hours of the morn. My story is their story too.

There is no political aim in my writing. Nor is there any deliberate attempt to demean any individual or organization that I encountered or befriended during my time in Haiti. The vast majority of my memories I recall with great affection and some others with tremendous sadness. I am aware that this may not be the case for everybody reading this book. I have tried to portray my naivety and my growth in these pages as honestly and as accurately as my reminiscence allows. At the end of the day, this is just simply a story told from my point of view.

Haiti was never a warzone. And yet it was often more volatile than the politicians would admit, or the humanitarians accept. Some will say that the reports of violence there were tenuous and blown out of all proportion. Though one cannot doubt the surging resilient character of the Haitian people, there was a shadowy co-existing undercurrent seen only by those who dared to look.

I found myself privy to some of the most violent and vicious scenes of human killing I could ever have believed possible. On a daily basis I watched how people eked out an existence in places of absolute squalor and filth and how ultra-elite neighborhoods built in the lush rolling green hillsides seemed to turn a blind eye to the justifiable rage and revolt on the poverty stricken streets below.

For those of you about to read this book, I (and some of my colleagues) may come across as unemotional and at times unsympathetic to other people's misfortune. This was not the case and all I can ask you to do is, well, read on. This was our reality during those years; it was the craziness and the absurdity of our work and environment that added to the hilarity, silliness and heartache of our lives. In a world that pushed our patience and, sometimes, our sanity to the limit, it was our friendship and loyalty to each other that made the everyday pressures more tolerable.

This was the world we shared with a city of more than two million people.

It was Port au Prince. It was Haiti.

We despised it. We grudgingly embraced it.

We sometimes even feared it.

But truth be told. We loved it.

This book is dedicated to   the children of Haiti.

Particularly to the orphans.

May you always be loved, nurtured, and never forgotten.

A History of Haiti:

Today, Haiti is known as the poorest country in the Western Hemisphere. As cliché as that might be, it is a land that has been plagued by natural disasters and economic strife.

Christopher Columbus landed on Haiti in 1492. He named the island "La Isla Española" which we know today as Hispaniola. While there, he established the first European (Spanish) colony.

Initially, the island's people, (called the Taino) welcomed the new Spanish arrivals. However, relations quickly deteriorated under colonial control. The European colonizers enslaved the natives. Eventually, the Taino were all but annihilated by their colonizers. The Spanish imported African slaves around 1517 as a replacement to the Taino.

French settlers eventually arrived in the seventeenth century. After a period of fighting, Spain released the western third of Hispaniola to France. The French-controlled western territory became known as Saint-Domingue, and the eastern portion remained under Spanish rule as Santo Domingo. France invested heavily in developing agricultural plantation. The French government benefited immensely from its natural resources of gold, cotton and sugar. They had also sanctioned the exportation of slaves from Africa (mostly western Africa) to work on the plantations. The slave system on the island was merciless. Plantation owners overworked their slaves and many died from disease and malnourishment.

By the late eighteenth century, the population of Saint-Domingue was more than half a million people. The vast majority were African slaves. Twenty-four thousand were free people of black or mixed race, known as affranchis (later to be called mulattos). Slave revolt was continuous but had little effect in France relinquishing any powers to the black slaves or affranchis.

Then in 1801, a former slave called Toussaint l'Ouverture, became such an influential figure in the slave's revolt that that a new French government with ideas of "equality to the colonies" gave him the title of *"governor-general for life."* L'Ouverture reinstated the plantation system that had fallen during the revolt. However, his rule still relied on forced labor to maintain the nation's crops.

France, who was experiencing her own period of revolution, saw Napoleon Bonaparte, its new dictator, restore French authority in the former colony. In turn, Toussaint l'Ouverture was deported to France, where he died in captivity in 1803. The Haitian Revolution continued under his lieutenant, Jean-Jacques Dessalines. With war mounting in Europe and continuous revolt by Haitian soldiers, Bonaparte decided that many of the distant French colonies in the New World were more trouble than they were worth. On January 1st, 1804, Haiti became the first free black republic. The new government renamed their country as "Ayiti", meaning "mountainous."

Dessalines was assassinated north of Port-au-Prince, on the 17th October 1806 while on his way to suppress a mulatto rebellion. Two candidates emerged as worthy replacements: Henry Christophe, who had served in the military under Toussaint, and Alexandre Pétion. Both men ended up ruling separate regions of Haiti. Christophe to the north and Pétion in the south.

Pétion died in 1818 and was succeeded by General Jean-Pierre Boyer. During this time Christophe had lost the support of his troops and his people in the north. Also in his early fifties, his health was failing. Rather than lose his power, in 1820, Christophe committed suicide. Boyer saw an opportunity in the north's fallen leader and stepped in, reuniting all of Haiti under his rule.

France had never truly recognized Haiti's independence and still felt that a debt was owed to them because of their loss of troops and the former colony itself. Boyer knew that France's discontentment was a risk to Haiti and her new found independence. He wanted to settle the matter rather than run the risk a repeated acts of conquest by France.

The two countries agreed to a financial settlement priced at 150 million francs. This was later reduced to about 90 million, but not until 1838. Today, it is the equivalent of around $20 billion US. With Haiti plunged deep into debt and irreversible economic turmoil, she had gained her status as a sovereign state, but at a cost which would echo through the ages.

Boyer's rule lasted until 1843, when the poor economic situation was worsened by an earthquake. The disadvantaged majority rural population rose up under Charles Rivière-Hérard in late January. On the 13th February 1843, Boyer fled Haiti to Jamaica. He eventually went into exile in France where he died in Paris in 1850.

This would be a pattern to be repeated time and again for the next sixty years. Between 1843 and 1915, almost two dozen men ruled over Haiti. Many were assassinated or overthrown in violent coups. Most of them were ousted because of forming corrupt governments and using Haiti for their own personal gain.

In July, 1915, rioting and political unrest in Haiti urged the U.S. government to intervene. They sought to establish a 'temporary rule' by which they would bring the small Caribbean country into the twentieth century as a 'civilized nation.'

One of America's primary goals was to encourage foreign investment into Haiti's economy. It was intended to stimulate the growth of the country and help create a middle class, thus eradicating the 'rich versus the poor' culture that had been existence for over a hundred years. By 1918, the American government had helped implement a new constitution for Haiti.

The American occupation was initially welcomed by the vast majority of Haitians. The rich elite saw it as an opportunity to reestablish their control of the country's stability, and the working class saw it as an opportunity to end the oppression they had been under for so long. The result was not what either class of citizen expected. A strong and educated middle class were on their way to competing for power over Haiti which was disconcerting to the wealthy elite. The working class continued to be exploited for arduous labor to build roads and buildings. A rebellion against the American occupation briefly arose, but it was suppressed by the U.S. Marine Corps in 1920.

By the time the U.S. pulled out of Haiti in the summer of 1934, it had overseen many advances in the sociopolitical structure. The country now had a workable system of roads, railways, new hospitals and schools, and increased access to clean water. When America withdrew from the island, security was left to the Haitian Gendarmerie (later to be called Garde d'Haiti). It was a non-political military force formed by US Naval and Marine officers to maintain law and order and ensure that the constitution remained in place.

In October 1930 Haiti elected Sténio Joseph Vincent as President. In 1935, just one year after U.S. occupation ended, he began to amend the constitution to suit his needs and reigned over Haiti in an authoritative manner.

In 1937, claiming that Haiti was harboring his former Dominican opponents, Rafael Trujillo, the President of the Dominican Republic, ordered a brutal attack on the border. The result was the slaughtering of what was estimated to have been more than twenty-five thousand Haitians. Trujillo had 'persuaded' the Haitian Garde officers to lead a coup against their president. When a number of these coups had been suppressed, Vincent expelled all military officers suspected of disloyalty. The Garde d'Haiti had been established as a type of neutral guardian of Haiti. The action of its officers showed that the Garde was far from a neutral body.

In 1941, Vincent intended to run for an unconstitutional third term in office. The American government made it very clear that they would oppose any such action. Not in a strong enough position to resist, Vincent consented to hand the presidency over to Elie Lescot.

It was believed that Lescot would be a worthy successor and help lead Haiti successfully into the latter half of the twentieth century. However, once in office, he showed himself to be very similar to Vincent. Lescot quickly moved to take complete control of the country, naming himself as head of the Military Guard and appointing a circle of wealthy white and mulatto Haitians into senior government positions. Haiti's black population saw these tactics as insulting and provoking.

After America was dragged into World War Two, Lescot declared war on Germany and her supporting countries. He also conveyed his support to the Allied Forces. His government offered safe haven to European Jews and Arabs who were fleeing to the Americas in search of a new beginning. In 1942 Lescot claimed that in a time of war, it was necessary to cease a peacetime constitution and had the parliament give him unlimited executive powers. This led to an almost fascist regime of censorship and in no way was any political opponent allowed to speak out about Lescot's governance without facing reprisal.

Lescot lost all popular support when his dealings with Trujillo became public knowledge. By 1946, his endeavors to suppress the opposition press ignited fierce demonstrations that gave way to a revolt across Port-au-Prince. Another significant disadvantage to Lescot was his white and mulatto-dominated cabinet.

Lescot ordered the predominantly black Military Guard to break up the demonstrations but his order was rejected. He had lost the respect and command of the Garde. Lescot and his cabinet felt they were now completely isolated. In fear for their lives, they fled into exile. Their discontent paved the way for a Garde-led coup. The Garde now ruled Haiti by junta until August of 1946, when Dumarsais Estimé was elected and appointed as president.

Estimé was born to a poor family. He was the first black president of Haiti since the US occupation ended in 1934. Estimé seemed genuinely concerned with the welfare of his people. As part of his vision of a prosperous country, his education policies included the building of schools in the provinces and professional training for teachers.

Desperately short of funds to finance his reforms, Estimé issued an extraordinary call to the Haitian people to make monetary sacrifices and help raise collateral. He believed that before things could get better, Haiti needed to face its international debts. This would play an integral part in securing economic independence. Inspired by his vision of a sovereign nation, the vast black population responded positively (if only for a while). Five million of an extraordinary internal loan of $7.6 million went towards debt repayment.

However, Estimé's presidency ended in 1950. He had faced relentless opposition from the Haitian elite. His introduction of an income tax had turned public opinion against him. Finally, he, too, sought to unconstitutionally extend his term in office. The move caused public unrest and prompted the Garde to reestablish their junta. Estimé gradually lost his grip on power. He signed a letter of resignation and was exiled to Paris in May 1950.

The presidency was given to a former junta leader, Paul E. Magloire, throwing the balance of power back to the military and elite. During Magloire's presidency, Haiti became a favorite spot for US and European tourists. His anti-communist position also gained favorable reception from the US government. He was eventually overthrown because of his economic corruption (using state funds for private gains). In 1954, when Hurricane Hazel ravaged Haiti, relief funds were stolen. Magloire's public support suffered. In 1956 when Magloire overstayed the end of his term, the Haitian people took to the streets in strikes and demonstrations. Magloire fled the country, and in the year that followed, Haiti came under the brief rule of three different provisional presidents. One stepped down from office. The others had to be removed by the army.

During this time, a doctor named François Duvalier emerged as a potentially suitable presidential candidate. He had been appointed Director General of the National Public Health Service under President Estimé. Duvalier was seen by the ordinary Haitian citizen as a genuine individual. Also, the military liked his candidacy. He won with a landslide victory in the election of October 1957 after his only opponent, Daniel Fignolé, had been sent into exile.

Once sworn into power, Duvalier began to show his corrupted tactics. He established a new constitution in 1957 that furthered his own power. He manipulated the ranks of the civil service and the army; weaving a network of men who were completely loyal to him into senior positions. Duvalier turned the National Guard into an elite unit that would help secure his reign of power. In 1959, Duvalier commissioned a rural militia, the Milice Volontaires de la Sécurité Nationale (MVSN, English: National Security Volunteer Militia) to work as a national personal army just like his National Guard. Haitians christened the militia after the Haitian Creole mythological Tonton Macoute (Uncle Gunnysack). Tonton Macoute was a bogeyman who kidnapped boisterous children by putting them in his gunnysack (macoute) and taking them away to be eaten. This superstitious fable alone helped to solidify the Tonton Macoutes fear and intimidation throughout the country. Though it was more of an auxiliary force rather than a traditional army unit, the Tonton eventually doubled their numbers in comparison to the national army. Their blind obedience to Duvalier gave him complete power over Haiti and her citizens.

Duvalier employed many of the same tactics used by previous dictators. Bizarrely, this did not hinder his rise in popularity. As he was originally educated as a doctor, he was well aware of Haiti's medical needs. Through this he could win the hearts and minds of the poorer classes who saw him as 'the gentle doctor.' Affectionately, Duvalier became known to the masses as, "Papa Doc."

Also, Duvalier harnessed his interest in voodoo, appointing priests and witch doctors into government positions. This accentuated his mystique and invincibility as 'president for life.'

After failed negotiations with the United States, President John F. Kennedy withdrew American financial aid to Haiti. Duvalier would not hold himself accountable to Haiti's poverty and would not admit the fact that he was an egomaniacal dictator.

In 1971, François Duvalier died and left his position to his nineteen year-old son, Jean-Claude. Nicknamed "Baby Doc." Jean-Claude was as ineffective as his father to bring Haiti out of oppression.

In 1978, African Swine Flu was rampant among Haiti's pig population. Baby Doc had every pig in the country culled and accepted American pigs to be sent in from the US as a replacement. This caused widespread hardship among the peasant population as it had been less expensive for them to feed their own hogs.

The outbreak of AIDS hit Haiti in the 1980's. This had a direct impact on national medical facilities. The stigma of AIDS also affected tourism from abroad. This drained Haiti's economy further. Haiti was quickly approaching the end of the twentieth century. The prosperity of its people and its future waned in the balance.

In 1986, Duvalier fled the country. Like many of his predecessors, he relocated to France.

In November 1987, the first attempt at a new election ended when dozens of voters were killed by the Tonton Makoute in the capital. However, in January 1988, Leslie Manigat was elected into office. He was suspected of voter fraud. Manigat was ousted by Lieutenant General Henri Namphy in June, who was himself overthrown by Lieutenant General Prosper Avril in November of the same year. Avril failed to bring stability to the country and so stepped down from office in 1990.

Haiti's interim government sought help from the international community in organizing the next election. Foreign observers sent to Haiti by the United Nations General Assembly helped ensure that the elections were free and fair. This was said to be the first honest elections ever to be held in Haiti since its birth as a republic. Jean-Bertrand Aristide, a Catholic priest, was elected as the new leader.

In September 1991 the army performed a coup against Aristide, led by Army General Raoul Cédras, who had been appointed by Aristide as Commander in Chief of the Army. In an attempt to force the coup leaders to step down, the United Nations initiated a trade embargo on Haiti. The economy of the country was already crippled. These harsh measures were eventually successful. Under "Operation Uphold Democracy", a force of twenty thousand U.S. troops was peacefully deployed to Haiti to ensure stability. With strong relations alongside President Bill Clinton, Aristide returned to Haiti from exile and took office in October 1994. He soon saw to the disbandment of the national army and in its place, a police force was setup.

Aristide successfully held office for his five year term until René Préval took over in 1996. Préval became the second democratically elected head of state in the country's two hundred year history. Préval, had once been Aristide's prime minister and was a strong advocate for economic restructuring. Elections were held in 2000 and Aristide was once again elected into office. But once again, it would not be without incident.

In February 2004, the assassination of gang leader Amiot Metayer sparked a violent rebellion. Aristide was blamed by many as being responsible for the assassination. The National Revolutionary Front for the Liberation of Haiti was formed by Buteur Metayer, brother to the dead gang leader. The rebel force quickly took control of the north, including the second largest city in Haiti, Cap Haitien. They eventually waged conflict on the streets of Port au Prince. The country was in anarchy and the situation volatile. Fearing his own life, Aristide was flown out of the country by the U.S. on the 28th February 2004. Later it would be argued if Aristide did in fact resign from office under duress or voluntarily. There were also claims that he had been 'kidnapped' by the United States. The subsequent instability made it almost impossible to hold new elections. Law and order was lost. Haiti was on the brink of collapse.

On the 30th April 2004, acting on the recommendations of the Secretary-General, the Security Council, established the United Nations Stabilization Mission in Haiti (MINUSTAH), which took over on 1st June 2004.

MINUSTAH was originally created to support the transitional government while keeping the peace on the streets of Haiti. Also, to assist in monitoring, restructuring and reforming the Haitian National Police (PNH) and to help with comprehensive and viable disarmament of gangs. Initially, the MINUSTAH mission comprised of 6,700 military personnel, 1,622 police, 550 international civilian personnel, 150 United Nations volunteers and about 1,000 local civilian staff.

Finally, with law and order generally restored, in 2006, Préval was reelected.

By 2010, although still facing major challenges on many fronts, Haiti was well on its way toward a more favorable future. This was achieved in no short measure by the combined efforts of the Haitian authorities, the United Nations, and the international community, spearheaded by former US President Bill Clinton and Digicel CEO Denis O'Brien.

Violence had largely been removed from national politics. Also, kidnapping had vastly decreased and crime was at a more manageable level for the relatively young national police force. The economy was growing, foreign investment was beginning to arrive and positive constitutional amendments promised sustained economic growth in the years to come.

President Préval was in the midst of his second term when the devastating earthquake of the 12th January 2010 hit Haiti. Though Préval survived, a large number of senior governmental officials did not. The Presidential Palace was destroyed. Amongst the devastation, vital infrastructure necessary to respond to the disaster was severely damaged or in some cases, nonexistent. This included all hospitals in the capital; air, sea, and land transport facilities; and communication systems. The earthquake had also damaged the control tower at Toussaint L'Ouverture International Airport. Damage to the Port-au-Prince seaport rendered the harbor inoperative. The earthquake had struck in the heart of the most populated area of the country. By the 24th of January, at least 52 aftershocks measuring 4.5 or greater had been recorded. An estimated three million people were affected by the quake. Death toll estimates were uncertain. It was thought to be about 250,000 to 300,000 (this varies between different organizations).

Préval quickly came under criticism for not reacting effectively and in time to the natural disaster. Because of how near the earthquake was to the upcoming elections of 2010, Préval extended his term in office by three months. Some opposed this, but Préval was supported in this decision by both national and international governments. An interim government was too big of a risk to Haiti's security at such a time. Nobody wanted to lose the stability that Haiti had fought to achieve for so long.

Elections ran from October 2010 into 2011. Michel Martelly was elected Haiti's next president after a run-off against candidate Mirlande Manigat (wife to former president Leslie Manigat). Martelly was an extremely successful compa (Haitian music) musician and was known throughout the country for his music. No matter his popularity, the new president was taking office in a post-earthquake nation with an exacerbated health problem now on its hands.

Beginning in October 2010, Haiti was witnessing cases of cholera in the region of the Central Plateau, stemming from a tributary on the Artibonite river. No cases had been recorded in Haiti for more than a century. Cholera quickly spread into many towns and villages sharing the Artibonite's banks until finally reaching the capital Port au Prince. By the end of 2010, more than 3,500 people had died with thousands hospitalized.

Scientists eventually determined that the strain of cholera responsible for the outbreak was consistent with strains found in Southern Asia. Many health organizations believed that the strain may have been introduced into Haiti by UN peacekeepers from Nepal who were stationed near to an estuary on the Artibonite. It is currently estimated that up to 9,000 people have died since the outbreak.

In August 2011, Martelly declared that he wished to reinstate the nation's military. This plan was met with controversy and suspicion. Many were concerned about bringing back a military which had been responsible for many atrocities in the past.

In September 2011, Martelly formed an advisory board that included business executives, bankers, and politicians such as former President of the United States Bill Clinton. This he hopes will improve business and further stimulate the economy in Haiti.

He is quoted as saying that "Haiti is open for business."

President Martelly issued a statement on the 10th of June 2014, setting parliamentary and local elections for October 26th, 2014. These elections have since been cancelled. Their cancellation has led to mass protests where Haitian citizens are now demanding the resignation of President Martelly.

PROLOGUE

As soon as I stepped out onto the main road I felt as if my heart was going to burst out of my already heaving chest. Everything, everywhere, was covered in dust. It was so thick that I could only see about twenty meters in any one direction. Car alarms wailed irrepressibly while panic stricken people ran up and down the street like headless chickens. A lot of them were crying hysterically. Others appeared to be injured. Blood pumped from cuts and gashes on various parts of numerous bodies; mostly legs and arms. Many of the wounds appeared superficial at a glance. There were no police present and no control. Mass hysteria intensified the chaos.

I felt my forehead thumping profusely. My legs felt weak from the eleven story run and the dash across the yard. Seeing an abandoned white Honda Civic across the street, I ran over to examine my head in one of the wing mirrors. There was no laceration. Just a mark. I stood up straight and took a better look at what was happening in my vicinity. The roadway and surrounding routes were in disorder. Dozens and dozens of abandoned cars were choking up the sidewalks and roads. I coughed violently with the copious amount of concrete dust my lungs had ingested. The powdered concrete that hovered above our heads continued to block out the sun. I coughed up dirt as more people arrived. They had come from further up the street. Their traumatized screams added to the horror unfolding before me. Many cried for God to come and save them. Some people even dropped to their knees , in the middle of the crowded street and reached with both arms to the skies. In Creole, French and English, they cried, 'Why God? Why?' Tears rolled down their ashen faces, mixed with the blood and gray residual powder of fallen concrete.

I continued to look around, absorbing the scene. Surrounding buildings had fallen. Some were obliterated, and others only partially collapsed. The three story Canape Vert hospital, to my left had buckled into itself, like a poorly controlled demolition. I wondered how many people were in there: patients, nurses and doctors.

More and more people arrived from further up the street. More bloody faces and injured bodies. Only these people looked a lot worse. They were arriving to our location for treatment. Obviously they hadn't realized the disastrous demise of the hospital.

A violent trembling ran through the ground underneath my feet. It was fierce, like as if a colossal ogre was angrily trying to punch a hole through the ground from far below. The shaking only lasted a few seconds but the magnitude was ferocious. More dust rose into the air. The roars of a helpless city reverberated for miles around. Shock and distress increased amidst the helpless and the scared. I heard somebody say that the end of the world was upon us. It sure felt that way. Whatever the case, I had to get to a safer location. In the hundreds, perhaps over a thousand, faces that I could see, none of them looked familiar to me. I had to leave, for fear of my workplace collapsing. Even when I wasn't looking at the eleven story building directly, I could still make out its prominent pose with my peripheral vision. If the beast were to shake our world in its rage one more time, there was the possibility that the Digicel building could come hurtling down. If this were to happen, nobody would be able to out run the waves of bricks and mortar that would follow. I could not spend much longer, looking for a familiar face. I just simply couldn't stay there.

It was coming on quarter past five when I spotted one of my colleagues from the call-center. It was Nancy. I called out to her but she could neither hear me nor see me amidst the pandemonium. I could see that she was trying to make a call from her cell phone. I walked towards her, cautious of my surroundings as I paid heed to the badly damaged walls of neighboring structures.

'Nancy,' I said as I tapped her on the shoulder.

Nancy raised her head from her Blackberry and looked at me. She hugged me and cried a little. I guess she was just grateful to see a friend. We were both captive to the unfamiliar terror that surrounded us.

'Paddy, I cannot get through to my husband. What about my son? My husband is supposed to pick him up from school.'

'I know, Nancy,' I said. 'I know. The network is probably down. It's the earthquake. Have you seen any of the guys, Nancy? Did you see Claude or Lisa or anybody?'

'No, Paddy,' she said. 'I'm sorry. I haven't.'

Her breathing was short and rapid. I was still switched on and running on the leftover adrenaline that ran through my body.

'We have to go, Nancy. It's not safe here.'

'There's no network, Paddy,' she said as she fumbled with her phone. 'Oh please, Jesus. My family.'

The ground rumbled and the city screamed as another aftershock hit. I thought about that invisible monster far below us. I knew my time was up for hanging about. I had to get to a safer place before nightfall.

'Let's go, Nancy. I know a place not too far from here. We'll contact your family soon. But we have to go *now*.'

Nancy put her phone in her left hand and clasped my arm with the other. In my mind, she was my responsibility to evacuate from the eleventh floor. As we started to make our way up the street, I felt even more responsible for her.

Somewhere above the shroud of gray dust the sun was already setting. What we did and where we went in the next hour would determine our safety for the night. Our destination was clear in my mind. We had to get to Canape Vert apartments; home to many of the Digicel ex-pat staff and their families. Beside the apartment buildings was a large open spaced garden. If the apartments had collapsed, it would not have affected the garden area which was free from any solid constructions. From there I would be able to hook up with the security staff. From where we were, it normally took four minutes by car to get to the apartments. I'd never had to walk it before. I drew a quick breath, stared at the route ahead and we began our ascent.

As we walked, I couldn't believe what I was seeing. Fallen debris from collapsed walls and houses lay everywhere. Badly injured victims screamed out of fear and a need for mercy. Tumbledown houses had buckled under the pressure. Collapsed walls claimed possession of the road.

'Watch your step, Nancy,' I said. 'Watch the bricks and metal.'

She had her phone out again and was desperate to make contact with her family. It was a wasted effort on her part.

'There's no network right now, Nancy,' I said. 'You've got to watch where you're stepping and just keep moving forward. Okay?'

She nodded at me then looked to the road under her feet.

My throat was still burning from inhaled particles of dust. Each breath I drew was heavy with the polluted air. The deeper my breath, the more chalky dust I inhaled.

Nancy was struggling more than me, but there was simply no time to stop. We had to get to Canape Vert before nightfall.

With each careful step, the howling cries of the badly injured increased in both pitch and volume.

'Just look down at where you're stepping, Nancy,' I said. 'Don't worry about anything else.'

I'm not sure she if she was listening to me. Her hand struggled to keep a hold of me. Her palm continued to sweat in mine as I increased the pace of our ascent.

'Maidais! S'il vous plait! Maidais!'

I stopped for a second to see who was screaming. It was impossible to ignore the tormenting cries. They were so close. To my right I saw a woman, lying half buried under the fallen front wall of a house. Her legs were trapped beneath the rubble. They no longer appeared to be a part of her. The only thing connecting her upper body to them was a minute sliver of flesh on her right hip and lower back. Her innards streamed down from her abdominal region. Blood seeped into the cracks and grooves of the tarmac. Her life was slipping away before my eyes. I noticed that Nancy was looking away. The blend of light gray concrete particles and blood only added to the shear horror of her hellish end. I imagined that the collapsed house was once her home. Home to her family. Less than a half hour ago she was probably preparing dinner in the kitchen while waiting for her kids to come home from school and maybe her husband to return from a day's work. Now she lay dying on the side of the road. Her body, ripped in two, was surrounded by other scenes of carnage and mayhem.

'I'm so sorry,' I whispered. 'I cannot stay. I have to go. There's nothing I can do. I'm so sorry. What can I do? There's nothing I have that can help you.'

Her cries became muffled as Nancy and I continued our uphill march. But the woman's cries were soon replaced by more. Many more.

Men cradled badly maimed babies and children in their arms. The alarming high pitched screams of little kids pleading for a dead mother or father to wake up added to the insanity. Cries, screams, pain and anguish filled the road, and the sky. Perpetual suffering on only one of a thousand streets throughout Port au Prince tonight.

The top of the road eventually came into sight.

'Not too far to go, Nancy,' I said. 'Two hundred meters and we'll be at the T- junction.'

She was exhausted. I could feel that she wanted to stop. If only for a minute or two. I wanted to also. But I just couldn't take that chance. Not yet.

'We're almost there, Nancy. Okay?'

She nodded, barely looking at me. She was too breathless and shell-shocked for words. I was mindful that I was taking her away from the direction she had originally wanted to go. But this was not the time to wander down through the streets. Darkness was coming and God only knew what else.

Finally we reached the T-Junction. It marked the end of the tarmacked section of the road and the beginning of two derelict tracks.

Our turn was to the left. It was a dirt road that stretched for more than five hundred meters, leading down towards a small residential area and then finally onto the back gates of the Canape Vert apartments. We quickly rounded the turn only to see debris from other fallen homes. The remaining section of the road ahead was no more than four meters. It was more of a concreted dirt track than anything else. The entire path was covered in heavy rubble. Twenty-five minutes ago, this had been a small neighborhood of about twelve neatly built houses. Now those homes were left to nothing. The rooftops and the rear walls had toppled onto the center of the road. I noticed a rusted bath tub and a water tank hanging to the rear of it all. Electrical cables had fallen close to battered concrete pillars and jutting rebar. The entire scene looked like the back drop to an artillery barrage. We could not turn back now. We had come too far to return to the madness below.

Behind the tumbled households I got my first glimpse of Port au Prince. A large ashen cloud of smoke and dust had materialized over the entire valley. Displaced fires still burned throughout the hundreds of streets below. It was impossible to contemplate that more than a quarter million people now lay dead.

Even though I was fearful, I was grateful to be alive.

Chapter One

HAITI CALLING

THURSDAY, 30TH NOVEMBER, 2006

WATERFORD, IRELAND

Bill was sitting in the chair next to his bed when I came into the room. In front of him was a small wooden table with a large bottle of 7up and beside that an empty glass. It was the type of glass with those indented grooves at the base that you might sip a whiskey from. Over his left shoulder and beside Bill's bed was a large window. The curtains had not yet been drawn and Bill stared outwards as the harsh rain of an Irish winter's night tapped furiously against the window pane. Each night I arrived the curtains were always the same. That was how Bill liked them. And each night I would find him sitting there, by his bed, gazing into the darkness outside.

His short, thin frame looked fragile and lost in the oversized pajamas the ward sister had given him. At the age of eighty-five, Bill was alone in life. His wife had passed away eight years before and he had buried his only son, who had died in a car accident that spring.

I pulled up a nearby chair and sat down beside him. I watched as his attention turned from the window, his frail and wrinkled hands reached out to open the long green plastic bottle. Bill fumbled with the stubborn cap before noticing me. Then he smiled as he continued to wrestle with it, almost like he knew his problem had been solved.

'It's not coming off,' he said.

'I can see that alright, Bill,' I said, swaying back on my chair. 'They can be damn stubborn things them caps. Can I give you a hand with it?'

'Do please,' he answered in his soft voice.

I poured Bill a half glass of 7up and watched him raise it towards his thin, dry lips. Bill clasped the glass with both hands. The tips of his emaciated fingers were interlocked to ensure the vessel did not drop. After a couple of sips, he slowly lowered the glass and gently placed it back on the table. Bill gave his lips a shaky wipe with the side of his wrist. He then looked about the room before leaning towards me.

'Why does that woman keep staring at me from over there? She doesn't live here.'

Each night he would ask me similar questions and each night I would attempt to explain to Bill where he was.

'You're in the hospital, Bill. That lady over there is in the hospital too.'

'Oh,' he answered. 'And how are you keeping?'

Bill was a gentleman. His tone and mannerisms set him apart from many of the other, more aggressive dementia and Alzheimer's patients I had worked with for the two years prior to him. It had been almost a month since he was admitted, and I had spent the best part of that time caring for him.

For two years I had been working in my local hospital as a care assistant for a nursing agency. My duties ran from eight at night until eight in the morning. Most of my time was spent working with patients like Bill. I was usually sent to the medical floors where the regular nursing staff could not keep a watchful eye on such patients every minute of the night. I would 'special' them which basically meant that I would spend a twelve hour shift with any one particular patient. I'd ensure that they were comfortable and clean. Wash them after their supper time. If they wore pads (adult diapers) then I would change them when they needed changing and help them to take medication that the nurse had administered.

I saw men and women like Bill as people, not patients. Giving them my time and the care that they deserved was a privilege. I enjoyed the work but being a care assistant certainly wasn't my calling. At 26 I still longed for a more adventurous life.

By ten o'clock, all the visitors to the hospital ward had left. Most of the lights had been turned out in the six bed ward where Bill slept. The dim forty watt bulb of his bedside lamp gave enough light without disturbing those patients who were trying to sleep.

Almost every night for the past three weeks, I had helped Bill shuffle onto the side of the bed from his chair and settle him comfortably up onto his pillows.

'Everybody is gone now,' he whispered.

'They're all gone home, Bill,' I said. 'Now you should try and get some sleep.'

The old man placed his right arm out over the bed sheets and raised it towards me. With both my hands, I clasped his palm between mine.

'Will I see you tomorrow?' he asked.

'Of course you will, Bill. Don't you worry about that, just get some rest now. I'll be here if you need me.'

His grip relaxed when I told him this. He did not want to be alone and I was glad to be there for the old codger, even if it was only for one more night. I just didn't have the heart to tell him that in a few days I would be leaving for a small country on the other side of the world.

Earlier that day I had received a call from a man in Dublin. It was in relation to a job advertisement I had stumbled across in the classifieds section of an evening newspaper. It said they were looking for ex-soldiers with close protection training for 'prestigious overseas contracts'. Normally security jobs in the classifieds were for shop floor security guards, construction site night watchman or even hospital security. I was surprised.

'Patrick, I read your CV in my inbox this morning,' said the man from Dublin. 'My name is Martin Brady. I run a security company based in the Caribbean. How long did you serve in the army?'

'Just short of four years Martin,' I said. 'Honorable discharge.'

'Would you be available for interview on Friday morning?'

It was the call I had been waiting for all year.

'Absolutely, Martin,' I said. 'That's not a problem.'

We agreed to meet in a Dublin café the following morning . . .and then it hit me. I had to throw it out there and ask him.

'Martin, I realize this might be a bit out of place,' I said. 'But I have a friend here in Waterford also. He's ex-army, overseas experience, honorable discharge and CP (Close Protection) trained with me. His name is Mick Dowling and I couldn't recommend him enough.'

There was a pause and I hoped I hadn't messed things up by being so impulsive.

'Very good' said Martin. 'Can he be in Dublin tomorrow with you?'

'Yes!' I said. 'No problem. He'll be there.'

I called Mick straight after I hung up the phone to Martin. He would want to hear this. It was the call that both of us had been waiting for. He was as excited as I was to hear the news.

Mick had been my best friend since high school. He was a well-built fella. Standing five foot ten, he was stocky, robust and full of life. Mick joined the navy reserves soon after some of us told him about it and by the time school was done, we had both enlisted in the army. During our time in recruit training, Mick had always excelled as one of the top guys in our platoon. He was extremely methodical and a deep thinker with a wry sense of humor.

By 2002 we ended up serving in different units. It wasn't until late 2005 our paths crossed again when we both signed up for the same Close Protection training course in Denmark. It was something I had been thinking about for some time. And when the finances were right, both myself and Mick were on our way to Copenhagen and Bosnia for several weeks of CP training. The skills we acquired in that time, added to our military experience. We hoped that they would be enough to gain employment in the private security sector. Or 'the circuit' as it is known.

However, finding employment on 'the circuit' was practically impossible without the right contacts. Had we served in the British Army, it probably would have been easier to find work in Afghanistan or Iraq (which is where we originally wanted to go). Now here we were, with the distinct possibility of a job overseas.

As soon as I got home from work the following morning, I grabbed a shower, packed a small bag and waited for Mick to come and pick me up in his silver Skoda. The meeting wasn't until midday in a small café just off of Grafton Street. It was a beautiful morning in the city when we arrived, with a bite in the air and frost on the pavements. The sky was blue and cloudless as the winter sun shone down on an icy, dry Dublin city.

Mick and I met Martin Brady as we walked into the café. Martin was well spoken and seemed quite friendly. We made our way into the café and pulled up a couple of chairs. He offered to buy us a late breakfast. I wasn't particularly hungry but accepted the offer. As the three of us drank coffee and ate our bacon and eggs, Martin initiated the 'chat' by asking us about our time in the military, our CP training and our family lives. He had been a sergeant in the infantry himself so I was sure that he would see us as two professional young men. Once the food was eaten and table cleared, he asked to see any documentation that we had brought. It felt like an eternity as he studied our course reports and military discharge books. And so with 'informal formalities' over, the votes were in.

'Okay, lads,' said Martin. 'Ye don't have any actual experience in the CP world but your course reports read well and ye do seem like two switched on fellas .My company is called 'Vigilance Security Services'. We operate out of a small country in the Caribbean called Haiti. Ever heard of it?'

Martin could see by the blank expressions on our faces that we were unsure.

'Okay. No problem,' he said. 'Our client is a prominent telecommunications company in the Caribbean region. It's called 'Digicel' and the CEO is a man called Denis O'Brien. You've probably heard of him. He is the guy who practically kicked off the entire mobile phone phenomenon in Ireland over ten years ago. He has since set up operations in Jamaica and Haiti. Your duties down there would include protecting his executives, engineers, technicians and their families. These people all work for Digicel and they will be depending on you to take care of them.'

Martin went on to describe current team strengths and the fact that they would be desperately undermanned due to team members going home over the Christmas period. The job description was brief. The main threat explained to us was kidnapping. Martin Brady was offering us a provisional contract of ninety days and should we perform well, a second contract might be offered down the line.

With smiles and handshakes, we accepted his proposal to visit his offices and read over the proposed contracts.

'Alright, good men,' he said. 'My building is out by the airport. Have you got a car nearby?'

'I'm driving,' said Mick.

'Okay, follow me out the road and you can read the contracts. If you are still happy after that, then we'll set dates as to when you go.'

The office was in a block of business units in a fairly remote area bordering the airport grounds.

'What the hell are we doing?' I said.

'He's probably gonna whack us and stick our bodies in a fucking dumpster,' said Mick.

When we parked up, Martin brought us into his office block and told us to head upstairs and take a seat in the briefing room. The briefing room was spacious. From the navy colored carpet to the bright blue painted walls, everything looked new. There must have been fifteen desk chairs all facing towards a projector screen at the front of the room. Attached to the walls were various maps and printed articles. There was one large map by the bathroom door but I couldn't make out what country it was. I guessed it was Haiti. We sat down at a large wooden office desk over by a window. Martin came in and handed us each a copy of the contract.

'There's a lot in the contract guys,' he said. 'Take your time to read through it carefully. If you are happy with what you've read then we'll sign them when I get back. I'll be an hour so that should give you plenty of time.'

We probably spent the best part of forty-five minutes reading over about thirty pages of legal jargon, life assurance, beneficiaries, accident and injury etc. The contract stated that we would serve ninety operational days in Haiti and one month off if a second contract was to be offered. Three months work. It didn't sound like that long a time.

Once finished, I went over to the wall that held the large colorful map. It had been catching the corner of my eye all through reading the contract. On it was the island of Hispaniola, home to Haiti and its neighboring country, the Dominican Republic. There was a smaller map in the top corner showing Haiti in relation to the United States. I couldn't believe that it was so close to Miami. The other sheets on the wall were medical notices about dehydration and malaria. I had never even considered malaria up to that point.

It must have been half past two by the time Martin returned.

'Well guys, are you happy?' he asked as he closed the office door behind hm.

Before his return, Mick and I had already agreed that we would sign.

'We are indeed, Martin,' I said.

He handed us a pen and watched as we signed our respective contracts.

'How are you guys set, if I were to ask you to fly out next Tuesday?'

We were stunned. It gave us less than four days. It was a hell of a lot sooner than either Mick or I had anticipated. I would have preferred another week. So too would Mick. But that's how it was offered. Haiti was the type of opportunity we had sought for so long and we were not going to let it slip by for the sake of inconvenience.

'Yep,' I said. 'That's okay'. Mick nodded.

'Good stuff,' said Martin. 'You'll need to pick up your tickets in the travel agency that we use in Kilkenny.'

Luckily for us, Kilkenny was on our route home so we wouldn't lose too much time. Martin gestured towards the office door and we made our way back out to the almost empty car park.

'Okay lads. I'll give you a buzz in an hour to confirm that the tickets are sorted. You'll need to speak to a girl in the travel agency called Linda. She will have them reserved for you and confirmed once she has seen your passports. Go home and sort out your kit, your lives and your families. I'll talk to you later.'

As we drove back home to Waterford, we both knew that we would have to say goodbye to everything. It was a hasty deployment unlike anything we had ever done with the army. There was no 'blue/ green umbrella' of the United Nations to protect us. No pre-deployment training with your buddies back in the Battalion to rely on. We had each other and the guys who were already operating in country.

Mick seemed to know more about the geography of Haiti than I did. I really hadn't a clue.

'It's like Africa', Mick explained. 'Fucking overpopulated and underdeveloped. Years of corrupt governments and economic hardship for the ordinary people. Basically Africa.'

These were just words to me. But Mick knew what he was talking about. He had spent the best part of his childhood growing up in Lagos, Nigeria. And in 2004, he had been part of the UN mission into Liberia after the former President Charles Taylor had been ousted. Mick had spent six months on the ground there. He knew what unstable, impoverished African countries were all about. All I knew about Haiti was that they spoke French and that my French was crap.

I'd always associated the Caribbean with that of a paradise destination for holiday makers and honeymooners. White sandy beached islands surrounded by tropical blue waters, all the while happy Europeans and Americans sipping on fancy cocktails and enjoying everything that upmarket beach resorts and hotels had to offer. How the hell could a Caribbean island be like a poverty stricken African nation? How on earth could people be killing and kidnapping in a tropical paradise?

Stopping in Kilkenny to pick up the tickets took an hour and a half. The sun had already set by the time we arrived into Waterford City. My head was still trying to process everything that had just happened and all the shit I had yet to sort out before I got to the airport on Tuesday morning. There were a lot of loose ends to tie up for the both of us.

The hardest part of all would be explaining all of this to my mother. I came from a very close family. My mother especially would be heartbroken.

I went out to the backyard and greeted her with a big hug as she came down from the garden with a wash basket full of clothes.

'I need to talk to you about something, mom,' I said.

She looked at me with grave concern. It was as if she already knew.

We went inside and I began to explain to her about why I had gone to Dublin and what had happened since eight o'clock that morning. The tears welled up in her eyes.

'I don't understand, Patrick', she said. 'Why do you want to go off to these dangerous places? You have a good job with the agency in the hospital. What could you possibly want with a place like Haiti?'

I tried to explain but I was stuck for words. The right words at least. I had such an overwhelming urge to go that I struggled to formulate it into an reasonable explanation. I told her that I had to take the chance and that Mick would be with me. We would take care of each other out there. My reasons probably came across as feeble. But my reasons were my own, even if I barely understood them myself. My sister Karen was saddened also. It was as if I was going against the grain, hurting those I loved the most.

That night I met Mick and some of the lads in town. We knocked back pints as our mates wished us a prosperous journey and a safe return. We went to all the old haunts and enjoyed the Guinness and whiskey in good fashion. It could easily have been farewell drinks for me alone. Thank God it wasn't. We were headed down an unknown path together and I was glad that it was Mick who was coming with me.

Chapter Two

GOODBYE IRELAND

MONDAY, 4ᵀᴴ DECEMBER, 2006

WATERFORD, IRELAND

Mick and I arrived at the office block for about quarter to ten on a rainy Monday morning. It was bitterly cold as we stood outside sipping coffees and waiting for Martin to arrive. But this time we were greeted at the door by another man: Andrew. He was tall, stocky and slightly balding. His demeanor was less relaxed than Martin's. This gave him an unsettling edge.

Andrew told us to take some paper and pens from his office and head up stairs to the briefing room. The majority of the brief comprised of slide show pictures of Port au Prince and other areas that we would be operating in. I could see that the streets of the capital looked incredibly busy. I thought about what Mick had said. The squalor and poverty were evident in each slide.

Haiti appeared to consist of hundreds of thousands of people all living on top of each other in streets congested with archaic vehicles, small numbers of roaming dogs and pigs and sporadic piles of abandoned garbage left to rot by the roadsides. The streets looked smaller than they actually were because of the immense market areas surrounding them, barely leaving enough room for people to walk on the sidewalks.

'Haiti was the first African slave colony to gain independence,' explained Andrew. 'But in reality, after two hundred years of that independence Haiti has been left as a highly volatile country with continuous political unrest. The vast majority of the population have been used and exploited by decades of corrupt governments and military dictatorships. Rioting is common place down there and kidnapping is the name of the game, especially since 2004 when Jean Bertrand Aristide was ousted from presidency. The United Nations have boots on the ground for over two years now. I think it numbers about ten thousand or so. Their mission is called MINUSTAH (Mission des Nations Unies pour la stabilisation en Haiti). This country will be your new home for the next ninety days gentlemen.'

Andrew explained about the Vigilance security teams and how they operated, but it was the streets of Port au Prince which made up the vast majority of his brief. His description of some areas, in particular a place called Cite Soleil, suggested a warzone.

'Expect to see bodies on the streets. Life in Haiti is cheap. Stop your vehicle for nothing down there. Absolutely nothing!'

'But what if you are just stopped in traffic?' I asked.

He gave me a discerning glare.

'Just push straight through it,' he replied.

It sounded like anarchy down there. I wondered why, if things were so bad, I had never seen Haiti on the news before. I felt nervous about the entire process, mostly due to my ignorance of the country. I had no clue who the hell Aristide was and why he had been ousted. Maybe all this was beyond me and maybe we were being naïve about it all. I suppose like many young lads, our naivety was outweighed by our desire to prove our self-worth.

I did get the feeling, however, that Andrew was boasting a slightly ludicrous image than that of the reality. I was under no illusions that he reveled in the sound of his own voice. The brief went on for an hour and a half. A lot longer than Mick and I had anticipated. I was keen to know more but I knew that would come from the guys already there. We had already eaten into precious hours and still had to get back down home only to get back up to Dublin airport later that night.

It probably took me twenty minutes to shove everything I would need for three months into a rucksack and a small day pack. I wasn't sure if I had enough, but it would have to do. Mom and dad sat waiting for me in the living room. I dropped my bags by the doorway in the hall and went inside to see them. Their mood was somber. From the redness of my mother's eyes, it was plain to see that she had been crying and was just trying to keep a brave face while I was still present. My dad simply sat in his green leather arm chair, occasionally glancing in my direction while he rolled himself a cigarette. His attention was fixed more on the smoke he would soon enjoy. I watched his fingers roll the loose tobacco into the paper with smooth precision. The tips of his index fingers had been blemished dark brown from years of smoking. Dad was old school and showed little by way of emotion. I didn't really know what to say to him except that I would be fine and not to worry about me.

Just before midnight, Mick rang to say that he was waiting for me outside in the car. I shook hands with my dad in the living room and gave him an awkward hug. My mom on the other hand was another story. I hugged her so tightly that I could feel her sobbing as we embraced. I had been to so many places down through the years but this was the saddest parting I'd ever experienced. I hated the fact that I was missing Christmas with them. I hated the fact that I was leaving so abruptly. I hated not being able to assure them that I would return safely in three months. But most of all, I hated whatever part of me was driving my life down this risky and uncertain path.

I picked up my backpack and gave her one last kiss on her cheek before turning away. My mother stood by the front door as the car made its way up the road and gradually rounded the corner and disappeared from sight.

'Shit isn't it?' said Mick. Obviously he had done the same not long before me.

'Yeah,' I said.

'You got your passport and tickets?' (It might sound arrogant to ask such a question but given the day we had, it made sense.)

'Sorted Mick. All good mate.'

I tried to take my mind off of it all and concentrate on our second drive to Dublin in one day.

'How are things with you Alan?' I said. 'Cheers for the lift man.'

Alan was a tall, thin lad. He was Mick's older brother by about three years. Generally he was a quiet, reserved type of guy until you got to know him. I always respected him for the way that he kept himself to himself.

'Alright boy. No bother,' he answered. 'Ye are some men for doing this. There's no way I'd have the balls to do what ye are doing.'

It was the first time that I had stopped and considered that there might be some bravery involved to our escapade. If so, it was easily outweighed by the fear and apprehension in my gut.

We arrived on the outskirts of a dark, rainy Dublin city at about three o'clock in the morning. Alan pulled the Nissan Primera up outside the departures terminal of Dublin airport. We still had hours to kill before the flight but had been grateful to escape an uncomfortable redeye bus ride.

'Best of luck to ye,' said Alan as we shook hands. 'Drop us a line when ya can.'

About five hours later we boarded the Aer Lingus flight bound for JFK International Airport in New York.

The sun was not long up as the airplane taxied down the runway. I gazed far out into the distance at the cars driving along the narrow roads outside the airport perimeter. I wondered where some of them might be off to on a cold and sunny December morning. Maybe a mother was dropping her kids off to school or a father on his way home after working a night shift in a factory somewhere. I envied them. Maybe one day that would be me. I felt a million miles from it all.

Flight EI105 sped down the runway at a tremendous speed. She gradually winged her way into the air until all that was below me were fields of green. Soon Irish pastures were replaced by blue Atlantic waters. I looked at Mick. He wore a cheeky smile. Finally I felt myself accepting this adventure, however it might unfold. We were headed into the unknown. We were finally on our way.

Chapter Three

PORT AU PRINCE

WEDNESDAY, 6TH DECEMBER, 2006

JFK AIRPORT, QUEENS, NEW YORK

The Comfort Inn shuttle bus dropped us off outside the American Airlines Terminal at about six thirty on a freezing Wednesday morning. Snow blanketed every inch of ground as far as the eye could see. New York, Queens was a winter wonderland. The only areas resistant to the white powder were the roads and sidewalks where busy men in snow ploughs had wiped them clear in the sub-zero temperatures throughout the night. I was relieved to step into the warmth of the airport terminal.

We checked in at the American Airlines desk and then got the tedious task of security checks out of the way. I noticed the amount of Haitians standing in the line. They were returning to their homeland. Many of them were wearing exuberantly bright shirts, t-shirts and blouses. All speckled by a few pale white Americans and Europeans like me within their ranks.

Mick and I had enough time for some breakfast in the little restaurant opposite our departures gate before we were due to board our flight. The first group to board was nine elderly Haitian ladies in wheelchairs. Dressed in their best bib and tucker, these old, heavy looking women sat comfortably in their chairs as they were wheeled down the passageway by airport attendants. I'd never seen that done in any other airport before. Not for so many people at any one time at least.

It seemed like every person boarding the flight had packed all their worldly goods into boxes and bags of varying shapes and sizes; large old leather suitcases, extra suitcases and lots of large blue plastic bags. Some Haitian men had five or six baseball caps aptly placed on their heads. Even some of the younger men were wearing two or three hoody tops. I wondered if they'd forgotten where they travelling to with all the winter gear. Little did I know that I was already being exposed to Haiti and all its unusual and brilliant peculiarities. There was a method to their madness. I just didn't know it yet.

What was more baffling was the amount of white people heading to Haiti. There were dozens of couples with young children running about at their feet. Why were they taking such young children to a country that only two years ago had been in a state of anarchy and civil unrest? More and more questions were darting through my mind. But the answers did not follow. I knew I was definitely leaving my comfort zone.

I tightened the strap of my seatbelt as the plane ripped down the runway. From my cabin window, I managed to get one last splendid view of New York City. I clenched my toes as I felt the plane jump and shake through cold pockets of air. My eyes were drawn to the incredible sight of skyscrapers and the unmistakable landmark of the Empire State Building. The Statue of Liberty was just a tiny green figurine far below, holding her torch overhead. Whatever happened in the months ahead, I hoped I would see this view again.

Ever since we had cleared the Miami coastline, I had been mesmerized by the intoxicating blue Caribbean waters with its tiny islands all scattered randomly throughout. Their white sandy beaches surrounded by electrically translucent pools of blue.

Eventually the turquoise waters gave way to the green jungle canopy of mountainous terrain. The captain declared that American Airlines flight AA837 was beginning to make her descent into Toussaint Louverture Airport.

I was finally getting my first glimpse of Port au Prince. The first thing I noticed was the city's harbor with about a half dozen oil tankers laid up in the bay. Most of the city lay beneath a shadow of dark, green mountains on either side. To the south-east, the mountains appeared to lose their natural shades of green. White and ashen box shaped houses sprang up like gatherings of sugar cubes all carelessly tossed out upon a pool table.

The last image to spring into view was a large zone of shanty towns surrounding the northern and western sides of the airport. There were hundreds of buildings. Some had roofs with rusted corrugated tin while other structures appeared a lot more solid with concreted roofing. I braced myself for impact as the plane's wheels screeched onto the tarmac followed by a pounding thud.

When I stepped out and onto the tarmac, my face was suddenly whacked by the humidity that lingered all around us. My eyes struggled to adjust to the Haitian afternoon sun as the sky appeared to be more of a bright white than that of a deep blue. The massive aircraft engines spurted out puffs of dark gray smoke as they gradually wound down. I couldn't help but cough slightly as the jet fumes hit the back of my throat.

Mick and myself sauntered through to the main arrivals building. A local band of three men all wearing distinctively red and white Digicel t-shirts, played a lively song on their array of instruments. I was surprised to see one of them playing an accordion. He must have been about forty years old and he sat there on a small wooden chair, smiling and swaying from side to side as his fingers danced about the buttons of his instrument. I had never associated accordions with third world countries before. It all felt quite surreal.

Customs seemed to take forever to clear. I had written my stay in Haiti as ninety days but the customs lady never asked me what my business was in her country. Mick had already cleared customs when I joined him at the carrousel to pick up our luggage. The baggage area was absolutely choc a bloc with people as we waited for our gear to arrive.

'He's definitely Irish,' said Mick. He discreetly gestured towards a tall, thin white figure further down the carrousel line. 'I saw him in New York waiting to board. Reckon he might be with us.'

Mick was always that bit sharper than most for spotting things early. He had proved that time and again on the surveillance stage of our security training the year before. Even throughout Army recruit training (boot camp) he was always acutely aware of his surroundings. Mick undoubtedly remained the most switched on man I knew.

An airport assistant helped us find our bags. Throwing our kit over our shoulders, we paid him $10 each. An outlandish amount of money for such a simple task but one I was happy to pay. The cheeky bugger looked dissatisfied and reached his hand out gesturing for more money. He wanted $20 more from both Mick and I. We smiled at him then walked away to join the line of people heading out towards the arrivals door. Hundreds and hundreds of Haitians stood in wait for family and friends just beyond a green barrier fence positioned about seven meters from the arrivals doorway. Our eyes scanned desperately for somebody to recognize us. Just a wave or a nod to acknowledge our arrival would suffice. Finally I noticed the guy that Mick had pointed out to me at the carrousel. He was standing outside chatting to another, much bigger man. They stared at us and some eye contact was made. We took the chance and walked outside to them.

'Alright lads,' said the man who had shared the same flight as us. 'Vigilance Security is it?'

'Yeah,' said Mick.

'I'm Liam,' he said. 'And that's András. I saw you boarding the plane in New York. Ye had that lost look standing by the carousel inside so I had a feeling ye must have belonged to us. Well boys, welcome to Haiti.'

We shook hands with both men. András was tall and big-bellied, with a husky eastern European voice. I was surprised by his fluent English. Liam was tall also, but thin with it, and he sported a tan that gave him the air of a weathered athlete.

'The car is just over there,' said András. He pointed towards an area fifty meters away from where we stood.

A Haitian man with a goatee opened the boot of the white Nissan Patrol. Once our bags were inside, we boarded the car and made our way out of the airport grounds and onto the main road. Mick and I sat in the back with Liam while András sat upfront with the driver.

András informed us that he had been unaware of our arrival and that it had been Liam who noticed us on the flight. I think Mick was as unnerved by that fact as much as I was.

'What would happen in that case?' I asked the two experienced operators.

'Ah, you'd just have to wait longer I suppose,' said Liam. 'Most sheriffs are shite when I go on leave. I always have to clean up their mess when I get back.'

'What's a sheriff?' I asked Liam.

'He's the man who makes shit happen. He basically runs the operations room from the Hexagon. That's the building where we are based out of. Don't worry mate. You'll soon get the hang of it all. So where are you boys from?'

'Waterford,' said Mick.

'Were ye in the army back home?'

'Yep, 3rd Battalion and 5th Battalion,' I answered.

'I was 2nd for eight years,' said Liam. 'Then I fucked off and joined the Brits.'

Our driver remained quiet and completely focused on the road in front. So too did András. I noticed how much his head bopped from left to right as he continually scanned the streets and buildings around him. He still managed to drop the odd comment or two in our direction.

'We have to make a quick detour to the Aciérie switch,' he said. 'I need to pick up an engineer over there and drop him back to the Hexagon.'

We moved swiftly down through the city's main road (Route Nationale One) and though there was a lot of traffic in front of our vehicle, we continued to make steady progress.

'So much for having to ram vehicles out of the way,' I said to Mick.

The driver eventually took a sharp turn off to the right and onto a very rough and dusty dirt road. After about two hundred meters we reached a gateway where two Haitian guards stood on duty, both of them armed with what looked like old rusted shot guns.

The switch was situated in a massive warehousing facility used by a multitude of national and foreign companies. Yellow fork lift vehicles buzzed about, loaded with an assortment of drums and containers moving to and fro both in front and behind us. The switch itself was situated behind a mass of security fencing. The security guard on duty checked András' I.D. He was a skinny guy who wore a faded brown shirt with dark brown pants and dust covered black boots. He had a sleepy look about him and didn't seem to care too much for his posting. The guard handed the I.D. card back to András, then opened the gate to allow our vehicle through.

'This is a relatively well secured facility,' said Liam. 'But you can never be too sure with some of the robbing bastards around here.'

There was a slight pause before he continued.

'Did ye see the shantytowns next to the airport as we were flying in? Well that's Cité Militaire and Cité Soleil. Both are situated directly behind the walls of the switch. They are two of the biggest shitholes down here and they are the kind of places you don't want to end up.'

By this stage I was sweating as the afternoon sun pounded its heat into the back of the Patrol. But there was no time for a break or to stretch the legs. The Digicel engineer was soon in the vehicle and we promptly left the Aciérie area bound for the Hexagon.

The Nissan left Route Nationale One bringing us onto a series of small, winding streets.

'We always take these back streets,' said Liam. 'If we took the main route back up to the Hexagon every time we went to the airport then then we'd make ourselves more of a noticeable target.'

Dust and stones kicked up indiscriminately as the Patrol pushed onwards through the backstreets. The Nissan felt as though it was taking more than a fair beating from the rocks and stones underneath her wheels as we were bounced around in the back.

'These roads are fairly shite for our cars,' explained Liam. 'Especially armor, but they allow us to move much faster than getting jammed up in traffic on Delmas.'

The conditions of the buildings and houses either side of us were also poor. Decrepit houses painted in bright whites and blues with many other structures left in their natural dull, gray, cemented color. Women washed their clothes in old plastic basins and battered rusty buckets as their children played within their view. Skinny little kids with short black hair were running about with carefree and happy faces.

Eventually we broke back on to a main road and fell in line with the rest of the slow moving traffic. One minute the driver would put his foot down and move at a steady speed. Then we would hit another row of traffic and wait patiently for another stretch of open road. I was beginning to wonder about the contents of our brief as explained just two days before back in Dublin, but I decided to say nothing. Sometimes the best tactic is to keep your mouth shut and ears open.

It had just gone three o'clock when we arrived at the Hexagon building in the uptown area of Petion Ville. It was the tallest building in Petion Ville, standing ten stories high with an underground car parking facility made up of three levels. In front of the building was a small car park that could hold up to twelve vehicles. This space was used exclusively by Vigilance.

András told us to leave our gear where it was while he checked in with the operations room (sheriff's office) as to what he should do with us.

We waited by the car for him to return. I noticed a bunch of European-looking men lounging around outside the main doors of the Hexagon. Liam shook hands with most of them. Some sat lazily on deck chairs enjoying the heat of the late afternoon sun. Others spoke quietly in a small huddle smoking cigarettes and drinking coffee. They looked like a bunch of modern day cowboys.

When András returned he told us to hop back in to the Nissan.

'Okay guys,' he announced. 'You will be living in team house three. But first I've been told to take you to meet the boss at team house two. He is waiting to speak with you.'

Chapter Four

TEAM HOUSE THREE

WEDNESDAY, 6TH DECEMBER, 2006

PETION VILLE, HAITI

We drove out the gates of the Hexagon and turned right heading further up into Petion Ville. The streets here looked slightly less run-down compared to downtown. Petion Ville was the main affluent hub of Port au Prince. Its streets were made up of banks and supermarkets along with plenty of businesses and restaurants. As wealthy as the area was, every street corner we came to had old disheveled men and women begging for money and food. Some of them were on crutches. Ragged women with hard, leathery skin and small groups of children dressed in shabby t-shirts and dusty, faded shorts waited for cars to stop at the traffic lights, before pleading for hand-outs. When we came to a stop, three young boys approached our vehicle. The smallest of them tapped on my window and stared. He couldn't have been more than eight years old. I looked straight at him but the boy avoided eye contact.

It was frustrating to see people living in such conditions, but I knew I had to form a hardened shell around my feelings. If I didn't toughen up to what I was seeing, I would not be effective in my work. I had to remind myself that I was not on a humanitarian mission here.

When the lights changed to green we drove out of Petion Ville and up into the mountainous region of Montagne Noir. The team houses were situated halfway up the mountain. András dropped down through the gears of the Nissan to gain momentum on the steep hills. He contended with a series of jagged, potholed, winding roads that led further into the mountains. I had to pinch my nose to pop my ears on several occasions so as to equalize with the rapid change in height.

As we entered the gates of team house two, a skinny security guard came from the side of the property to open the oversized black gates. He was followed by two large black Dobermans. When we drove through, András halted the Nissan right beside the front door of the house. He pulled up the handbrake on the Patrol and kept the engine running.

'Okay guys,' he said. 'I will leave you here. I must return to the Hexagon.'

We thanked him and grabbed our gear from the rear of the car. The two black Dobermans came sprinting towards the vehicle. I'd been bitten on the ass by an Alsatian as a kid. Ever since then I was wary of excitable dogs.

'Get down ye fuckers,' a voice roared from inside the hallway of the house.

Whoever it was definitely had an Irish accent. A smiley figure of a man wearing a Liverpool soccer jersey came out and ordered the dogs back into the house. They didn't hesitate for a second. Both Dobermans ran inside.

'Don't worry lads,' said the man. 'They won't bite you, unless you're gonna rob the place.'

I wasn't sure if he was serious or not.

'You're Waterford boys I heard. My name's Ricky McGuire, from Galway. My friends call me Mac.'

Like myself and Mick, he was of medium build and height. About four or five years older with jet black hair and sporting a darker skin complexion, Mac had obviously been in Haiti for quite some time. All in all, he seemed to be a friendly sort. We introduced ourselves to him before he helped us carry our bags into the hall of the team house. I could hear the car drive away from the main entrance and out the gates.

'They'll be grand there lads,' said Mac as he dropped one of our bags by the door. 'The country manager will be up in a while. He's just down at the Hexagon at the moment with two other new lads. They flew in earlier this morning.'

Mac brought us through to the kitchen of the house.

'Ye haven't been up to team house three yet?' he asked.

'No. Not yet, Mac,' I said.

'Ah no worries. You'll be up there soon enough. That's where you'll be living with the rest of the bodyguards for the next three months.'

Mac put the kettle on and pulled out a box of Barry's tea from a cupboard. The two dogs sat outside the kitchen intently staring up at him. As big as they were, they knew he had the last say.

'That's Julius and Caesar,' he explained. 'Don't worry about them biting you. They don't mind the bodyguards but by fuck they'll go for anyone else who comes through those gates. Can I offer you a cup of tea boys?'

Mac was a really chatty type of fella. But he spoke incredibly fast and with a low tone so we had to almost stretch our ears out just to pick up on what he was saying. When the kettle boiled, he made us two piping hot cups of tea. I felt as if I was visiting a neighbor's house back home.

'Did they say if you'll be on the houses or out in the cars?' he asked.

'Cars I think,' answered Mick. 'Martin Brady told us that you were stuck for operational bods out here.'

'Ah good stuff,' said Mac. 'It's always good to see Irish boys coming out here. There are ten of us here at the moment including yourselves.'

'Are you on the cars as well, Mac?' I asked.

'Nah mate. I'm basically the Quartermaster of the security operation down here. I sort out everything from food supplies to bedding. I have a young Haitian fella called Baptiste who works with me, although half the time I can't find the fucker when I need him.'

Mac paused pensively as he sipped his tea.

'He's better than most. But your patience would be pushed thin down here at times. Haiti can be a hard place to get things done.'

We were still drinking our tea when we heard a car horn from outside the gate.

'That's probably them now,' said Mac.

I heard the nails of the Dobermans' paws scrape across the marble tiles of the hallway as they bolted towards the front door. From where I stood by the small kitchen window, I could see a green Nissan Patrol pull up outside the house with three white men and a local driver inside. Mac leaned over the sink and peered out the window.

'Yep,' he said. 'That's them now. The guy getting out of the front is Colin Rawes. He is acting as country manager for the moment. Until we get a replacement anyways. We better go out and say hello.'

Colin Rawes wore a faded pair of combats and an oversized green shirt that did little to hide a WELL developed pot belly. He was clean shaven with a tightly trimmed-haircut. The two boys who had sat in the back couldn't have been more different. One guy was bald and skinny while the other was tall and robust with short black hair.

The three of them walked through to the hallway where we were standing while the driver remained in the Nissan with the engine off. He was probably too afraid to get out of the car with Julius and Caesar eagerly staring up at him from where they sat.

'Alright boys,' said Rawes. 'I'm Colin Rawes, country manager. What's the names?'

'Paddy Doyle,' I said as I shook his hand.

'And you?' he said quite sharply turning to Mick.

'Mick. Mick Dowling.'

We shook hands with the other two new arrivals. They appeared to be quiet and anxious just like us.

'Right then fellas, follow me through to the living room and we'll have a quick chat about how things work around here.'

Colin went on to give us a brief about dress codes and personal appearance. He also spoke about how we were to show respect to the clients and their families. He didn't go into too much detail about the operational side of things. The team leader would take care of that. His talk lasted no more than ten minutes. It was more of a meet and greet than anything else. I was glad as I just wanted to drop my bags at the end of my bed space and finally relax.

'Right so fellas,' said Rawes. 'The car outside will take you up to team house three and I will see you down at the Hexagon at some stage tomorrow.'

We shook hands with Mac and thanked him for the tea. With that we threw our bags in the back of the green Nissan and headed for team house three. The other two lads introduced themselves as Victor and Peter. Victor was the smaller, bald guy. He was from France and had been a tactical police officer for ten years. Peter was from Poland and had served with the French Foreign Legion back in the nineties but had been working 'the circuit' in France ever since. A few weeks later he would tell me how one year, while he was working on 'the door' of the Cannes film festival, he had to refuse entry to a five foot nothing

Australian pop singer as her name was not on the list. Peter would go on to become a very close friend. There wasn't much time for a chat as our new home was literally just around the corner of the management residence.

When we passed the main gate, the first thing that drew my attention was the beautiful green lawn to my right. The grass was short and it was lavished with massive palm trees and exotic plants. Next to the garden was a swimming pool, which had a sickly green glow to the water and didn't look all that enticing to swim in. The property itself was impressive, on the outside at least. It had an old French colonial look to it with whitewashed walls two stories high and long narrow windows with brown wooden shutters either side. More than a dozen marble steps, about five meters in width, led up to three large archways that followed on into the main room. Up over the archways was a balcony whose roof was supported by three big pillars. I almost tripped on the steps as I carried my bags into the main hall.

We were met inside by the team leader, Iván. He was a stocky Polish guy in his late twenties. Iván had been part of the operation in Haiti since the early days of 2005. He was smiling wholeheartedly when he saw Peter. They hugged like two long lost brothers. Iván too had been a legionnaire. I guessed that was how they knew each other.

'Guys, you are most welcome to team house three,' he said. 'Or as we like to call it, home.' Iván offered to help us with our bags and show us to our rooms. He told Peter and Victor to remain behind while Mick and I followed him out a back door, through the kitchen and out to an open spaced courtyard that was surrounded by a corridor of rooms.

'There are six rooms back here and three bigger rooms upstairs,' he explained. 'This room is free.' Iván opened a door to the smallest two person room I had ever seen. It was very basic with two single beds, a bathroom and a

Chapter Five

FIRST DAY

THURSDAY, 7TH DECEMBER, 2006

TEAM HOUSE 3, PORT AU PRINCE, HAITI

It was about quarter past five when I woke the following morning. The gentle light of the rising sun beckoned me from a sound slumber. I was still exhausted from our travels. In the distance I could hear bedroom doors opening and closing throughout the house and the sounds of flip-flopped feet traipsing about on tiled floors. Showers were running in neighboring bedrooms while low monotone voices reverberated in the small courtyard just outside our room.

Mick was already awake and sending a text message home to his family. I took a quick shower and had a shave before I rustled through my backpack for some fresh kit. We had not yet fully unpacked our gear because we wanted to give the room a proper cleaning before settling in. Combat trousers, t-shirts and buttoned shirts were the requested dress code. I wore an old pair of desert boots which I'd kept from my army days. Mick was kitted out pretty much the same.

There was a fresh pot of coffee on the boil when we went into the kitchen. Six bodyguards were in the main living room, all eating breakfast. One by one I shook hands with them. Apparently shaking hands was seen as a sign of respect for your fellow colleague. To greet each other as such was to become a daily routine. A lot of the guys were from countries like Poland, Slovakia, Czech Republic and Hungary. Many of them had broad shoulders, tanned complexions and stocky builds. I felt somewhat intimidated by their rugged appearance.

'Welcome to Haiti boys.'

A large figure of a man in his mid-twenties walked towards Mick and I.

'Dave Carney. From Offaly,' he said. 'The lads here call me Elmo. When did ye get in?'

'Eh, late yesterday evening,' I answered.

'You boys must be wrecked. It takes a few days to get into the swing of it. The two days of travelling kind of fucks you up. So I hear you boys are on the cars with us this morning. None of that residential shite. Sure ye might as well ride down to the Hexagon with me.'

Elmo spoke with Iván then took a set of car keys from the dining table. A couple of the other guys threw their cereal bowls into the kitchen and followed us out to the car with Elmo. We sat in the back with a Hungarian guy who had introduced himself as Kinga. He was probably the biggest of all the bodyguards we'd met that morning. He had colossal biceps and broad shoulders. His eyebrows and eyes drooped ever so slightly, giving him a sort of sad look. It was a tight squeeze sitting beside Kinga in the back seat, but we managed. A quiet French man called Jean Luc sat in the front with Elmo. The rest of the morning team travelled down Montagne Noir to the Hexagon with Iván.

I had to pop my ears again as we descended the hills. We drove past dozens of Haitians who were slowly making their way up the hilly roads of Montagne Noir.

These people worked for the wealthier classes; gardeners, drivers, housemaids and laborers. An old woman of about ninety hung clothes out on a washing line next to the road. I was surprised by the amount of activity at such an early hour.

When we drove into Petion Ville, the streets were already full with traffic and people. Hundreds of young boys and girls all dressed in their school uniforms waited patiently for the doors to open to a four story school in the town center. I was surprised by the immaculacy of their appearance. Their white shirts and blouses were blinding in the early morning sun. I thought about when I'd gone to school at that age with kids who looked like their shirts had been dragged down the street by their dog before they put them on. Here was a poverty stricken country whose children were dressed like model students going to a private school. On another corner, Haitian artists were hanging their pictures up on concrete walls beside a long stretch of roadway while florists set up flower stalls next to a small park.

'This is Place Boyer,' Elmo told us. 'It's a main market area in Petion Ville. There have been two kidnappings here this month already.'

'Is the kidnapping really that bad here?' I said, regretting the question the second I'd asked it.

'Yeah, it's bad alright,' answered Elmo. 'Especially at Christmas time. What they do is kidnap children or family members of a local businessman then set a ransom for their release. But at Christmas time they offer a lower price for their freedom. A bit like the January sales back home.'

We laughed, but in reality what Elmo had said was unsettling.

'Yeah, I've been down here six months straight now,' he added. 'Seven more days and I'm outta here. It's time for me to get back to some fucking reality for a while.'

He sounded relieved to be returning home to Ireland. I couldn't help but feel disappointed that he was leaving us. Though I'd only just met him, it was plain to see that Elmo had a wealth of experience from his time in Haiti. He was the type of guy who would set you straight if you needed anything. Particularly when you were one of the new lads like myself and Mick. Men like Elmo had been few and far between throughout my time in the army. He said he was only going home for two weeks and though it was a short time, I already looked forward to seeing his return.

'NGO's are kidnapped also,' said Kinga.

'NGO's?' I asked.

'Non-Governmental Organizations, charity workers. A lot of them think they are special down here. Some of them say they are doing God's work and that they cannot be touched. But they can. The kidnappers like them the most because they won't fight back.'

Once we reached the Hexagon, Elmo parked up the Patrol and the rest of us made our way into the operations room of the Hexagon.

The ops room, or sheriff office as it was called by everybody, was the hub of all security operations. The room was no bigger than the kitchen of a council estate house. To the back of the office was a desk. Behind it hung a wooden board with about two dozen sets of keys dangling from it. On the desk was a computer and some log books. This was the sheriff's work space. Armed with a cheap looking cell phone and a clip board, he practically ran the entire day-to-day operation throughout a twelve hour shift before handing over to the night sheriff. Liam was sitting in the sheriff's chair. His day had already begun since six o'clock. Liam had little time for pleasantries as he scrambled through telephone numbers on his phone and looked for a sheet of paper on his clipboard.

'Ah for fuck sake,' he said. 'The fucking morons around here. I leave for four weeks and they fuck this operation right up.'

I had no idea what he was referring to but I got the impression he wanted more than one of us to hear his misgivings.

'Alright guys. Get your weapons and sign for them. Kinga, you're straight up to Kilo Eight. You're fucking late as it is so get moving mate.'

Kilo Eight was the call sign for a client's residence. All houses had call signs.

I couldn't understand how Liam was under such tremendous pressure at half past six in the morning. He got up from his chair and began to pace up and down the white tiled floor searching for another number on his mobile.

'And you as well Viktor. You're fucking late and all. The client is supposed to be picked up in five minutes!"

Viktor was one of the older guys on the team. He must have been in his mid to late forties. Polish by birth, he had been a career legionnaire for twenty years. Viktor looked every bit the man who had spent the best part of his life living out of a bag. Tall, lean and snaggle-toothed, with a deep brown tan that only years of living in hot, sunny climates can give, he came across as a dogged and gnarly individual.

Viktor muttered something in Polish as he cleared his pistol and pushed in a magazine before holstering the piece. With that he grabbed his day sack and headed straight out the door.

Me and Mick were last to take pistols out of the small arms case beside the sheriff's desk. They were Glocks and I was happy to take one as it had been the pistol I'd trained with on my Close Protection course in Denmark.

'I'll put you out on a couple of short missions this morning and give ye two English speaking drivers if I can,' said Liam.

I cleared my pistol into a nearby sand bucket just to make sure it didn't have a round in the chamber. I had not had enough time to buy a holster before we left Ireland so

I just slipped the pistol down the side of my trousers and tightened my belt to hold it in place, covering it with my shirt. Liam saw me doing this but he didn't seem to care. I took out my notepad and wrote down the mission details.

'Alright, Paddy,' he said. 'I need you to go to Bravo three, pick up Mr Yasseer and bring him here.'

'Bravo three?' I asked.

Liam looked somewhat pissed off that I didn't know the location.

'Did they not give you boys an orientation after you arrived yesterday?'

'No, Liam. Nothing like that mate,' said Mick.

'Prince!' yelled Liam as he looked towards the office door. 'Prince!'

A few seconds later a well-dressed Haitian came running in to the office.

'Show Paddy to his car and driver, Prince. He's headed for Yasseer house.'

Liam handed me a Motorola radio that was sitting in a charger. I clipped it onto my belt and headed out to the car park with Prince.

'Hi', he said as we hurriedly headed out into the daylight of the car park. 'Are you Irish?'

'Yep,' I answered. 'And my French is shit.'

He laughed and told me not to worry.

'I will give you Raymond in 657 (car number). He is a good guy and speaks very good English.'

Prince explained to Raymond where the mission was for. They spoke to each other in their native Creole. Dressed immaculately in a yellow checkered shirt and brown trousers, the short skinny driver looked at me with a sheepish smile as he listened to his supervisor.

I got into the Mitsubishi Montero and shook hands with my new driver. We then drove out the gates and turned right. We were headed for an area called Morne Calvaire. This was the mountainous region next to Montagne Noir. It was another area full of Haiti's wealthy elite. By now the morning's traffic was absolutely hectic. Dozens of bright, multi-colored taxis made up the vast majority of the traffic.

'Interesting taxis you have down here,' I said.

Raymond smiled.

'Yes, we call them tap-taps. Some tap-tap is like a bus. But many are old pickup trucks with a roof from a small boat.'

His voice was squeaky and he sounded almost distressed as he talked. He appeared to have a continuous smile across his gaunt face.

'Why do you call them tap-taps?' I asked.

'Oh yes,' he continued. 'We call them this because if you want to get off, you must tap a coin on the roof. Or if you want to get on, you tap on the window to see where he is going. Tap-taps, you see?'

I turned the air-con unit on as there was a strange odor in the car, like smelly socks or a stinking wet dog. The sudden rush of cold air through the interior began to dilute the smell almost instantly.

Morne Calvaire was very similar to Montagne Noir apart from the fact that her roads were not as steep. Both hills were adjacent to one another with some dead ground in between to separate them. Palm trees stretched out towards the street from behind high rise walls.

'They are very rich people who live here,' said Raymond.

'It certainly looks that way,' I replied.

'This is like Hollywood for this people,' he added. 'They have everything in the life.'

We waited outside Mr Yasseer's residence. I stepped out of the Montero to stretch my legs and take a look around. The house was not much to look at from out front but from the side I could see a beautiful garden with a swimming pool to the back. Its water was crystal blue, not frog pond green like the one back at the team house. A gardener was already busy weeding a flower bed while a housemaid walked out to hang clothes on a washing line. I heard the front door open. Out stepped Mr Yasseer. He was a large man of about thirty five. Far too heavy for his age and already quite bald, he looked much older. I said good morning and opened the car door for him. His breathing was noticeably heavy as he shuffled about on the seat attempting to make himself more comfortable. I signaled to Raymond to start the car and reverse her out onto the road so we could swing around and head back down the mountain. Given the short space of driveway and the road outside, it was a difficult maneuver but the smiley Haitian handled it with the minimum of fuss.

'Where are you from?' asked Yasseer as he texted on his cell phone.

Judging by his tone, it sounded like he had asked the same question of other bodyguards.

'Ireland,' I answered as I continued to view my arcs.

'There are a lot of you guys here. I'm from Lebanon.'

'Whereabouts?'

'The south,' he replied, still engrossed in his texting.

'But whereabouts?' I repeated. This time he took his view away from the phone and looked towards me.

'Do you know Lebanon?' he said. 'Do you know Ain Ebel?'

I smiled as I glanced back over my left shoulder.

'Indeed I do. I was stationed in South Lebanon back in 2001. Not long after the Israelis pulled out.'

Yasseer placed his phone into his shirt pocket. He was more interested now in sparking up a conversation than returning to his texting. For the remainder of the drive we spoke about other various towns and villages surrounding his home. Yasseer was happy to chat about this. I referred to other villages I had patrolled through as a young soldier. I couldn't recall all of the names, but he was able to identify each of them by my descriptions.

When we arrived at the Hexagon, I dismounted the car and opened Yasseer's door. Yasseer asked me my name and we shook hands. The conversation had been a good ice-breaker and gave me a chance to gauge what type of an individual he was. Raymond parked the car and I made my way up the steps of the Hexagon.

'Making friends already,' said Elmo. 'He's alright that fella. Bit of a strange fish, but alright. Did ya throw him the Lebanon card?'

'I did actually.'

Elmo laughed.

'What trip did you do?' I asked.

It turned out that Elmo and me had been on the same United Nations mission in 2001, only we were with different companies within the Battalion. He'd been based thirty miles away from me with the Battalion Mobile Reserve while I'd been posted out on the border to Israel.

Raymond came back over and handed me the keys.

'I better drop these into Liam,' I said to Elmo. I was still the new guy and I didn't want to piss off the sheriff by not telling him I was back.

'Grab me a coffee when you're in there, Paddy. Two sugars, no milk,' said Elmo as I walked through the front doors.

'Will do,' I answered.

When I walked into the sheriff's office, Liam was even busier than when I had left him. He was sitting at his desk scribbling onto a transport log sheet.

'I have another mission for you in about ten minutes, Paddy,' he said.

'No bother, Liam. I'm here,' I said as I poured out two cups of coffee and went back out to the main steps for a cigarette.

The front steps of the Hexagon seemed to be the local hang out for the security staff. Elmo looked very relaxed as he leaned into a corner and looked out into the yard. I could see why lads would rather lounge about outside than sit in an operations office the size of a dog shed.

I handed Elmo his coffee and lit myself a cigarette.

'Most of the missions are fairly run of the mill,' he explained. 'But don't be fooled by these mundane runs. It's a busy town down here. A fucking crazy town actually.'

Whether he knew it or not, he had my full attention.

'Oh yeah?' I said.

'Yes mate. Six weeks ago I was on a mission from the airport. I'd just dropped off a client and was on my way back. We usually return through the back streets in Delmas. We were only off the main road about five minutes when I drove up to a PNH (Police Nationale d'Haiti) checkpoint. Five cops. They stopped my vehicle and told me to hand over my pistol, then took me out onto the road. There was nobody around. The whole thing felt completely wrong.'

Elmo paused and took a slug of coffee. Though he was telling the story in a very cool manner, I could see that the events were still fresh in his mind.

'The senior officer told me to walk between two parked cars and get down on my knees with my hands behind my head. The next thing, all I could hear was my Beretta being cocked by the left side of my face. The senior cop then asked me what could I give him to get out of this situation. I asked him to let me take my mobile phone from my pocket. If he'd let me make one phone call I would sort him and his boys out with free mobiles and credit. He said okay and I called a contact of mine in the cops. An Inspector. A good guy. Within seconds this fucker had me back on my feet apologizing for the inconvenience.'

'Fucking hell, Elmo,' I said. 'You must have been shitting yourself.'

He gave a slight chuckle as he looked down at his coffee cup.

'When I heard the gun being cocked, I thought that was it. Just another dead statistic.'

'And did you get them? The mobiles I mean.'

'Nah, I tried but I couldn't get them. So now I just pray that I don't bump into any of those cops again. The main thing here is, Paddy, keep your eyes open buddy and never get too cocky about what you are doing down here. A simple situation can turn complicated very quickly.'

I stubbed out my cigarette and headed back inside to the office with Elmo.

'Make friends with a couple of cops when you get the chance,' he suggested. 'And learn some French if you can. It will make life easier for ya here.'

Liam already had the keys in hand when I walked into the office.

'Alright, Paddy,' he said. 'Take Raymond again and head for Bravo six. It's up in Morne Calvaire as well. Pick up Mr John and bring him down here.'

I scribbled the mission details in my notepad and took the car keys from Liam, then headed back out to the car park. Once Raymond started the engine, we headed back for Morne Calvaire. Home for many of the Digicel clients.

Chapter Six

CARREFOUR

SATURDAY, 9TH DECEMBER, 2006

TEAM HOUSE 3, PORT AU PRINCE

The sun was rising from behind the distant mountains to the east. A UN Huey helicopter buzzed lazily above the awakening city. The white chopper made a sluggish sound in the blue sky. The whomp, whomp, whomp of her blades created muffled and mechanical echoes against the jagged contours of Montagne Noir.

From where I stood in the front garden of the team house, I had a complete bird's eye view of Port au Prince. Thousands of sprawled out buildings down below looked like specks of light grey concrete. Our team house offered a welcome retreat from the claustrophobic streets of the overpopulated sweat box that was Port au Prince.

'Those things will kill you kurwa,' said a voice behind me as I stubbed out my cigarette.

It was Cerek. He was a Polish guy about the same age as me. I had only spoken to him a handful of times over the few days I'd been in country. The stocky, energetic Polak had been a medic during his time with the French Foreign Legion. He knew the causes and cures of almost every tropical disease from malaria to dysentery and could treat anything from headaches and stomach cramps to back pains and diarrhea. He was nothing short of a walking medical dictionary.

'Kurwa, you have another for me?' he said grinning broadly.

I handed him a smoke to have with his coffee. Cerek quickly lit the cigarette and took the first plume of smoke into his lungs with one deep breath.

'Breakfast,' he said, releasing the smoke into the cool morning air. 'So what you think this place kurwa?'

'Yeah, it's okay,' I answered. 'I'm happy to be here mate.'

Cerek looked at me with his piercing, yet friendly stare. 'This place is very far from home for people like you and me kurwa. When I go to my home, I can never explain this kurwa country to my family. But for me, I like it here.'

Practically every word that came out of the ex-medic's mouth was 'kurwa', which is the Polish word for 'fucker'. But for Cerek, this was a term of endearment and affection as much as it was used to criticize and scold. Everyone and everything to him was 'kurwa'. The more I would get to know him, the easier it would become to distinguish what context the word was being used in.

'Don't worry kurwa,' he said. 'We will take care of you here. We take care of everybody. Our job is to keep the client happy inside the kurwa 'blan bubble.'

Slightly bewildered, I smiled with my head bowed and said nothing. I didn't know it at the time, but what Cerek meant by the 'blan bubble' was the world that nearly all ex-pats in Port au Prince lived in. Blan was the Haitian word that referred to white people. It was used more in reference to one's social status than actual skin color. Most white people were seen by many Haitians as extremely privileged. Whether one was actually wealthy didn't matter. You had a foreign passport to come and go as you pleased. From the long line of UN and NGO cars parked outside top class restaurants in Petion Ville every Friday and Saturday night to the array of Nissan Patrols (many UN and NGO) coming and going from the Petion Ville Club (the PVC club) on a Wednesday evening. This was the world that so many ex-pats lived in. Right or wrong, it was detached from the reality of the country and I was part of that culture whether I liked it or not.

The boisterous Polak had done two tours in Haiti already and was now almost halfway through his third. He seemed like the kind of guy who thrived in such environments. It was as though he was more at home in Haiti than he could ever have been in Poland. His magnanimity charmed me almost straight away.

Iván, Mick and some of the morning crew were coming down the steps to one of the parked Nissans in front of the house. Saturdays meant fewer missions and a later start so Iván left a handful of the team in the house on standby. Most of our missions that day were to take the client's wives and kids to the markets. Elmo was flying home the following morning so he got to enjoy his last full day in the Caribbean by soaking up the early morning rays.

If there could be anything worse than going shopping with your wife or girlfriend, it would be having to go shopping with somebody else's wife or girlfriend. All that waiting around and with none of the fringe benefits. Most of the team hoped to finish work later that morning.

There was a new sheriff in the office when we arrived. His name was Joseph but everybody called him 'the Captain'.

'Good morning guys,' he said as we entered the office. Joseph was in his early forties and had been an officer in the Slovak army. He had a neatly trimmed haircut and looked young for his age.

'Please all. Take a pistol and radio and wait for your mission.'

This time I was first in the door and first to sign out a pistol. There was an assortment of various makes but once again, I signed out a Glock without thinking twice.

'Good morning,' said Joseph as he organized some papers on his desk.

I placed my hand out in front of me to introduce myself. He shook it but immediately returned to the paperwork on his desk.

'Okay guys,' he said. 'I am very fucking busy this morning. You know what I mean?'

Nobody acknowledged him.

'Fucking shit,' said Viktor as he cleared and loaded his pistol. 'Hey Irish. Do you smoke?'

I nodded yes and went outside to the front steps of the Hexagon.

'This fucking Captain. He is always the fucking same way this guy,' he said, lighting his smoke.

Viktor drew a long, slow drag before pulling the cigarette from his lips and looking at it with a brooding appreciation.

'You know I smoke this shit for too many years now. I'm going home in four days. This will be my last packet in this place.'

We spoke for a while on the steps of the Hexagon. I saluted a couple of the local drivers that I had worked with during my first few days. Some of them acknowledged me with a smile or a simple wave. The language barrier was still there with most, even though I was making best efforts with my poor high school French.

'How many languages do you speak Viktor?' I asked, changing the subject. I had noticed him the day before with an Arabic dictionary.

Each day, Viktor would sit quietly in the sheriff's office waiting for his next mission. While all the younger guys were chit-chatting about cars, sex, weapons and wars, Viktor would simply read his book, giving the impression that he was miles away in thought. But if something was said that grabbed his attention, from out of nowhere he would add his ten cents worth, which was usually a discerningly cynical comment. He was a grumpy motherfucker and I liked him.

'I speak Polish, English, French, some Spanish and I am learning a little Arabic.'

'Where did you learn English?' I asked. 'The Legion?'

'Hmm, no. Australia.'

He went on to tell me about how he had stowed away on a ship as a young man in search of a more prosperous future.

'Me and one other guy planned this for one year. We brought along some chocolate bars for food and some water and managed to board a ship bound for Australia. But we ran out of food after a week or so and had to come out of hiding to find some more. The motherfuckers found us when they came to port in South America. They sent us home.'

'So if they caught you and sent you home,' I said. 'How did you get to Australia?'

Viktor took a few more drags. I wasn't sure if he was smiling as he pressed his lips around the butt.

'Simple,' he said. 'We just brought more fucking chocolate bars the second time. Within that same year we made it to Sydney and I stayed for eight years. I even became a citizen.'

Many of the legionnaires like Viktor had incredible stories about life and adventure. In comparison, though I had travelled alone and with the army, I couldn't help but feel my life had been sheltered compared to these men. Listening to their stories, I yearned to be tested by my own choices and my own actions. Not by university exams or physical feats. Green and foolhardy, I prayed that Haiti would be *that* place where I would find myself being tried and tested. The time was coming on seven thirty when the Captain finally prepped me for a mission.

'Okay, Paddy. Have you been to Carrefour yet?'

I had no clue what or where the hell he was talking about.

'No, Captain. I only got in on Wednesday.'

He turned his attention towards a large map of the city hanging on the wall behind him.

'Okay so, we are here. This is the downtown area and this area here to the south is Carrefour. It's a pretty fucked up place. It is very poor area and with high crime rate. Extremely volatile region actually. But not so bad like Militaire or Soleil. Better to take some vests with you,' he advised, pointing to a batch of bullet proof jackets in the corner.

Hearing this, one of the guys sniggered.

'What's the mission?' I asked, notebook in hand.

'You will take two technicians, one is local and one is ex-pat, to our telecoms site in Carrefour. The switch is down and needs repairs. You need to stay with the technicians throughout the mission until they are finished.'

'Any idea how long it will take?'

'It will take as long as it will take. Probably three to four hours.'

The Captain reached under his desk and pulled out a medium sized, bright orange medical bag.

'Take the medic pack with you also,' he said. 'You might need it. If you experience a security situation down there just call me.'

This time somebody else sniggered.

Luckily Iván had issued me, Mick and the other new guys with cell phones the day before. We carried Motorolas but their range was limited to a couple of miles. 'Just call,' I thought. I knew that if anything happened in Carrefour I was miles from home, and from help.

Once I was in the car park, I checked my vehicle for fuel, oil and a jack. The car was armor but of the lowest level. When my driver, Reginald, saw me throw a bullet proof vest on my seat, he became nervous.

'I take one also, Mr Paddy,' he said.

'Why, Reginald?' I asked. 'Is Carrefour a bad place?'

'It is not so bad place but it not so good place.'

I told Reginald to run inside and grab a vest as quick as he could. The clients would be here shortly. By the time he reappeared, the two technicians had arrived. They were deep in conversation about the problem with the telecoms site and sounded like they were arguing over what work needed to be done with it. One man was Haitian and the other Indian. Both were well dressed. Probably too well dressed for the area we were headed to.

'Good morning gentlemen,' I said.

They ceased chatting and looked at me puzzled by my interruption.

'My name is Patrick. I will be your security escort to Carrefour this morning.'

'You are new,' stated the Indian man. Wearing a checked shirt with dark slacks and a protruding pot belly, he looked a jolly, easy going type of guy. The other technician was much skinnier and wore similar clothing.

'Do you know the location of the site?' I asked.

'Yes we know,' smiled the Indian.

He looked happy and eager to be getting out of the office environment for the morning.

They loaded their technical kit in the rear of the car and without any further ado, Reginald started the engine of our lame looking armored Isuzu Trooper.

The Saturday morning traffic moved steadily as we descended from the relative safety of Petion Ville and continued towards Delmas.

Delmas was an area on the suburbs of the city that linked Petion Ville to the downtown district via a road called 'AutoRoute de Delmas'. It was this roadway which interlinked many of the regions from uptown Petion Ville to the downtown areas. Though too underdeveloped to be called a highway, its purpose was exactly that.

For the first time since my arrival I was getting up close and personal to the heart of the city. Never had I seen so many market places strewn with such a variety of goods and produce. There were hundreds of Haitians buying and selling on every available corner. Toothbrushes, soaps, cups, plates, mangoes, bananas, vegetables, flip flops, nuts, car phone chargers, fish, sweets, chewing gum, meat and rice. In fact, space was so limited that many of the vendors had to set up shop just below the curb of the sidewalks, spilling their wares onto roads already crammed with fume ridden clap-trap cars and commandeering tap-taps. It looked chaotic and wonderful at the same time.

A good forty minutes had passed by the time the markets gave way to barren, unpopulated roads. Fewer people moved about their Saturday morning business. We were nearing the Carrefour area.

This satellite zone was made up of more basic concrete housing, consisting of old, wooden French colonial homes. Many of these elegant constructions looked weathered and weak, their fragile wooden pillars and broken window shutters showing signs of ageing under sundried cracked coats of paint, evidence that they had long since outlived their colonial heyday. An irrigation system ran adjacent to the road we were travelling on. What should have been a system of free flowing water in a concrete reservoir was in fact a stagnant river of indolent shit that ran sluggishly through hefty mountains of garbage. Enhanced by the mid-morning sun, a smell of absolute filth began to filter in through the air-con system. Reginald tried to steer the car with one hand as he used the other to block his nose. It was impossible to ignore the stench. I fumbled with the off switch to the air conditioning unit. A cloud of dust rose behind the wheels of the car as we entered the dried dirt roads of Carrefour. I began to feel an uneasy sense of seclusion. This was the furthest I had been away from the Hexagon since I'd arrived in the country.

'Do you know where the site is exactly?' I asked the Indian technician.

I was not interested in any bullshit at this point, only solid facts.

'Yes, yes, I know,' he assured me once again smiling. 'We need to turn off and take a left just up ahead.'

I had little confidence in his words and decided that now was as good a time as any to put on my vest.

The left turn took us off of the dusty battered main Carrefour road and down into the maze of tiny streets with houses on either side.

These were very basic buildings. Probably no more than two rooms in each. Yet altogether, they were home to thousands of Haitian families. The dainty looking armored car twisted and turned her way further along the narrow winding alley ways. Turning left, turning right and turning left again, we soon lost sight of the main road.

We drove past children playing outside their homes and women walking slowly, heavily laden down by food baskets and water buckets on their heads. The men had a more leisurely morning. Most of them stood outside their homes talking to other neighbors on the street. They watched on as our wine Isuzu Trooper trundled past. Everybody was curious as to our presence. We stood out like a sore thumb. Our vehicle was too big for the narrow roads. There was no more than half a meter of space available either side of the car. People had to press their bodies against walls so as not to hit them with the wing mirrors. We were definitely screwing up a neighborhood's morning routine.

After about three minutes of driving over rocky earth and mounds of dirt, I could see the signs of stress on Reginald's face. He was not a happy driver. His worry mounted as we interrupted ten grown men playing a game of football in the middle of the road. They had no choice but to stop playing and let us through. They were lean, muscular looking fellas. As they stared straight in through our protected glass, I could see the discontent in their faces. Also, to say nothing of the fact that I was the only white asshole sitting in the car, awkwardly staring back out. I hoped that by my wearing shades, they would not pick up on the apprehension and anxiety in my eyes.

The entire scenario felt wrong. This car and I did not belong here. We were displaying wealth, arrogance and incompetence in an impoverished neighborhood. I grinded my teeth out of sheer frustration. Once we were out of their way, the men continued with their game.

The two technicians looked out towards the rooftops from the rear windows of the Isuzu. They muttered something amongst themselves while their beady eyes strained to identify where we might be. We rounded another narrow corner. I felt the blood rush from my head, giving me a sickly feeling in my stomach. The road we had rounded onto was blocked off by a column of large boulders. They looked as if they had been put there by locals and looked completely out of place. We had spent ten minutes driving further and further down into a maze of poverty and we still weren't where we were supposed to be.

Reginald looked at me gravely. 'We cannot go forward, Mr Paddy.'

I stared at the boulders and glanced left and right at the severe shortage of turning space.

'Yes, Reginald,' I said. 'Thank you for that information.'

'This is not the way,' stated the Haitian technician. 'Let me ask this person.'

Before I could say or do anything, the stupid son of a bitch had opened his car door to ask a passer-by where the telecoms site was located. I was fuming but given how badly things were going I had little choice but to allow it.

When the local man had told him, he closed the door. At that point I removed my glasses and turned around in my seat.

'Gentlemen, you told me twice already that you know where the switch is located. You both clearly have no bloody clue.'

They looked at me like two school boys standing in front of a headmaster.

'If you ever open a car door without my permission again, you can bloody walk home. I am responsible for the safety of my clients, my driver and this vehicle. Don't ever pull that stunt again.'

'Okay,' the Haitian man acknowledged. 'But I know where we are going now.'

'Yeah,' I said. 'You know now because that man told you. But can you tell me how my driver is supposed to turn this bloody car around in the mean time?'

No answer. They both sat there quietly. I had upset their Saturday morning outing. Part of me was sorry for speaking so abruptly to them. But the fear of not being in control of the situation was enough for me to stick to my guns.

For what seemed like an eternity, we backed the vehicle up the narrow lane to make our way back to the initial left turn off. Eventually we were back to interrupt the soccer game once again. The young men now appeared extremely vexed as Reginald reversed the vehicle through their make shift court. I couldn't blame them. We looked ridiculous. Like a bunch of idiots pretending not to be in a difficult situation. Beads of sweat formed on Reginald's brow as he reversed the Isuzu all the way out through the maze. For a man under tremendous pressure, he performed amazingly. Not a scratch to the car. I was glad he was my driver.

Once the vehicle was facing the right direction, Reginald made no bones about dropping her into second and getting out of the immediate area as quickly as he could.

Five minutes later we arrived at the telecoms site. It was only then that I realized we had driven in the wrong direction. The switch was located on the roof of a three story building on the other side of Carrefour. Reginald parked up outside the building. I scanned the street as the technicians grabbed their equipment from the rear of the car. A few curious children gathered a few meters away watching us as we made our way inside.

From the roof of the building, I could see for miles around. The area we had been lost in looked even more confusing from up top. I was relieved to be out of there. But we were still miles from home base.

By now the sun was beating down hard as the tech guys set up lap tops and assortments of wires and clips. I had no sunblock in my grab bag so I put on my baseball cap to protect my shaven head from the rays.

As they worked on the switch problem, a small crowd of men gathered below us to the east. I was almost sure that some of them had been the soccer guys from earlier. They stared directly up at us. I suppose by now the entire neighborhood was aware of our presence. Though the men posed no immediate threat, I still felt on edge. The sooner these guys finished their work, the better.

After three long hours on the roof, they began to pack up their kit. I was drenched in sweat from the bullet proof vest, but happy that their work was finally done.

From our three story structure I had been able to see what road we needed to take to get back out safely onto the main dirt road. Soon, we were loaded up and on our way back to Petion Ville.

The small crowd of shady looking men had a menacing air about them. We drove past them and once again they stared in at us with malice.

I could see the relief on Reginald's face as we left Carrefour and put the car back on solid tarmac.

'Happy to go back to the Hexagon, Reginald?' I asked.
He looked at me with a big smile.
'Yes, Mr Paddy. I am very happy.'

Chapter Seven

CONTACT! CONTACT! WAIT OUT!

MONDAY, 26TH FEBRUARY, 2007

HEXAGON, PORT AU PRINCE

I had learned that the best missions to take were the long ones: the jobs that took you far outside the smothering, traffic ridden confines of Port au Prince and out into the lush, green countryside of the central plateau. Those missions appealed to me more than the mundane morning pickups and midday restaurant runs.

Having had my morning smoke with a cup of coffee out on the steps of the Hexagon, I headed inside to the sheriff's office, grabbed my keys and ran my first mission of the day. The usual pick up of the usual clients. Liam smiled at me when I got back.

'The very man,' he said. 'How would you like to go on a long one?'

'Jesus Liam,' I said, throwing my plastic cup in the bin. 'I didn't know you felt that way.'

'C'mere you funny fucker,' he answered. 'Ben Smyth needs to head out to Cange today. They're looking at a potential site out there for a switch. Seeing as how you're always looking for long missions, you can go with him.'

There was really no better way to kill a Monday than an all day mission out in the boonies. I was more than happy to take it.

Preparing the car was second nature at this stage. I just about knew each one simply by somebody calling out the registration number alone. Today I was taking 0705, one of the older Nissans Patrols. She had more wear on her than most. A few dents and scratches here and there, but the old white 'soft skin' had never given me trouble. Ralph, my driver was a pretty solid individual too. He was one of the originals, the first batch of drivers hired by security in 2005. Though he was overweight, he always came to work looking well, which must have been difficult for him as he lived in very basic housing. Some homes in Port au Prince comprised a room and a wash basin. Ralph came across as a bit of a joker, always laughing and with a good sense of humor. I saw him as one of the better ones on the team.

I had a half hour to kill before Ben Smyth, the site acquisition officer for Digicel, would be ready to go. Cange was an eighty kilometer drive to the north-east of Port au Prince. Given the road conditions, that meant at least a two hour drive there. Ralph and I checked everything from fuel gauge to oil level and spare tire to tire pressure. Medic bag and breakdown kit were in place. A quick run to the supermarket for snacks along the way, one last morning coffee with a smoke, a fast piss, some minty chewing gum in the gob, open the car door for the arriving client and away we went.

I always enjoyed the drive out of Port au Prince. I liked the countryside and the people. Their temperament differed from city folk. They were always curious to see what the 'blan' was up to when we drove into a town or village. Normally the children were the first to arrive, then the elders, all with smiling, curious faces.

Once the car was clear of the city, we found ourselves in a lunar landscape. The remote, dusty mountains of

Morne á Cabrit stretched far out in front. The sandy white dust kicked up around the Nissan as Ralph kept his eyes on the road for potholes, rocks and other debris. Ben Smyth multi tasked in the back seat. He checked emails on his Blackberry and explained what the general schedule was for the day. Ben was from Wales originally and had been working in Haiti since 2005. He was of medium height and had a full head of jet black hair. I'd often made small talk with him on the Hexagon steps or when dropping him home to Canape Vert. This was my first long mission with him since I'd arrived. He was always quite specific in what he needed to do and that always saved a lot of time wasting for us security boys. Ben was a nice guy.

'Once we get to Cange, we will meet up with a couple of local officials to review the proposed site,' he said in his soft tone.

I looked at Ralph. His entire attention was concentrated on the road ahead. He leaned his upper body towards the steering wheel. This made him look like somebody who was still learning to drive. I knew he was deep in concentration. Ralph's vision was occasionally blinded by oncoming buses when their wheels threw dirt and dust into the air. They were old American school buses painted with a multitude of colors. Their tyres weighed down the road, laden by far too many people on board. They even had folks sitting on the roof and holding on for dear life as the aged passenger carrier ploughed towards the capital. Ralph slowed down until the dust passed and he had a clear line of sight of the road once again. But he never relaxed his posture or focus.

Not long after, we broke onto tarmac and began to climb up the winding tracks of Morne á Cabrit. As I looked out of my window, I could see Port au Prince stretched far off in the distance. I could even make out Petion Ville with Montagne Noir and Morne Calvaire extending upwards to meet the blue morning sky. Cange was at least another hour and a half away. Ralph relaxed into the drive once we hit the quieter roads leading into the central plateau. Ben was still busy on his smart phone and organizing some paperwork. I just sat back and enjoyed the drive.

We arrived in Cange by eleven o'clock. The sun was high above us and I could feel the rays beating down on my body as soon as I stepped out of the vehicle. I sprayed on a little sun cream before offering the bottle to Ben. I had long since wised up to all the necessary kit I needed to carry. And factor thirty was one of them.

It was a small village in the center of a valley. It had about twenty homes, a local police station and a market place. Everything here was pretty basic. The houses were made of brick and concrete. Some of them had small porches directly outside the front door and corrugated tin for roofing. Like those Hollywood films about Iraq and Afghanistan filmed in Morocco or Jordan, they could equally have shot a movie about Eritrea or Ethiopia right here and no viewer would be any the wiser.

A few houses down, I noticed two men and some boys chopping a fallen tree. We were all stifled by the dead heat of the late morning and yet these men relentlessly continued chopping and sawing up timber. All I could do was wipe the sweat from my dripping brow and admire their resilience.

We walked across the street to one of the market stalls. The young man working there was selling ice cold bottles of Coca-Cola at less than seventy cents a pop. A more than fair price to quench everybody's thirst. The teller was about twenty years old and had a cheeky grin about him. He was skinny and wore a bright red Digicel t-shit. There was also a large Digicel umbrella covering the stall, so we took some shelter from the sun underneath it and waited for Ben's people to arrive. Across the street, two policemen were watching television with the door and windows to the station left open. One officer sat back into his chair while fanning himself with a piece of cardboard. The other was leaning by the doorway looking back into the room at the television.

Not long after we finished our drinks, the local town representatives showed up. They were accompanied by a Haitian civil engineer that Ben had also arranged to meet. Part of the deal for acquiring the sight was that Digicel would build a road linking up another, smaller village on the far side of the south facing hill to the main road leading into Port au Prince. Tap-taps and cars would eventually be able to pass through that area saving the local villagers a daily commute of about three miles, while also providing a far more reliable phone signal in the area. Digicel had been in operation just two years in Haiti. They were still popping masts up around the island every month. The Irish owned telecoms company, with its distinctive red and white logo was steadily outperforming any competitors sharing the same turf. Earlier that month, I had visited Digicel projects in neighboring towns and villages with clients. The CEO, Denis O' Brien (most of the security guys referred to him as DOB), was sponsoring the development and construction of local schools and health clinics throughout the entire region. Digicel was proving to be more than just a telecoms company. It was winning the hearts and minds of the Haitian people. Though I had never met DOB, it was hard to ignore his efforts of long term investment in the country and the people. Most of the bodyguards spoke highly of him also. Elmo had told me a story of how he had once been part of a convoy that drove Denis O'Brien down into one of the slum areas of the city. They were visiting a proposed site where a school was to be built by Digicel funding. The problem was that the area needed both an elementary school and a high school and, according to Elmo, the project leaders couldn't make up their minds on which one to construct. When O'Brien and his entourage stepped out of the cars to view the proposed site, the Irishman took one look around and said, 'Fuck it. Build the two.' I don't know if it happened exactly like that, but that story had earned the businessman a lot of respect within the security ranks. Particularly with the Irish boys.

We drove off-road behind the other car before finally having to trek by foot to the suggested area. Ralph remained behind with the two cars as we walked on down through another valley and eventually made it to the correct place.

Already, local and senior villagers had gathered. They had seen our small group cross over the hills to get there. Haitians were definitely proving to be some of the most curious people I had ever come across. As Ben spoke to the village elders with the representatives, I was approached by an aged farmer who offered me a drink from a plastic soda bottle. Inside the bottle was some kind of local plant that had been fermenting into a sickly green colored concoction. His wrinkled, wiry fingers screwed the cap off. He then held the bottle out and gave it a little shake, gesturing for me to try some.

'Non merci,' I answered.

The man began to laugh. The clever old sod probably knew I would say no. Some of the onlookers found my rebuttal funny too. Inside that bottle looked to be the seeping remnants of a decomposing green plant mixed with broken twigs. I offered him a cigarette to go with his 'exotic cocktail'.

'Merci, merci,' he said as I lit the smoke for him.

The old man offered me a swig of his home brew one last time. I smiled and declined the offer once again. Then we shook hands before he walked back to the giggling bystanders.

It was almost four o'clock by the time Ben had completed his report. The late afternoon was still bright and hot as Ralph drove us out of Cange and on towards Port au Prince. The day had been very relaxed and enjoyable. This was probably going to be my last long mission before I went home in a couple of weeks. All in all, I must have been out on twelve other similar long missions since being in Haiti. If this was to be my last before going home, then I wasn't doing too bad.

The drive back was slower than I had anticipated. The plan had been to make it back to Petion Ville before sun down. By half past five, that idea was unfeasible. As we started to descend the rocky dirt roads of Morne á Cabrit, twilight had already set in. Thousands of lights flickered far below in a city that was home to more than two million people. I felt anxious about the fact that we were still so far away and had so many miles to cover in the darkness.

The city limits was rife with evening traffic upon entering. We moved slowly as there was no way of passing the long line of cars in front. I decided that the best way to get back up to Petion Ville was to go around the city rather than through it. Usually the fastest way back was up through Delmas, but that could take hours from where we were. The best of a bad lot was to take a left turn for Tabaire, pass by the newly built American Embassy and up onto Rue des Frères, which in turn would bring us into Petion Ville. I didn't exactly fancy the idea. Our intelligence reports had told us that Rue des Frères was notorious for kidnappings and crime. But to be fair, the same could be said of almost any area of the city. At that late hour of the evening, I thought it was the quickest and smartest way to go. Darkness would be our ally.

When we finally reached Rue des Frères, I immediately regretted my decision. Traffic here was so slow that the Nissan could only move about twenty meters every five minutes. It was beyond frustrating but all the road rage in the world would not help us here. We just had to sit, wait and ride it out.

By half past six we had made very little progress. I racked my brains trying to come up with an alternate route. And that's when I heard the first shot.

'What the fuck?' I muttered.

More shots rang out up ahead. Sharp, loud cracks that only live ammunition can make. At first I thought that there was a logical explanation for it. But that thought lasted all of two seconds. I looked at Ralph. With his two hands clasped to the wheel he stared wide eyed straight back at me. Ben dropped down as low as he could on the floor behind my seat. I could hear him swearing under his breath. Instinctively, I wanted to get as low as I could in my seat as well, but I needed to see what the hell was going on. From what I could see of the road ahead, people were running downhill screaming and panicking. Drivers and passengers abandoned their cars to join those running for their lives.

A volley of shots and tracer rounds zipped past overhead. It sounded much closer than the first batch. I kept as low as the car would let me, which didn't feel low enough. My eyes were drawn to the red tracer fire flying overhead. More and more people were running down Rue des Frères. The cracks of gunfire were getting louder every few seconds. I could make out at least three different sounds of gunfire. Whoever was shooting was getting much closer. A fire fight had broken out and we were in the middle of it. With no possible way to back up, I knew it was time to abandon the car.

'Ben! Can you hear me?' I shouted as I opened the lock on my door and on his.

'Yes! Yes!' he yelled.

'On three I want you to open your door, keep low and get out of the car. You have that?'

'Yes!'

My heart was beating like a racehorse. I held my firearm at the ready. I had already cocked it without even realizing. Conscious that it was a Glock 40 and the safety was built in to the trigger mechanism, I kept my trigger finger running down the side of the weapon. There were still a lot of people running down the road and I was soberly aware of not wanting to shoot an innocent person.

'Okay, One! Two! Three! Go! Go! Go!'

I quickly opened my door and stepped onto the street while trying to keep low and keep aware of my surroundings. Ben was slow in stepping out, all too slow. I rounded his open passenger door as fast as I could, grabbing him by his shirt and pulling him into the nearest alleyway I could find. There was no sign of Ralph, but I had every confidence in his survival abilities.

Semi-automatic weapons were still firing out on the street. So too were pistols.

The alley I had run us into was extremely narrow. About thirty people were seeking refuge there already. I knew that the tracer fire probably came from UN weapons, but what I wasn't sure of was who was firing those weapons. If one of the shooters came upon the alley, there was nothing to stop him from mowing down half the people hiding down there.

The gunfire decreased, giving way to a lot of shouting and general confusion.

'We can't stay here,' I said to Ben. 'It's not safe.'

He nodded, trying to catch his breath.

'Come this way,' a voice said from up above us. I looked up to see a young Haitian man peering down from the second floor of the building to my right. The whiteness of his protruding eyes was like a guiding light. The house smelled of fresh cement and was probably still under construction. Above my head was a small wooden beam. We would need to grab a hold of it and haul ourselves up if we were to join the young man on higher ground. And higher ground was definitely what we needed.

'Okay, Ben, you go first mate,' I said.

The Welshman was in his early thirties and a strong individual compared with many of his colleagues. I pushed his feet up from below and he managed to haul himself up with relative ease while the Haitian chap helped him the rest of the way. In all my concentration of helping him, I hadn't noticed that I'd placed my foot into a plastic water bucket which was right next to me. My boot was soaked instantly but it was too dark to see exactly what liquid it was that I'd stepped into. Now it was my turn to move. I was never a great candidate for upper body strength, but at that moment it did not matter. The mere rush of adrenaline and fear was enough for me to haul my ass off of the ground. Ben and the Haitian boy helped me get my leg over the side and onto the beam. We were only one story above the mayhem and confusion directly out on the street in front. One story high was still better than staying out on the main road.

I moved Ben into the center of the room, careful not to step or fall on the various lengths of rebar spearing up from the floor below. The shooting had all but stopped by now. The young man who had helped us stood peering out of a large window space facing out onto the street. Voices could be heard yelling up and down the road. I was still confused as to what exactly was going on out there so I made my way to the window for a better view. When I got there, I crouched down and looked out. I could make out about thirty men. They looked to be soldiers, armed with rifles. I was fairly certain they were UN, but I had no idea of their nationality.

Also, there were four other people taking refuge with us on that darkened second floor. Two of them were texting while another was making a call. The problem was that the light from their cell phones was illuminating our position and I still had to clarify what the hell was going on down there among the abandoned vehicles and swarms of armed soldiers. Also there was the fact that Ben and I were two blans, alone in a very remote part of town. Any assistance from the security QRF (Quick Reaction Force) was at least a half hour away. There had been kidnappings in the surrounding neighborhoods and I was not about to walk out on to a dimly lit street to wander home.

'Keep down my friend,' I whispered. 'Thank you so much for helping us. What is your name?'

'Claude,' he answered. 'My name is Claude.'

'Okay, Claude. My name is Patrick. Really, thank you for helping us. But what I need you to do now is tell these people to switch off their phones. I need to keep watching what's going on outside from this window space here. But I cannot do that safely if we are lighting up this floor. Can you do that for me, Claude?'

Claude looked fearful, yet excited. His breathing was heavy and he was sweating in the warm climate of the evening.

'Yes, Patrick. Okay.'

He turned to the others and instructed them in Creole to switch their mobiles off. Everybody was still nervous. The voices on the street were increasing now. I had to contact the sheriff's office for an armored vehicle as soon as possible and I still had no clue as to where Ralph had taken off to.

From where I was observing, I could identify the outline of the soldiers. They were all wearing camouflaged uniforms, possibly desert type. Armed with long barreled rifles and wearing blue helmets, they moved between parked vehicles blocking the road and then onto the sidewalks both left and right. More of them were further up Rue des Frères, searching between buildings and alleyways. They were searching for somebody or somebodies. I could distinctly hear them speaking in Arabic, and that's when I became a little more nervous.

One of my biggest concerns in Haiti was the use of so many conscript soldiers from poorer armies. The word on the street that December was that a MINUSTAH taskforce had been sent into Cité Soleil to weed out hard core Haitian criminal gang elements. Apparently, the operation had not gone entirely to plan and had resulted in the killing of twenty nine residents and left thirty three people injured. If these figures were true, then it was nothing short of a proverbial 'clusterfuck'.

Having said that, the UN did have some very demanding tasks in which some of their finest troops were deployed. The MINUSTAH mandate had clearly upped the ante on their hard arrest strategy of gang members since I'd arrived. February had been a busy month, with one mission seeing several hundred UN troops storming Cité Soleil and resulting in a major gun battle. Cerek had told me that he had sat back on the roof of the Aciérie switch, just behind Cité Soleil and enjoyed the fireworks on that particular evening of operations. Even though I had a lot of respect for the UN, I had zero confidence in facing the barrel of a gun belonging to any conscript soldier. As far as I was concerned, the only soldiers worth deploying on Port au Prince's gangland frontline were the Brazilians. Well trained, well-disciplined and with years of experience in Brazil's Favelas (ghettos), these were the boys for the job.

Out in front of my street was a platoon of Jordanian UN soldiers shouting at one another while trying to cordon off the immediate area with the assistance of the Haitian National Police. Slowly moving down the street, they were beginning a house to house search. From my subtle vantage point, it all seemed extremely unorganized. I worried about what might happen if they were to find me and Ben. Plus the fact that I was armed would not help the situation. Nervous trigger fingers clearing a blackened out house. Suddenly you see a man with a gun. Black or white, it's a bad combination.

I quietly beckoned Ben to keep close to me then pulled out my phone to call the sheriff's office. Covering the light with my hand, I waited for the receiving end to pick up.

'Good evening sheriff's office,' said Mick answering the phone.

I spoke as loudly as I could allow myself.

'Mick it's Paddy. Can you hear me?'

Mick could barely make out what I was saying with the loud jovial chatter of bodyguards behind him.

'Hello? Hello?' he said. 'Can you speak up please?'

'Mick, it's me, Paddy, real message, real message. Contact, mate. I've been caught in a contact.'

This time he heard me.

'Shut the fuck up! Hey, hey, shut up will ye.'

The office fell silent. I could imagine the lads looking at Mick and wondering what the hell was his problem.

'Alright, Paddy. Go ahead. What's the situation?'

'I'm with Ben Smyth down on Rue des Frères. There's been a small fire fight on the street involving the UN and PNH. I'm in a building. Not sure exactly where. I think it's about three hundred meters down from the main gas station on Rue Des Frères. I think it's the Tiger gas station. I've abandoned the car. It's outside but there's no sign of my driver. Suggest you send armor down here to pick us up, Mick. Do you have that?'

I could imagine Mick scribbling all of it down on a piece of paper, phone in one hand and pen in the other while the clueless faces of clients looked in at him from outside the hatch.

'Yeah, Paddy, I've got that. Can you give me a more precise description of where you are?'

I paused for a few seconds trying to picture the area as I would have seen it by day. The problem was that it all looked the fucking same. All I had to go on was the vague memory of a Tiger gas station somewhere further up the street. I could only hope that I was right in what I had told Mick.

'That's all I have, Mick. We're in a building that's still under construction on your left hand side as you make you way down Rue des Frères. We're laid up on the second floor. Just tell whoever it is coming down to ring me as soon as he is on his way.'

'Alright, lad,' he answered. 'Iván is on the way now. He'll call you in a few minutes. Keep your phone handy.'

'Cheers, Mick,' I said. 'Oh, and tell management that Smyth is fine. We are both okay. But it looks like the UN is doing house to house so tell Iván to get a move on.'

By now the Jordanian soldiers were no more than fifteen meters from our doorway. Two by two, they searched buildings and alleyways.

'Is the front door to this locked, Claude?' I asked.

'Eh, I don't know, Patrick. I don't live here.'

Fuck! It was too late.

'Everybody lie down and be quiet,' I whispered. 'The soldiers are coming. Just lie down and be quiet.'

I dropped to the floor, took the magazine from my pistol and emptied the round already in the chamber. Then I left the action to the rear and took my weapon license and I.D. from my pocket.

'Ben, mate. Take out your Digicel I.D card and hold it outwards in your hand. If these guys come in and search us, we need to identify ourselves when they approach us.'

Ben did so and we waited. I could hear the soldiers' boots tapping on the pavement outside. It sounded like they were walking past us. Very carefully, I peered back out of the open window. They had walked by and were now clearing traffic to move on up the street. People were beginning to get back into their cars. As quickly as the street had turned into a makeshift turkey shoot, everything was now returning to normal.

I placed the magazine back in my Glock and let the action spring forward allowing a round back into the chamber. My training had never taught me to do such a thing as to disarm myself in a potentially hostile situation, but the situation as I saw it, was unique in that the immediate threat had become jittery peacekeepers and not hardened criminal gang members.

I pulled my cell phone from my pocket and called Iván to give him a situation report. I also needed to find out how long before he arrived.

'I think I know where you are,' said Iván. 'Is there a shitty hotel near to you?'

I knew exactly what and where he was talking about. The same hotel was about a hundred meters after the gas station and on the same side of the street as me. I had to be near it.

'Yeah, Iván, I am fairly certain that I'm just down the road from that hotel. About two hundred meters down.'

'Okay,' he answered. 'Traffic is moving slowly here. I'll call you back as soon as I am passing the Tiger station. Just try not to be kidnapped until I arrive.'

'Thanks, Iván,' I said. 'I'll see you shortly.'

I looked at Ben who was right by my side. He seemed calm and collected, but a little unnerved by the event. I was very lucky that it had been him who was with me. Anybody else and they might not have been so calm and responsive.

'They're on the way, Ben. They'll probably be about another fifteen minutes.'

I paid closer attention to the pungent smell that was coming from my leg. Even Ben was looking at me funny as I rubbed my hand on my damp trouser leg and wet boot.

'Ah for fuck sake!' I said as I took a whiff of my hand. 'It's fucking piss. When I was pushing you up on the beam, I stepped in a bucket. I thought it was just water.'

We both laughed. If a pissy leg was the worst of our concerns then we weren't doing too badly.

Not long after, I could see the silver Prado make her approach from up the street. I rang Iván and told him to look for the shining torch I was holding from the second story building twenty meters in front to his left.

'I see you", he answered. 'Come on down.'

Traffic had returned to normal as we walked out onto the busy street. In the darkness of the late evening there was nothing I could see to indicate a shooting had occurred less than an hour before. I shook hands with my team leader. To my surprise, Mick was with him. I also spotted Ralph, who was sitting on a wooden box outside our safe haven. He had been there for about five minutes, waiting for me to return.

We got into the armored Prado, made a U-turn and headed back towards the Hexagon. Ralph was two cars behind us in the Patrol.

'We heard the shots from the Hexagon,' said Mick.

'What's that smell?' asked Iván.

'I stepped in a bucket of piss getting up to the second floor,' I explained.

Mick and Iván looked at each other and laughed.

'Jesus, Paddy,' said Mick. 'I can't take you anywhere can I?'

When we got through the Hexagon gates, Colin Rawes and Nicholas Brady were there waiting for us. Nick was Martin Brady's son. He had been in the army back home and had recently taken over security operations from Rawes. They would need me for debrief and to hand in a written report. As far as I knew, this was one of the few incidents of its kind since the company had been in operation. The entire event would no doubt be treated as a very big deal. My elation of doing my job was soon passing. All I wanted to do was change my pants and go for a beer.

Nick and Rawes spoke with Ben Smyth on the steps of the Hexagon. It was all pats on backs and manly handshakes. Rawes of course was the loudest of them all with his usual distinct and bogus career laugh. He barely glanced at me as I walked past him on the steps. Nick shook my hand and said he would see me inside in a minute.

The debriefing between Nick, Rawes and I went on for about fifteen minutes. I described the entire event to them with as much detail as I could while it was still fresh in my mind. Arms folded, Colin Rawes didn't ask much. He just stood there listening and observing. When I told them about my removing the magazine from the weapon system, it suddenly dawned on me that I had just shot myself in the foot, metaphorically speaking. They both looked at me like I had just committed treason.

I tried to explain to them why I had done what I'd done. At that point Nick told me to write up my report and head home for the night. I had only known him for a few weeks, but the young operations manager was a decent guy. I only hoped that he would appreciate my actions during the incident.

The report took me about forty minutes to write. Elmo sat next to me, full of questions. The burly bastard teased and taunted me as I tried to concentrate on my typing.

'Did ya get scared?' he asked. 'Is that why ya smell of wee? It's okay, you can tell Uncle Elmo.'

I smiled and tried not to laugh as I struggled to continue writing.

'Elmo, fuck off and let me get this shit done. We'll get a feed and some beers in tonight.'

'Jaysus,' he answered. 'Will ya hurry up so, Jessica Fletcher. It's not a fucking murder mystery novel you're writing.'

As soon as I was done, Mick managed to give me and Elmo a car to get back to the team house. On the drive, I told him about the entire incident. I knew that my weapon situation would be a topic of conversation that night between management. Even if it was, I still believed that I had acted correctly.

'One fucking week to go,' I said as Elmo drove us up Montagne Noir. 'They are sure to give me a Spanish Holiday for this.'

A 'Spanish Holiday' was a one way ticket home. The catch was that you never knew you were on a Spanish Holiday until you actually got home. If they called you up, then you were welcomed back to work for them. But if you didn't receive a call, then it was bye, bye and thank you for playing.

'Not necessarily, lad,' he answered. 'You did your job and got the client back safely. Nick will see that. I know him a long time. He's a good guy. If it was up to Rawes then yeah, pack your sombrero.'

We both laughed. Elmo always had a way with words.

One of the larger sized 'Tap Taps' downtown

(Courtesy of Bright Harbour Productions)

Very early morning at Toussaint Louverture Airport

(Photo by author)

Men fishing the beautiful waters of the Haitian coastline

(Courtesy of Bright Harbour Productions)

Sun burst over the Central Plateau

(Courtesy of Bright Harbour Productions)

Remnants from a time long gone.

An old French colonial maison in Port au Prince

(Courtesy of Bright Harbour Productions)

Author meeting a family in northern Haiti

(Courtesy of Photojournalist Bryan Meade)

Security convoy moving through the back streets of Delmas

(Courtesy of BG)

One of the poverty stricken areas of Port au Prince

(Courtesy of Bright Harbour Productions)

A basic school house in the Central Plateau

(Photo by author)

A scene of 'local justice' on the hills of Montagne Noir

(Courtesy of Mick Dowling)

A 'Blue Force' security car after an attack by gang members

(Photo by author)

Author with Cerek, the magnanimous ex-legionnaire medic

(Taken by Pavlov)

Chapter Eight

SHERIFF:

SUNDAY, 8TH APRIL, 2007

TOUSSAINT LOUVERTURE AIRPORT,

PORT AU PRINCE

Returning to Haiti had been much easier than I had anticipated. I was happy to have been home in Ireland for a month, but the itch to get back to my friends in the Caribbean wasn't long raising its head. At twenty-seven years old, I was sure that I'd found my place. In three short months, solid friendships had been formed and I could finally say that I was making a living from working in a hostile environment. Stepping off the big silver bird of American Airlines, I was once again walking across the hot asphalt of Toussaint Louverture Airport.

I stepped outside from arrivals where hundreds of people were waiting behind the green fence. This time I wasn't so nervous like I had been four months before. I spotted an airport attendant pick up two suitcases belonging to an American newcomer. The American, wary of being taken for a ride, was trying to grab his bags from the attendant. A lot of new arrivals were often afraid of their baggage being stolen. The heat and humidity added to the hectic atmosphere, making it hard to move or even think without sweating.

Sándor, the Hungarian, was there to pick me up. It was hard to miss him amidst the scores of people. His stocky build and black Oakley glasses made him look like a badass. With Sándor there was another bodyguard whom I did not recognize.

'Oh, Peggy! Welcome back,' he said.

I shook Sándor's hand then walked with him to the car.

For some reason the stout Hungarian had decided to call me Peggy halfway through my tour in Haiti. In turn, I christened him with the name Sandie. He found this hilarious. After a few weeks, both names just stuc43k.

'Peggy, this is Piroska, he is Hungarian guy also.'

'Hi, Piroska. How are you doing? How are you enjoying Haiti?'

'Yeah,' he said with a smile. 'It's an interesting place. My friends call me Piro by the way'

Piro was a broad shouldered guy with a shaven head. His pale white skin had been burnt red from his first week or so under the Haitian sun. He asked me if he could help me with one of my bags. I gave him my backpack as we headed to the car.

'Mick isn't coming back Sandie,' I said as I opened the passenger door. 'Apparently they weren't happy with him.'

Sándor looked disgruntled.

'Fuck. I heard something about this but I wasn't sure if it was true,' he replied. 'It is big bullshit eh.'

'Yeah, mate. Big bullshit is right.'

The drive back up through Rue de Delmas and into Petion Ville was far from nostalgic. I still had a long way to go before I would succumb to the warmth of Port au Prince. I looked out through the window of the armored Prado. People were still sitting on corners, selling their wares and going about their business. On our second set of traffic lights, two young boys, no older than ten, began to wash the windscreen of the Prado with a grimy piece of rag. Everything was as I had left it. There was still dissociation within me for the way people were living here. I still saw Port au Prince merely as an operational environment. By doing so, I could rationalize my being here in the first place.

'So, what's the news Sandie? Who's here and who's gone?' I asked.

'Liam is finished,' he said. 'He left two weeks ago and is not coming back. Cerek is in the home (on vacation). Oh, and Elmo is finished in Haiti.'

'Where is Elmo then?'

'Trinidad,' replied Sandie. 'They sent him there to take care of some big boss.'

'For good?'

'I think so, yes.'

'The lucky fuck.'

'Not much more has changed, Peggy. Except you are sheriff now.'

We both laughed.

'Yeah, Sandie,' I said. 'Thanks for reminding me.'

'Don't worry, Peggy,' he said. 'When Cerek gets back maybe they will put you back on the cars.'

When we drove in the gates of team house three, I felt as if my month back home had never even happened. I grabbed my bags from the rear of the car and headed up the steps to the house. Some of the lads were casually lounging around the pool. Judging by their tans, I saw that any color I had picked up in my first three months had long since faded. Pavlov, one of the Slovak boys, threw me a wave as they saw me walking up the steps to the house. I didn't really know him yet. Pavlov worked as night security on the new Digicel construction project in Turgeau. He practically lived a separate life to the rest of the team when it came to work. From what I knew of

Pavlov, he was a smart, solemn yet unpredictably roguish type of guy. An ex-legionnaire so it really wasn't all that surprising.

'What room am I in, Sandie?' I asked.

'Oh, Peggy, you will be very happy,' he said. 'Viktor comes back tomorrow. There is a room you can share with him.'

Sándor walked through to the kitchen and on towards his bedroom as his almost Viking like laugh reverberated throughout the house. No sooner had he left the room than I could hear him stabbing jokes at Pappy, the old Haitian gardener.

****

Monday morning and I was already in the thick of the fray. With the jet lag of the previous thirty six hours still hanging over me, I wiped the sleep from my eyes as Ratko, the night sheriff, briefed me for my first early morning handover. He looked as sleepy as I did, but his twelve hour shift was over now, while mine was just beginning. Ratko was another ex-legionnaire just like many of the team. Standing no taller than five foot six and balding way too early for such a young age, he was of typical Slovak stock in being built like a brick shit house with a temperamental character to boot. He had a tremendous sense of humor also. Ratko reminded me of some sort of Eastern Bloc mafia kingpin.

The office looked smaller than I had left it a month before. New maps of the city had been mounted on the walls. Small, plastic multi-colored thumb tacks marked various locations throughout the capital. I had been told that some of these locations were new and we would be dealing with them on a daily basis from here on in; hotels, embassies and new housing locations of recently arrived clients. The time was just coming up on half past six in the morning and I had only dispatched the first two cars for the early pick-ups.

'A lot of new names, Ratko,' I said as I read through the new client manifest.

'Yeah, they start to bring family here now also,' he said. He sounded concerned. 'Too many families coming to this place now.'

I handed my Slovak friend a set of keys for a Nissan.

'Get yourself home, mate. I'll see you this evening.'

Iván soon arrived into the office with a fresh batch of pastries from the nearby French Patisserie. At about seven o'clock the sheriff's phone rang for the first time that morning. Chomping on a chocolate pastry, I looked at the small, cheap mobile ringing and vibrating with its electric blue screen flashing on and off. This was the beginning of my second tour in Haiti.

Eighty-nine calls and seventy-two missions later, my first day was over. I was mentally exhausted. After I got back to the team house, I sat in the main room eating a breast of chicken and some rice with Tabasco sauce. I wondered how in the hell I was going to work the sheriff job without burning out like some of my predecessors. It soon dawned on me that I might have made a big mistake accepting the job.

****

It was another Friday night in the sheriff's office. The last of the clients had just been dropped home from one of the late bar/ restaurants that they usually frequented at the end of a working week. I had been back in country for five weeks and this was my first week as night sheriff. I liked the peace and quiet of the late night and early morning and I had no ambition whatsoever to go back to working as day sheriff. As far as I was concerned, by taking the night sheriff position, I was a step closer to getting back on the cars.

In the corner of the office sat my trainee sheriff, Brian, who was pouring himself a mug of coffee. It was his third night of training and he was coming along fine. With the Canadian bodyguard Graham as country manager, there was a good chance of me getting out of the office. The deal was, if I could train somebody who could manage the job as well as I could, if not better, then I'd have found my replacement and I'd be back out on the cars full time. Brian was my meal ticket.

The QRF (Quick Reaction Force) sat in the office with us too. Codenamed 'Cobra One', the QRF comprised a senior bodyguard and a driver. Their job was simply to provide a presence and to react in the event of a problem with any of the client's residences.

Also there was Steve, who had just returned to the office having dropped the last client home. With a head of jet black hair and standing six foot tall, Steve was one of the big units within the security company. Quietly spoken, reserved and probably one of the few guys I'd call a true professional, he dropped the keys of the Prado into my hand.

'Alright, Steve,' I said. 'Any problems dropping him home?'

'No problems, mate, all good. It's quiet out there now.'

Steve looked tired. He had been on the move for more than twelve hours, having spent the last six watching from afar as his client drank himself into a stupor. We all drew the short straw from time to time.

I signed out one of the cars for both Steve and Brian to take home when the screeching of car wheels could be heard tearing into the building. We were stunned by the violent skids at such an early hour of the morning. Each man automatically reached for his pistol.

'What the fuck was that?' asked Brian.

'Fuck knows,' said Steve.

We cautiously made our way out to see what all the commotion was. A couple of uniformed 'Blue Force' security staff were scurrying about one of their Toyota pick-ups. Blue Force was another security company who shared the same building as us. Their Toyota pick-up was in pretty bad shape. It had been peppered with bullet holes. On closer inspection, they looked to be 9mm. Four had hit the windscreen head on. Even though the cracks spread out through the pane of shattered glass, it still remained in place. The two rear passenger windows and the driver's window had been completely shot out. More bullet holes were visible on the side panels. The pickup was soft skinned. Judging by the amount of blood spilled on the front seats, it was doubtful if the security staff had survived the shooting. The deep red liquid glistened under the white light of the indoor parking.

'What the hell happened?' I asked one of the security officers.

They were deeply distraught. He explained to us that two of their security officers were out on a routine night patrol in the Peguy ville area. As they were checking the residence of one of their clients, men armed with pistols came out of the shadows and opened up on them. The driver was killed and the second guard was critically wounded.

'What time did this happen?' asked Steve.

'About twenty-five minutes ago,' answered the security guard. 'They were brought directly to hospital in Canape Vert. We just brought this back from the scene.'

Erring on the side of caution, I decided to send both the QRF and a second armored Prado out to the scene. Digicel had a number of clients residing in Peguy ville, including the principal client in country, Madame Khedy, one of Digicel's senior staff. It was too serious a situation to let Steve go alone in the second vehicle, so I quickly grabbed a vest and got in the back of his Prado. Brian could hold the office and man the radios between now and my return.

The two cars moved at high speed through the quiet and empty streets of Petion Ville. The QRF car was in front. I sat with my Glock in hand while focusing on the red glow of her tail lights at every turn we made. We would arrive at the principal client's house (otherwise called Khedy's house) within seven minutes. Adrenaline was building up in my system. I concentrated on my breathing and what I would do the second I stepped out onto the road. If we happened to run into a similar situation as the Blue Force security guys, I would be exposed at the rear of the car.

When we arrived, both cars came to an abrupt halt. We stepped out and I covered my arcs to the rear. We sat, listened, watched and waited. Quietness and crickets were all I could hear. A cock crowed in the yard of a nearby house. The armed men had long since left the area. Most likely they slipped back down one of the many small mazes of alley ways that lead to the shanty towns on Rue Des Frères. After checking Khedy's residence and those of two other clients, we returned to the Hexagon. No gunfight tonight.

****

There was a meeting in the Hexagon that night for the senior Digicel staff. A couple of the bodyguards were sitting in the office, just waiting for a mission. Sándor sat on the ammo bin playing his portable video game console while Cerek was slouched back in my chair playing Solitaire on the sheriff's computer. Viktor was reading his books as he usually did. They were bored. So was I. The only difference was that my boredom would only last as long as the sheriff's phone did not ring.

'Let's go for a smoke, kurwa,' said Cerek, as he pushed the computer mouse away from his hand and headed for the door.

I grabbed a can of Red Bull from my bag and joined my friend outside by the steps. Caffeine and nicotine had become my daily diet out here as night sheriff.

'So,' said Cerek. 'We must make a small party this weekend before I leave.'

'Sounds good, kurwa,' I answered. 'Maybe we can get Pavlov to make it too.'

Cerek smiled before he pulled on the cigarette like it was his last. Pavlov, Cerek and I had become close friends. Once in a while, the three of us would manage to get a night off and head out for drinks. Breaks like that were rare so we always made the most of what we got.

We chatted some more before a client arrived on the steps and asked for a car home.

'I can take him kurwa,' said Cerek.

I gave him a set of keys for a Nissan that were already in my pocket. He stubbed out his cigarette, called the driver and headed out the gates with the client. My friend from Poland always amazed me, the way one moment he could be full of laughs and revelry, then without a word of warning, his entire demeanor shifted into business mode when work came along. Cerek's serious nature meant that he didn't give even a slight wave or nod as he drove out of the car park. I sat on the steps to enjoy the last of my cigarette, allowing my mind to drift to the distant thoughts of Saturday night and the prospect sharing a few beers and whiskies with the boys.

CLACK! CLACK! CLACK!!!CLACK!CLACK!!

That was it, from zero to sixty. Bullets were fired and people were screaming. Somebody had fired five rounds in my vicinity but I had no idea exactly where. It was definitely somewhere close by. It sounded like they came from out on the street, no more than twenty meters away. First I crouched down then I ran back inside for the sheriff's office and past the open garage door where I was exposed. I did this as fast as I could, keeping low and throwing my upper body forward while putting one leg in front of the other. When I came bursting into the office, I ran straight for the weapons cabinet. Sandie and Viktor were already standing on their feet with weapons at the ready.

My heart was pounding as I caught my breath and loaded my pistol.

'Shots fired,' I said. 'Just outside the garage door.'

The garage shutter that the Blue Force security company were responsible for was open, allowing more than a hundred people to seek refuge from the shooter in our building.

Sandie, Viktor and I took up firing positions for fear of the shooter running inside the building with the crowd. Just to add to the confusion, dozens of Digicel workers came running down the stairwell to see what all the commotion was, oblivious to the fact that they were putting themselves in harm's way. Once the situation calmed down, the crowds dispersed back out onto the street. We checked the area but the police had already arrived.

'Maybe next time,' said Viktor as he placed his pistol back in its holster.

****

It was another hot and humid afternoon down at the airport. I was waiting for one of the senior clients to arrive in on the American Airlines flight from Miami. I took a mouthful from a cold bottle of Sprite that I'd just bought from a vendor across the street. It had been a few weeks now since they put me back out on the cars. Unfortunately it would be short lived but the opportunity to get out of the sheriff's office and back on the streets was long overdue and more than welcomed.

As always, hundreds of Haitians stood waiting in the midday sun for their friends and loved ones to return home. Peppered amidst the crowds of locals were about twenty missionaries. Normally these Christian folk came from the States. They flew in from Miami and New York to come and help Haitian communities. I often wondered what kind of lives they were living down here and how much they were really achieving. Their work may have been a calling from God, but down here they walked a dangerous line. Six months before, I too had been helping people who were less fortunate than me. I wanted to believe that these missionaries were doing something worthwhile, but my experiences in Haiti to date would not allow me to lower my defenses. As far as I was concerned, this was still a dangerous place to be.

I waited in the sweltering heat as more police cars arrived at the airport. An unarmed man had been pursued by another man firing a pistol about fifteen minutes before. The gunfire had sent people running in every direction. It was far enough away from where I was standing, so I thought it best to take a knee, smoke a cigarette and wait for my client.

****

Cerek, Pavlov and I had been relaxing by the pool and drinking some beers on my second Christmas Day spent in Haiti. I had even attended mass that morning with Pavlov. We may have come from different countries, but lapsed Catholic or not, I still wanted to go to morning mass. With most of the clients gone home for a few weeks, we had the entire day to wind down and enjoy.

'Lads, are ye up to much?'

It was Mac. He had driven up from the management team house earlier but I hadn't seen him for almost an hour.

'Not really, Mac,' I said. 'Why? What's up?'

'You won't believe what's out to the side of our house in the dump.'

I knew Mac long enough to know that he wouldn't waste our time. We jumped out of the pool and threw some flip-flops and t-shirts on.

'What is it?' I asked, wiping the water from under my nose.

'Hang on,' said Mac. 'You'll see.'

I tried not to slip as we made our way down a steep sandy hill where some wild dogs were already gathered. When we moved closer, the mongrels scattered, making it abundantly clear what they had been feasting on. The remaining corpses of two men lay head down and ass up in the dirt. They had been stripped of all clothing and, with bullet holes in their heads, it appeared to be an execution style killing. To top it off, their assassins had doused the bodies in a frugal amount of petrol. Rather than charring the remains to a crisp, only parts of their flesh had been cooked, sending an alluring barbeque scent out into the nearby hills.

No ambulances, no police and no investigation.

'Local justice,' said Mac. 'Happy Christmas.'

Chapter Nine

SOMETHING GOOD

SATURDAY, 5TH JANUARY, 2008

RUE KENSCOFF, PORT AU PRINCE

Rue Kenscoff was a main road that took us out of Petion Ville and Port au Prince. Raymond struggled for momentum on our uphill drive into the mountains. We eventually left the noise and pollution of the city behind us. Mile after mounting mile, fume ridden tap taps and rusty old cars became fewer. Busy shanty towns were replaced with small villages, which were placed across the gloriously lush hills of the rugged Kenscoff region. Monstrous white clouds sprawled out over an immense blue sky. Wave after undulating wave of rolling green hills stretched out towards the distant horizon, each one distinguished by small farms and dotted with pine trees. If I stared close enough, I could make out miniscule figures of country folk as they moved steadily across the jagged ridge lines.

I was escorting an Irish client called Jane to an orphanage in Kenscoff. The orphanage was run by another Irish woman by the name of Gena. I had heard her name mentioned a couple of times but had yet to meet her. Gena had been living and working with the poor children of Haiti since the mid-nineties. The orphanage belonged to a charity called 'Nos Petit Frères et Soeurs' (Little Brothers and Sisters of Charity). I was looking forward to meeting her.

Surrounded by farmland and lush pine, we pulled up to a set of large bright blue gates of the Little Brother and Sisters of Charity. From where the car was positioned, I couldn't see any of the buildings behind the wall. I'd been told that more than four hundred children were living there. It was hard to imagine so many kids in such a remote region. Though Gena was expecting us, neither Jane nor I had her cell phone number. I stepped out of the car and rapped loudly on the large blue gates, hoping that somebody on the other side was nearby to hear me. A few seconds later, a small latch slid open and a pair of beady eyes peered outwards.

'Can I help you?' said the voice.

I smiled and gave a slight wave.

'Yes,' I answered. 'We're here to visit Madame Gena for the day. We are from Digicel.'

The eyes remained unblinking and focussed as I produced my ID card.

'Okay,' he said. 'You can come inside. Everybody is expecting you.'

My driver, Raymond, drove the car forward, through the opened gates and past the young teenager who had opened them for us. We banked down a steep tarmacked hill and headed towards the courtyard. The compound was much bigger than I had imagined. There was a three storey building to my left with a large green triangular shaped roof overhead. It looked like it could have been the school house. To my right was another three storey building. On each floor, young teenagers leaned out over balconies chatting and looking at our car. What I had taken for the courtyard was a large circular platform with stone seating spreading outwards from the centre. It reminded me of the old Roman theatres. Within the central platform were a group of young girls chanting and singing while many of the other children sat, watched and listened to their eloquent Creole songs.

'Try not to kill the children, Raymond,' I joked. 'That would be bad.'

'Oh my God no, Paddy,' he said. 'I would never do this.'

He parked the car up on a nearby basketball court. The second that the car came to a stop, children swarmed towards us from every direction. They were beaming with excitement. Kids of all ages were singing, laughing and playing around the Nissan. This was something I had never seen before.

The second I stepped out of the Patrol, I was immediately surrounded by about twenty little ones, as was Jane. Some of the older boys ran to Raymond. They wanted to drive the car. My Haitian buddy looked somewhat stressed. Our arrival had certainly stirred quite the commotion. I could not understand a word they were saying as everybody was speaking all at once. I even began to wonder if I would ever break free of the five little boys hanging out of my arms and legs. They laughed and giggled as their wiry little fingers held to me like they'd been set with superglue. I noticed a smiling 'blan' woman approach our gathering. It was Gena.

'I see you're making new friends with us already,' she said.

'Yep, I think so,' I answered. 'I don't think I'll be breaking free anytime soon.'

Gena said something quite sternly in Creole to the children. I imagined it was probably along the lines of 'let this poor man go.' They did, well, all but one. He was the quieter one of the bunch. The little boy wore a red sweater and grey tracksuit bottoms. He had short hair and big, beautiful eyes. As he stared up at me with a smile, I was only too happy to hold his pint-sized hand.

I introduced myself to Gena and she asked me if I would like to visit some of the other parts of the orphanage before we had tea. Gena was a slim lady, not more than thirty eight years old. Her hair ran straight down past her shoulders. There was a refreshing femininity about her, but I knew that I should not be fooled by this. Gena was that rare breed of woman who had dedicated her life to something that many of us only wished we could. Apart from traits like compassion and understanding, it took a certain level of resilience and hardiness to stay and dedicate your life to a country like Haiti. Gena was simply one of those people. Haiti was her home. Gena, Jane and I took a walk around the grounds.

'So where are you from back home, Gena?' I asked.

'I'm from Mayo, originally,' she said. 'I came out to Haiti eighteen years ago on a project after I finished university. I never thought that I'd be here nearly twenty years later. But, here I am.'

The first building we visited was the treatments centre for the special needs children that required occupational therapy. Some had physical disabilities while others were both mentally and physically impaired. Each classroom had local assistants and a number of occupational therapists working with their designated groups. The building itself was basic, but that didn't matter, not in Haiti. Imaginative paintings adorned the brightly coloured yellow walls.

When we went upstairs, I realised that we had interrupted snack time. There were kids of all ages sitting in high chairs and at small tables. Their little faces were fixated on their next mouthful of food. Most kids could feed themselves while some had motor function problems. The carers continually attempted to catch their attention for the next spoonful. One little girl was fascinated by my presence. She constantly smiled at me as she happily ate her next spoonful of lunch. Her precious little face reminded me of a time before I had joined the army. I had worked as a volunteer in The Sacred Heart Centre back in Waterford. Their classes were full of little kids, just like these. But back there, they had parents, family. These little mites had nobody. Nobody but Gena and her staff to love them, teach them, and watch over them. Seeing these kids and meeting Gena made me feel that there was more to Haiti than what I was seeing. Working as a bodyguard had definitely shrouded my vision. Security was my job and that was what I was being paid to do. But I still couldn't shake the feeling there was so much more to this country that I really did not know.

Later in the afternoon, Gena treated me, Jane and Raymond to a wonderful lunch in the staff quarters. We were joined by other volunteers living at the orphanage. Some had come from as far away as Italy, Spain and even the North West United States. There was also another Irish woman working there. Her name was Maeve. She too was very pleasant, just like the others. Maeve and some of the other volunteers were staying in Haiti to work with the children for the next two years. I was struck by their dedication and selflessness. When a Mexican girl asked me what I was doing in Haiti, I became tongue-tied. I tried to explain as simply as possible what my job was, but the volunteer looked mystified. Her time in Haiti had nothing to do with security or kidnappings or shootings. She had come here out of love for those that could not take care of themselves. I think that she saw me as some kind of mercenary or gun for hire. If she had met half of the crazy bastards that I lived with, she might not have been far wrong.

The living quarters of the staff stood tall on the edge of a mountain ridge. After lunch I enjoyed a cup of Irish tea on the balcony with Gena, Jane and Maeve. I felt privileged to be sharing a cup of Barry's tea with three lovely Irish women so far from home. I looked out at the incredible view of the mountains and hills we had passed on the way up. The air was crisp and fresh unlike the city. I felt blessed, if only for an afternoon.

Before we left for Petion Ville, we visited the kindergarten where the infants were living. They all seemed so helpless and I wondered what would happen to them when they became young adults. Gena explained to me that once the children turned eighteen years old, they could no longer stay. Attempts would be made to find relatives that they might be able to live with, but that wasn't always the case. There was a disturbing possibility that many would wind up on the streets of Port au Prince searching for work. I looked down at my little friend who had never left my side. The prospect of him living on the streets deeply disturbed me.

It was time for us to make our journey back down through Kenscoff. The afternoon had simply not lasted long enough. Many of the kids came to the car to say goodbye. My little dude stayed with me all the way. Gena held onto him so I could get back into the Nissan. Just as I was getting into the car, a young Haitian chap ran over to me. He must have been about seventeen years old. He was tall and athletic looking and had a great big smile on his face.

'Hello, sir,' he said. 'My name is Michael. I heard you were coming to visit us but I was working on my project all day and I didn't have a chance to visit you. I just wanted to say hello.'

'No problem, Michael,' I answered. 'It's great to meet you. Maybe next time I am here we'll get a chance to chat more.'

Michael smiled.

'Yes. I would like that. Have a safe journey home.'

Visiting the orphans, Gena and her staff had opened my eyes to another side of Haiti. Little Brothers and Sisters of Charity was as much a breath of fresh air to me as the air that blanketed the hills of Kenscoff. My mission to

Haiti was almost over, but I hoped to return to Kenscoff again, if I could.

Chapter Ten

GAME OF CHANCE:

TUESDAY, 15TH JANUARY, 2008

TEMPLEMORE, CO. TIPPERARY, IRELAND

Dark, grey clouds filled the sky on the Tuesday morning I arrived at the Garda training college in Tipperary. Cars belonging to more than three hundred new trainees filled the lot. Even though I was early, precious few places remained as I had to make two rounds to find a place to park up. Grabbing my bags from the boot, I made my way to the front entrance of the college. I produced my letter of acceptance to a young, uniformed, female student Garda who was standing quite dutifully outside the guard room. She ticked my name from her list and pointed me in the direction of two other students in uniform who were gathered outside of an accommodation block. Once there, a tall, skinny senior student escorted me to my new living quarters. This would be my home for the next twenty weeks, from Monday to Friday at least.

We walked up two flights of stairs and down a long corridor where he showed me into a small room with a single bed and a desk.

'I hope it is to your satisfaction,' he said with a sly grin on his face. 'Everybody is to be over by the physical training hall by one o'clock. Make sure to be there.'

I still had twenty minutes to wash up and get my bearings.

'No problem, mate, thanks,' I answered as I dropped my bags on the bed. The student then put his peaked cap back on his head and went on his way to greet the next newcomer.

Out in the corridor, more people were still arriving. It was easy to know who was fresh in as all new students had been ordered to wear suits and ties on the first day. We would continue to wear them until such a time as being issued with police uniforms. It was similar to being back in the army, except for the absence of instructors incessantly shouting in your face and the constant dread of what the hell would happen next. I thought about Mick who was beginning his fire fighter training in Dublin that very same day. His first day was probably similar to mine.

There was a knock at my door.

'How's it going?' said a fair haired young man in a dark navy suit. 'John Callaghan is my name. Are you just in the door?'

'Hiya, John,' I said. 'How's it going? So you decided to sign up for this madness as well?'

It turned out that John had just left the army and transferred to the guards. He was one of many guys I would meet who had done likewise. Some of them I had even served with in Lebanon and completed courses with during my time as a soldier.

John Callaghan came across as a cheerful sort of bloke. He was full of stories and words of wisdom from his home county of Cork. Like most young men from his neck of the woods, he was fiercely proud of his county and extremely family orientated. It had been a long time since I'd made any new friends in Ireland and I could see that we would get on well for the five long months ahead.

At one o'clock, the three hundred or so potential police officers gathered in the physical training hall for an induction speech by the college Chief Superintendent. I was baffled by the amount of young faces there. At twenty-eight, I felt that I had done a fair amount with my life, even without a college education. Some of these youngsters looked as if they were straight out of school. And for many, they actually were. I was assigned to class KA3. The letters stood for Kilo Alpha, as that was the intake category, and the number 3 represented the third class of that intake. Our ranks were made up of young men and women from all over the country. Everybody was here for their own reasons but each with the same goal in mind: to complete the course and become fully fledged members of An Garda Síochana (sounds like 'she-a- cawna'). It consisted of five phases broken down over two years; phase one being of five months duration.

The first week was mostly administration. By the second week we had begun the main syllabus of our training. All students had to report in by ten o'clock on the Sunday night. Classes would begin at nine o'clock sharp the following morning. Lectures ranged from Legal and Policing studies, Garda Practices and Procedures, Criminal Psychology, French, German, Physical Education, Police Self-Defence and Irish. Irish was included as under the Constitution all guards must have a working knowledge of the national language.

By the end of the third week, our workload had increased to the point that I actually had to open my books and study for the first time since school. A continuous ladling of information ensued, which not only had to be learned word for word, but also embedded into our very psyche.

The guards was a lot like the army in that you had to queue for practically everything. Sometimes it took up to fifteen minutes from picking up a tray to placing a dinner on it. Procedure was the name of the game and nothing in the Garda College happened without procedure. Because we were cut off from the outside world from Monday to Friday, the college also brought with it its own inescapable culture. Practically all that people ever talked about was police related. The corridors were awash with blue uniforms. Day in and day out, everybody ate and slept 'policing studies'.

There is an old saying in Ireland that a guard is never off duty. This is true for the most part. Cops do tend to socialize within their own circles, whether talking cases they are dealing with or discussing files on their desks. It really can't be avoided due to the nature of the work and the identity that the uniform instils in both the officer and those around him/ her. From the day we were issued with uniforms, that sense of identity quickly began to take shape. There were times when I caught a glimpse of myself in the mirror and wondered what the hell I was even doing there. I soon stopped wrestling with the concept and embraced the training as best I could.

Students were allowed to drink alcohol up until ten past eleven at night in Polly's pub, just across the road from the college. There probably isn't a guard up or down the twenty six counties who hasn't been into Polly's at some point in training. Drinking wasn't entirely frowned upon by the college superiors, so long as you were in by the allotted time and up bright and early for classes the following morning. I never really bothered with the pints or the nights out in Templemore. Having to sign in and sign out, checking the time on your watch every ten minutes, to say nothing of the fact that you were up so early the next day, the hangover would not be worth it. Instead, my break away from the Garda culture was spent with a buddy of mine called Danny. We basically drank pots and pots of tea in his dorm while studying and watching the Australian soap 'Home and Away' on YouTube. I enjoyed hanging about with the short man from Kerry because he really didn't pay too much heed to the pragmatic culture of the college. At twenty-four, he was more of a free thinker than I had been at that age. Danny was a good pal and helped to keep me grounded amidst an ocean of blue.

For the next sixteen weeks, lessons and exams continued relentlessly and with less than two weeks to go in the college, everybody was anxiously counting down the final few days of exams and awaiting the news of where they would be stationed. A number of students were married and had families. They would be eager to know how far or close to home they were to be placed. I didn't really care where they sent me. Odds were I would be posted somewhere in Cork. That was often the norm with students hailing from Waterford. I was more concerned with finishing the final exams and getting the hell out of the college. Five months of running around like a 'blue arsed fly' had been enough. I was longing to see what the job actually entailed.

With the first week of exams out of the way and a May Bank Holiday weekend ahead, I felt as if I had plenty of free time on my hands before the following Tuesday morning exams. The summer had come quickly and as I drove home to my parent's house on a sunny Friday evening, my mind began to race with thoughts of phase two. Less than twelve days to go and we were out. Life was good, and all was going to plan.

Saturday morning brought with it a bright blue sky and a temperature that ranged in the early seventies. I decided to get out of my folk's house for the day and go for a drive. I had a load of study to contend with, but first I just needed to get away from it all. For a day at least. Sunday and Monday would be enough time for books.

There was a military exhibition in Co. Wexford. It was annual event held in the fort where my grandfather had worked for the Dept. of Defence. The exhibition was made up of hundreds of men and women who had an interest in past wars and conflicts. There were squads of men dressed as World War Two US Army Paratroopers while some other dudes were pretending to be German officers from a Panzer Division. They drove about the parade ground in old Jeeps, Land Rovers and motorbikes with sidecars. There was also a military museum set up on site.

I met a couple of people whom I knew from my time in the army. But most surprising of all, I happened to bump into Martin Brady. Being a retired army sergeant, he probably still had affection for things that went boom. We chatted for a while about Haiti and the lads. I'd been following the news on the recent food riots in Port au Prince from the month before.

Throughout April, while I was up to my neck in study, I would tune in online to watch what was going on in Haiti's capital. The level of anger and protest from the Haitian people practically shut down the entire city. Civil unrest was simmering away beneath the country's surface. Was it any wonder when they had a government that constantly toyed with commodity and fuel prices? And basic commodities at that; rice, the staple food source of all Haitian families, saw a price hike of up to fifty percent. Food prices had soared so high that people's patience was pushed to the brink. The situation was ludicrous given the fact that an average Haitian made no more than two US dollars a day. What followed was absolute bedlam on the streets of Port au Prince. The people had had enough and who could blame them.

'How are the boys managing with the situation?' I asked Martin.

'You know how it is down there, Paddy. It just comes with the territory.'

I spoke to him about the cops and what I was up to. But mostly, I turned the conversation back to Haiti. Nearly half a year had gone by since I'd left. A part of me still longed to be back with the boys, especially Pavlov and Cerek.

'It was good to see you again, Martin. Tell Nick I said hello,' I said as we parted ways.

'Yeah, will do. Take care and best of luck in the cops. If I get a parking ticket, I'll know who to call.'

I laughed and went on my way.

I left the military event late that afternoon and arrived back at the family home by tea time. Nobody was there. My mother was staying with my grandmother and my dad was probably out having a few drinks in her absence. Not long after, the house phone rang. It was my father, asking me if I could drop him and some of his buddies up the road to the local pub.

The moment I answered the phone was the onset to a series of events that changed everything.

I got in my car and drove the short distance to where my dad was.

'We won't be long more,' he said as he drank a short vodka at the kitchen table of his friend's house.

Quite often on a weekend, he would have a few jars over at his pal Dave's house on the far side of the estate. Somewhat begrudgingly, yet happy to be with my father, I sat there in the smoke filled kitchen and waited for them to finish their glasses so I could drop them to the Uluru bar less than a mile away. In all the time that I had been home, I had spent very little of it with my old man. I was just as happy to see him as he was to see me, to say nothing of the fact that he was proud of me for deciding to come home and join the cops. A barrage of questions was thrown at me about the college and where was I to be stationed.

'Why did you join the guards?' asked one of his friends. 'If I got a parking ticket, would ya let me away with it?'

The questions were becoming a little repetitious and all I wanted to do was drop them up to the pub, come home, have dinner and maybe read through a few notes before getting an early night.

I drove into the car park of the Uluru pub at about eight o'clock. For reasons I still cannot figure out to this day, I threw caution to the wind and decided to forget about my studies and the college for one night and enjoy a few pints with my father and his friends.

When the evening was near over, I knocked back what beer remained in my glass. My father had gone home an hour before and I had spent the remainder of my time chatting with an old school friend. The Uluru was my local pub and it felt good to see the familiar faces again. I had escaped my studies and the routine of the college for one night. The following day would be spent with my nose in the books. As I walked out of the pub, the car park and the main road out in front lay deathly quiet.

It had just gone one o'clock on an early Sunday morning. In that moment, idleness and complacency got the better of my judgment. Five pints in the space of more than four hours and I felt fine. I felt fine enough to open my car door and slip the keys into the ignition. I felt fine enough to go home. The car park didn't have a soul in sight. The orange neon street lights shone brightly as they stretched into a hazy summer night's mist. Starting the engine, I slipped the gear stick into reverse and backed out. I felt fine.

Less than a mile down a quiet country road, three minutes and I'd be home tucked up in bed. Driving out of the car park of the Uluru, I approached the awaiting roundabout. Then it appeared as if from nowhere. The all too distinctive front lights of a Ford Mondeo shone intrusively from behind. The interior of my car was lit up more than I cared for. Soon they were joined by a bright blue strobe light irregularly flashing in my rear view mirror, emanating from the dash of the car behind.

Less than one hundred meters later, I pulled my car off the road and stopped up outside the closed gates of a local factory. The area was well off the main road and dimly lit. As I turned off the engine of my Passat, I began to feel nauseous and weak. The lights of the Mondeo remained behind me throughout. I knew that most people normally just sat in the driver seat in these instances. Intrusive flashlights and 'high viz' jackets would disorientate the driver making them feel like some caged guinea pig. Instinctively, I stepped out, closed the driver's side door, and waited for the figures to emerge.

'Good evening Garda,' I said nervously, as two young officers in yellow 'high viz' jackets emerged from the unmarked police car.

'Have you been drinking tonight?' asked one of the men. His tone was unnervingly cold and formal.

I stood there, trying to grasp the situation that less than two minutes before, hadn't existed. I stood there outside those factory gates on that warm summer's night, wishing I was someplace else. Any place else.

Both officers were big men. I guessed the oldest was in his early thirties while the youngest, the one who was dealing with me directly, was about the same age as me. Both officers took it in turns to ask me questions. What was my name, where did I live, how many drinks had I had? As I stood there, in front of them, almost at attention, any feeling of tiredness or complacency had long since dissolved.

Even though I felt sick, I was never so aware of my surroundings or of every word that came out of my mouth. Apart from my boozy breath, I was fully alert and fully shitting myself. Aside from all that I was feeling, I knew there was still a slim chance of passing the Breathalyzer test. There was also an even slimmer chance of this situation being resolved right where we stood.

'Where do you work, Patrick?' asked the younger Garda. This was it, my last and only chance to reach out to the mercy and discretion of two men who wore the same uniform as me.

'I'm a student up in the college, Garda.'

'What college?' interrupted the older officer.

'Templemore,' I answered, fighting the urge to stare down at my feet in complete and utter embarrassment.

Both men were flabbergasted. If only they had any idea as to the thoughts spiraling through my head at that moment. I knew I had gambled and taken a chance. I also knew that my gamble had not paid off and the consequences as such were so dire that I couldn't yet begin to comprehend them. The only thing I was certain of was that my fate rested with these two men.

'What phase are you in?' asked the older cop. He sounded even more harsh and uncompromising in his tone.

'Phase one, Garda,' I answered. 'I'm halfway through my exams at the moment. We'll be finished them by Wednesday next week.'

Both men stared at me and at each other, baffled by the situation that confronted them.

They both gave me the proverbial bollocking that I deserved. I felt like a young recruit again, being chewed out by one of his corporals. One lesson that the army had taught me was never to argue back when you are in the wrong and to accept blame when blame was due. Attitude was everything and showing character to accept blame in the face of impending adversity was always the soundest way to go. I only hoped that my punishment here would not involve a formal arrest. Deep down, I prayed that they could see the regret and fear in my face. These two men held all the cards.

'You should know better than this, Paddy,' said the older Garda.

'I know Guard,' I said. 'I know I've fucked up really badly here lads. I don't know what to say. This is not who I am. This is not what I'm about.'

'Was it a moment of madness?' asked the younger officer. There was a sliver of empathy in his voice.

'Absolutely, Garda,' I agreed as I stood a short distance away from both men. 'I don't even know what I was thinking to even do this.'

The younger continued looking at me.

'Right, Paddy,' he said. 'I'm going to need a breath sample from you. You have twenty minutes before you have to blow into the bag. Do you understand?'

'Yes, Garda,' I answered. My legs were shaking from the fear.

So the three of us stood there for twenty minutes, twenty surreal minutes where we spoke about the Garda College, my classes, old lecturers that they had had at one stage or another. They even asked me if I enjoyed being in the guards. I tried to convey the human factor in all of my responses. Discretion rested in their hands, as did my future. When the twenty minutes was up, I blew into the white plastic tube attached to the Breathalyzer.

'Blow into the mouth piece as hard as you can until I say stop.'

He held the small machine up towards my face. I blew as hard and as long as I could.

'Now, Paddy, you might pass this,' said the young Garda. 'If you've only had what you say you've had to drink, there is a slight chance of passing.'

When I was finished, he took the machine from my mouth and waited for the result. I felt numb as he began to speak. He looked at me with a sorrowful stare. I had lost.

'I have formed an opinion that you have committed an offence under section 49(1), (2), (3) & (4) of the Road Traffic Act 1961 to 2006 and that you have consumed an intoxicant to such an extent as being incapable of having proper control of a mechanically propelled vehicle in a public place. I am therefore arresting you under 49(8) of the Road Traffic Act 1961 to 2006. In other words I am arresting you on suspicion of drunk driving.'

I understood only too well. I could verse the exact same statement word for word if needed. I understood what it all meant. And it was all bad.

'Can you lock up your car and hop in the back of ours like a good man?' he asked.

There was no need for handcuffs. They knew I was already broken.

When we arrived at the Garda station in Waterford City, I had shut my mind down and gone into some sort of automated state. I signed various forms during my processing, took an intoxalyzer test, sat in this chair, waited in that room, sat in that chair and waited in this room. Nothing mattered to me. Each place I moved to, I merely picked a point on the floor and stared at it intuitively. By now the word had spread to some of the other members in the station that a student Garda had been arrested. When I had completed the remaining processing admin with the duty sergeant, some of the younger cops brought me out back for a cigarette. I stood there listening to their words of advice and encouragement.

'You can still beat this,' said one girl. 'If you get a good solicitor the case could be thrown out of court.'

They even gave me the name of the best guy in town for such cases. I thanked them genuinely. Their compassion and concern, futile as it was, meant a lot. These were the type of people I wanted to work with.

Less than thirty-six hours before, I had been dressed just the same as them. Less than thirty six hours before, my life had been absolutely fine. I knew who I was and where I was going. But now, I was just a drink driver stood in a back car park of a police station on a Sunday morning in May.

The hazy orange glow of dawn on the far off horizon showed the makings of a beautiful day. I didn't want the day to begin. I wanted to drift away with the fading blackness of the night sky. I wanted time to go back so that

I hadn't even put my key in the car door. Better still, I just wished that I had stayed at home and never answered that fucking phone.

The arresting guard, the one who had been fair and impartial to me throughout the entire night, did me the courtesy of dropping me off at my parent's house.

'Promise me something, Paddy,' he said as we sat in the unmarked Garda car. 'Promise me you won't do anything stupid today.'

I sat there in the passenger seat, grateful for the ride home, but not so grateful for the arrest. It was funny. The junior Garda had shown the more empathy of the two. But he happened to be the one who made the arrest.

'I won't,' I answered quietly as I looked at him. 'I am the one who fucked up here. I drove the car when I shouldn't have. You just did your job. I'm the one in the wrong here so don't worry about me. This is my problem.'

I shook his hand and thanked him for the ride home, then went inside and headed straight upstairs. Collapsing onto my bed, all I wanted to do was drift away into a deep sleep and wipe my mind clean of that entire night. Sickness and loss filled my stomach as I lay there and stared into the nothingness. My eyes eventually closed, and for a while I could forget.

For the first time in my life I was in serious trouble. I had never been in trouble with the cops as a teenager, and now here I was, twenty eight years old, a student Garda under arrest for drunk driving. A course of events was now to unfold that would change everything. I fought to find logic and rationale in what had happened. There had to be some way to clean up this mess. I didn't have the answers or the connections. Worse still, nobody understood the sense of utter loneliness and despair that I was feeling. I'd never been a fan of 'tea and sympathy' from people. It doesn't solve problems. I had fucked up really bad. Yet deep down I still held onto the faint and desperate hope that somebody would see that I was really a good guy. I was meant to be a police officer. Even good guys made mistakes, but that didn't mean I deserved to be excommunicated from my friends and my career.

I returned to the Garda College the following Tuesday morning. Within a few hours, I found myself standing in front of the college Superintendent. She listened to me as I tried to explain how negligent and stupid I had been. How ashamed I was for letting myself, my family and my colleagues down. It was plain to see my regret, but the damage had already been done and even she knew there was nothing could be done for me now. Within twenty-four hours I would find myself suspended from training, seeking a Garda Union Representative, who, as it turned out, couldn't have given two shits about me. A suspension review board based in Garda Head Quarters Dublin also awaited me and a civil court case in the Waterford District Court was pending, which meant that I needed a solicitor to represent me. I would also probably lose my driving license for at least a year. It was all just too much to think about. For the first time in my life, I was truly scared.

Days slipped into weeks as I sat at home and waited for something to happen. Occasionally I was called back to the college for some paperwork or to meet with the Union Rep. But deep down in the pit of my stomach, I knew I was beat. They wanted nothing to do with me. I was a bad smell, but because I had rights I couldn't be booted out immediately. On the other hand, two Garda officers in particular were genuinely concerned. They did everything they could to support me. Even my classmates were amazing. Their loyalty and words of encouragement were second to none. But no matter what people told me about 'keeping my chin up' and 'it wasn't the end of the world,' I was in a world of hurt.

Eventually the phone calls from friends and guards stopped. The harsh realization that I would never be a cop was finally hitting me.

I had been called to meet with the college Superintendent again. Secretly I hoped that she was going to have some good news for me, but as it turned out, it was merely for some administration formalities. On the drive home, I decided that it was time to make the call I had been considering for more than a few weeks. I pulled the car into a layby about ten miles from home on a hot summer afternoon and dialed the number.

'Hiya, Nick,' I said. 'How are things? It's Paddy.'

It had been more than four months since I'd last talked to him. He sounded surprised to hear my voice.

'Alright, Paddy. What's the story?' he asked.

'Not good, Nick. I'm in a lot of trouble, mate.'

We spoke for a good half an hour as I explained the situation to my old boss and friend. I could hear in his voice that he genuinely cared. It was good to talk to somebody from my old life again. Nick knew my worth and knew what I was about. There were no explanations needed with him. From one ex-soldier to another, he could see I was backed into a corner and reaching out for help.

'When do you have your next court appearance?' asked Nick.

'About six weeks from today,' I answered.

Nick paused for a second.

'Are you ready to fly?' he asked.

'Yes, Nick. You give the fucking word mate and I'm there.'

'Okay. I'll get you down to Port au Prince by the end of the week. Just wait out and keep your phone handy.'

For the first time in more than a month, I felt a genuine sense of self-worth. I smiled as I thanked him, then hung up the phone and headed home.

I hated the police for forcing me to leave my family. The path I had chosen was now a dead end. There was no way out. Life for me in Ireland was as good as over. Here I was nothing more than a failed cop. With the Celtic Tiger taking her last few breaths, there really wasn't much call for a man of my caliber. I thought I had chosen a noble path, an honorable career in helping others. I found myself being labelled a drink driver, a loser, a waster. It was sickening.

'It's only for six weeks' I told my family. 'I'll be back before you know it. Maybe the guards will see sense. Maybe the judge won't be too hard.'

I tried to reassure them that I was making the right decision. I had to get away from this mess, if only for a few weeks. I had to start earning money again.

I said goodbye to my sister Karen at Dublin Airport. Baby Jack was there in her arms. Almost a year old and he was growing bigger every day. As Karen handed him to me, he looked at me and smiled. I kissed his plump, rosy cheeks and gave him one last hug. He was my little superhero. Karen hugged me and wished me good luck and a safe return.

'We love you, Patrick,' she said.

I loved them too. More than they could ever know.

I looked back one more time to see their faces before I rounded the corner for the security check. It was a terrible feeling. None of this had been part of my plan.

Aer Lingus flight EI105 accelerated down the runway one more time. Half a year had passed since last I had set foot on Haitian soil.

Chapter Eleven

SHELF LIFE

SATURDAY, 16TH AUGUST, 2008

HEXAGON, PORT AU PRINCE

The rain pummeled down from dark grey clouds far above us. It had been torrential and continuous since my return. Tropical storm Fay was already over the island of Hispaniola wreaking havoc for those who were much more exposed to the elements than us. We smoked cigarettes, drank coffee and watched the rain pound off the roofs and windscreens of the cars.

'How long has it been like this?' I asked Pavlov.

'Fuck kurwa. More than one week now,' said the gargantuan Slovak. Pavlov appeared to be much bigger since the last time I'd seen him six months before. I wondered if he was lifting heavier weights these days or perhaps he had begun to eat the damn things. True to form, Pavlov was still a gentle, mental giant.

'It is going to get worse before it gets better,' he said. 'They say that this season will be one of the worst for hurricanes.'

We stood quietly for a while, enjoying our vices.

'So, police is finished for you now or what?'

I had forgotten about the entire affair, even if only for a morning. A court case and a suspension review board awaited me back in Ireland. I had a window of five weeks before I had to appear in the Waterford District court.

'It's looking bad for me. They want me gone ole buddy. Maybe I can fight it, but I don't think I'm going to win this one.'

Pavlov looked at me with that familiar mischievous grin. I knew that he would be one of the last people to ever judge me. 'Well, Paddy, kurwa. Welcome home.'

It was as simple as that for my Slovak brother. A man of few words, he managed to bring a smile to my face on a miserably wet day in Port au Prince.

'You know you've missed all the excitement here just a few months ago?' he added.

'The food riots. Yeah, I heard it was pretty crazy alright.'

I peered out from under the cover of the terrace and let the rain hit my face.

'Well,' I said. 'Looks like it's time for a new story.'

We stubbed out our smokes and headed back inside to the sheriff office.

Hurricane Fay was only the beginning. Already villages and towns had to contend with uncontrollable flooding. Eventually, Fay was only classed as a tropical storm by American news reports. By the following week, reports were coming in that hurricane Gustav was on the way. The next couple of days were spent bringing client's families to supermarkets and hard ware stores. Everybody was preparing for the worst. The incessant showers showed little signs of breaking. Back home in Ireland we could sometimes find ourselves house bound by snow in winter. Here in Haiti, you're made housebound by hurricanes, assuming that your house doesn't wash away in the process.

A few days later, winds of up to one hundred and twenty miles an hour swept across the island. To their detriment, the coastal town of Les Cayes in the southwest, a place that was no stranger to hurricanes, failed to take proper defense measures. They never sandbagged the roofs and doorways of their homes. By Wednesday night, its townsfolk found themselves in an appalling situation. Rather than prepare for the oncoming storm, the locals had taken to the streets in protest at the radical hike in food prices. When Gustav ripped ashore with all her destructive power, the region was swamped. Roads and bridges buckled under her might. Farms were flooded and livestock killed in the surrounding areas. Hurricane Gustav was my first experience of the true forces of nature. Everybody hoped that it would be the last one of the season. How wrong we were.

Less than a week later the country braced itself once again for the 'big one,' hurricane Hanna. Unluckily, I found myself down at the Turgeau switch the morning she made her approach. The new eleven story Digicel building in Turgeau was nearing completion. One of the heads of the project decided at the very last minute to go 'check some things' at the site before Hanna arrived. Though the skies were a Caribbean blue that day, far off in the distance I saw one giant cloud unlike any other I'd ever seen before. It wasn't just dark, it was pitch black. By the time I left the Hexagon and arrived at the new building, the winds were already picking up. In my mind, I questioned why the client had chosen such a time to bring us down there. Could it really have been that important? As we drove through the main gate and onto the site, I asked him if he wanted to get out of the car and enter the building.

'No, no,' he answered as his spectacled eyes looked out of the rear passenger window. 'I just want to check that the windows are in place and everything is okay.'

I was stunned. How crazy could this guy be to want to check the windows of an eleven story building whose predominant exterior is made of glass? I'd thought that he'd wanted to come down here and press some buttons on a machine or a computer, but no, he came to check the windows.

Even the guard who opened the gate waited anxiously for us to leave as he continued to stare upwards as far as the top floor. The poor guy was probably troubled by the prospect of being sliced in half for standing out in hazardous conditions. I couldn't blame him.

When the client decided that the windows were 'still there' and everything was okay, we immediately got back on the road for Petion Ville. It was a good job too because I was on the verge of telling him that we were heading back anyways. I gave the local security guard a salute as he struggled to open the gate against the rising winds and hammering rains. By the time we pulled back out onto the street, the black cloud was covering Port au Prince.

As soon as we began to make our twists and turns along the back streets of Canape Vert, we quickly found ourselves blocked in by collapsing trees. I strained my eyes to see beyond the heavy rain splashing on the windscreen. At least two trees had already collapsed directly out in front. The rotted wood that came down had pulled a number of electrical cables along with it in the fall.

'Back up the car, Raymond,' I said.

As Raymond made the three point turn in the heavy armored Land Cruiser, another chunk of wood gave way, collapsing on the road directly behind us. When I turned in my seat to look out the rear window, I noticed the worried look on my client's face.

From behind an old abandoned car, a homeless man was taking shelter between a parked car and the wall. While Raymond, the client and I sat in the Land Cruiser out of the elements, this old Haitian stepped out from his place of refuge and began moving one of the thick, heavy fallen branches out of our path. A man who had nothing to gain, and everything to risk, put himself in harm's way so we could pass in this cumbersome automobile. I immediately dismounted the vehicle and joined the old-timer in his efforts. I pulled the branch out of sheer shame and frustration as I watched electrical cables dance about the street to my left. The trees and branches turned out to be much lighter than they had appeared. Once the last branch was out of the way, I gave the old Haitian the firmest handshake I could. In the wind and rain there was no time to stand around and chat. I had to get going just as much as he had to get back to his place of safety. As I told the man that I didn't have any money on me, he just shrugged his thin, frail shoulders as if to say, 'don't worry'. I was humbled by his selflessness. Drenched to the bone, I hopped back into the Land Cruiser. Raymond looked at me with the broadest smile. As if I had done something that was not part of bodyguard procedures.

'Hexagon please, Raymond,' I said as I wiped the rain from my face.

My friend smiled.

'Yes,' he answered in his squeaky tone. 'Hexagon.'

The hurricanes destroyed thousands of homes across the country, leaving tens of thousands more badly damaged. By the time hurricanes Fay, Gustav, Hanna, and finally Ike had passed, almost one thousand people had been reported dead. It was the worst hurricane season on record and another catastrophic disaster for the island. The strange thing about Hanna was that nobody could predict her path right up until the morning she made her debut.

One thing that I had forgotten in my six month absence was the fact that there was never a dull moment in Haiti. My five weeks came and went faster than I had anticipated. By the time I returned to Waterford in mid-October, I was the only one standing in the court house with a sun tan. This time as I sat in amidst the circus that is a modern day district courtroom, I didn't feel like the biggest clown there. Haiti was my secret. As far as the Garda College was concerned, I was sitting at home with my tail between my legs. As for the Road Traffic offence, typical of many district cases, the arresting Guard was dragging his ass. My case had been postponed until the first week of December. That gave me another five to six weeks of work back in Haiti. My friends and family still looked at me with worry and sympathy. I knew they meant well, but I was tired of been treated as a cripple. Back in Haiti, nobody gave a shit. To the boys, I was just 'Paddy the Irish guy.' My solicitor still thought that I had a case to fight. So did my family and friends. As much as I craved to return to my training, I wasn't sure if it was worth continuing with the case. It was too big a decision to make at the time. When the moment was right, I would know what to do. On the plus side, I got to spend five days at home with my family. Even though I had only been away for five weeks, life in Ireland was beginning to feel a lot different. I didn't truly feel like I belonged there anymore. I needed to get back to the basics of who I was, and being with my friends and having a mission. Haiti was where I could do that.

****

'So what's happened?' asked Pavlov when he picked me up at the airport on a sunny Tuesday afternoon.

'Big bullshit with police my friend, nothing new, same shit.'

Pavlov gave one of his hearty laughs as he opened the boot of the green Nissan Patrol.

'Welcome home Paddy kurwa. Finish this police bullshit. This is where you belong, with your brothers.'

I couldn't help but feel he was right. Maybe my life as I had known it back in Ireland had come to an end. Maybe I just hadn't realized it yet. I was caught between two worlds. There was 'Garda Paddy' and 'Haiti Paddy' and no way could I go on being the two. Eventually, I would have to choose. Nick Brady could only help me for so long. My being in and out of Haiti was probably keeping some other guy out of a job. The decision to quit the cops at that moment was still too big. I needed more time.

'You know that Colin Rawes is back since two days before,' Pavlov informed me.

'Oh for fuck sake. Please tell me you are joking.'

Rawes was not a hot favorite amongst the team. Nor was he too keen on my transient stays in Haiti this last while. Every so often he was sent in to check up on operations and ensure the lads were working to company standards. It was bullshit. The guys were always up to scratch. But that never seemed to stop our numbers from diminishing. Our original team strength from late 2006 had practically been halved. Many of the older guys had had enough and moved on to other projects. Cerek had left to go to Afghanistan. Ratko and Kinga had also left to go work in Iraq. Though still working with Vigilance, Viktor had been seconded to somewhere in Indonesia. Sandie and two other guys had also handed in their notice and went to work for another security company in Port au Prince. It was a much smaller company in comparison to Vigilance. But because it was smaller, the contract proved to be a more lucrative one. Opportunities were opening up within Haiti that still called for security personnel. Unfortunately, if any of the guys even hinted at leaving, they ran the risk of finding themselves out of a job. Losing even one of the good guys from the team affected the morale of those remaining. Nobody talked about it openly, but we all felt we were on a tightrope of sorts. Even I was conscious that this could apply to me at some point.

Over my time in and out of Haiti, it became clear that everyone had a shelf life. Not just security personnel, but ex-pats in general. Only those who had truly dedicated themselves to the country ever really stayed. By late 2008,

Haiti's security climate was slowly changing too. Although cosmetically it was difficult to see, Port au Prince was in a state of transition. The United Nations, in particular the Brazilian army and marines, had cleaned up and arrested the hard-core criminal elements of Cité Soleil and Cité Militaire. In the aftermath of the hurricanes, it started to feel like there was a glimmer of hope for Haiti.

****

It was still early morning but news had already reached the team house that something catastrophic had happened in Petion Ville. I poured myself a cup of coffee in the kitchen. I had been on the night shift and was still pretty fatigued. The former army corporal from Galway looked like a man with a lot on his mind. He paced about with a cup of tea in his hand and a cigarette in his mouth.

'Are you alright, Mac?' I asked.

'There's some bad news down in Petion Ville, Paddy. A school is after collapsing on a load of kids.'

'Fuck off! Where?'

'It's the 'La Promesse' school, just down by Munchees restaurant, happened less than a half hour ago. There's a lot of commotion down that way. I've heard reports of dozens dead. Kids, Paddy, fucking little kids, mate.'

I tried to picture the disaster. It was too much to imagine. What made it all the more visceral was the fact that the school and its students were no more than a ten minute drive from the team house. It was right on our doorstep.

'I've asked if we can form up volunteers to go down and help,' he said.

Mac had been a fireman in Ireland after his time in the army. Here was a situation where we might be able to help people in dire straits. We had to at least try and help. Mac, Piro, Pavlov, myself and two other lads grabbed medical supplies and took one of the Nissan Patrols parked outside the team house. We were adamant to get down to the collapsed school and see what the situation was.

Even though we were mobile and en route, we still had to get clearance from management. The word they were giving us was no. No way! Immediately we went to the Hexagon to have it out with the security operations manager. Graham, the previous manager, had since moved on and been replaced by a South African man called Cobus. Cobus was in his early fifties. He was a proper old soldier in that he was very approachable and generally a decent guy to the troops. I didn't really know him. All I knew was that he had been an officer with the fearsome South African Recces once upon a time and that he was a dedicated family man.

Finally, the word came down from Digicel management that our team could attend the disaster scene providing that we kept them informed of developments. However, the morning crew was to stay as day to day operations still had to continue. That was good enough for Cobus, and for our small team of medics. With the green light, we got back into the Patrol and made our way to the school.

We were no further than a half mile away when the streets in lower Petion Ville were blocked by hundreds and hundreds of people. Police checkpoints were everywhere. They had set up road blocks to keep back the multitudes of parents that came to find their children. The entire area was in pandemonium. United Nations vehicles and NGO groups flocked to the scene. Large UN APC (Armor Personnel Carrier) carriers lined one side of the street. The likelihood of our entry down to the school faded quickly.

A few seconds later, we neared the first Haitian police barrier.

'Put on some surgical gloves,' said Mac. 'Put on the gloves, roll down your windows and tell them we are medics here to help.'

We did as Mac instructed and quickly put the gloves on. When the cop looked over at our Nissan, all he saw were six grown men staring back at him while waving hands and wiggling fingers with surgical gloves and shouting that we were medics. He must have thought we were a bunch of mental patients on some sort of nutters' outing. Nevertheless, he let us pass, but warned that we would not get much further through the crowds by car.

With the Nissan safely abandoned at a petrol station, we grabbed the medic bags and made our way down to the collapsed school. It was quite a hike through the maze of back streets. The November sun was already beating down on us hard. Sweat ran down my face as I frog marched it along the rocky, narrow roadway. There were ambulances already there, but they could get no closer to the school than the final kilometer. Aid workers and UN soldiers were acting as stretcher bearers for many of the injured. Parents screamed and wept uncontrollably waiting for news of their missing children.

The scene was just as I had anticipated. What I didn't know, however, was that the school was a five story building with about five hundred students ranging from infants to seniors. It was a cataclysm. Five stories of classrooms had pancaked, creating a mountain of mangled concrete and metal. Worst of all, though there were at least fifty Chilean and Pakistani UN peacekeepers on the scene, nobody could enter the school. The mound of rubble and debris was near inaccessible and looked highly unstable. Professional rescue teams were needed immediately. As it would turn out, they needed to come from Guadeloupe, Martinique and the United States. To muster such assistance would take another twenty four hours. In the meantime, all anybody could do was remove the dead children who lay in the more accessible crevices and wait until expert rescuers with the proper equipment arrived.

As I spoke to some of the UN peacekeepers about what was happening, the faded cries of children far beneath the inner confines of the rubble were barely audible. It was like a distant murmur. From where we stood, none of them could be reached.

Soon the children's' cries were drowned out by a United Nations Huey helicopter hovering directly over the school. No doubt some UN general with his office of pen pushers were making their assessments for Kofi and the gang back in Geneva. What they didn't realize was that the down draft from the rotor blades was putting tremendous pressure on the buckled concrete floors. Dozens of people waved at the chopper to signal her to move away. The entire scene was ludicrous.

To add to the complications, the first Haitian attempt to send in heavy rescue equipment ended in disaster. A caterpillar crane that had been working on a construction site in uptown Petion Ville was dispatched to the scene. While the driver was making his way through Place St. Pierre, the breaking system malfunctioned and lead to the write off of three cars parked outside the local police station. The large, tank-like tracks of the colossal machine left one passenger dead and another injured. It was a testament to the sheer lack of resources the country had available for any form of crisis.

We worked as best we could with the United Nations forces. Eventually, military engineers arrived and there was little else we could do but move out of the way and let them do their work with what limited equipment they had. By the time we started making our way back, more parents arrived.

'My babies, my babies. Where are my babies?' screamed one distraught mother. Her husband held her tightly as he too was in a state of anguish. I tried to imagine what this would all look like back home in

Ireland. We had expected to arrive and treat the wounded. What actually awaited us was a crematorium locked away from the outside world.

A few days later, news spread that the director of the school had been arrested for the involuntary manslaughter of up to eighty five children. According to reports, he had built three extra stories onto a two story school without any architectural plans or construction standards in place. The hurricanes from August and September, along with the incessant rainfall, had softened the inadequate foundations and poorly extended construction. The covetous school director was a businessman. He probably just wanted more students to fill the rooms so he could line his pockets. That he most certainly did, and sent almost a fifth of them to their graves in the process.

****

I stood outside the courtroom waiting for my solicitor. This was my third appearance. Each time I came alone, and each time I was clean shaven, wearing a dark suit, ironed white shirt and burgundy tie. My solicitor told me that my court case would be postponed again until February 2009. When I asked him why, he explained that the arresting Garda was on his motorbike course in the Garda College and the member in charge (the Garda who processed my charge sheet) was going to Spain on vacation. Therefore my case would have to wait.

Enough was enough. The decision I had struggled with all those months before was now clear in my mind. Before we entered the courtroom, I instructed my solicitor to enter a plea of guilty. My career was over and it was time for me to move on with my life, no matter what the price. I received a two hundred euro fine, a one year's suspension on my driving license and a three year endorsement. And that was that. Case closed. As for my career suspension, I decided that I would rather resign than get the boot. That was my decision. No longer would I be judged and controlled by outside influences. The future rested with me. Not some crusty old Chief Superintendent in Dublin on a disciplinary committee. I had the upmost respect for my Garda pals who were going to make a career in the force and I wished them the best of luck. But my time was done. Two days later I handed in my kit and received a handshake and best wishes from the two officers who supported me throughout the entire ordeal. They asked me if I was sure I wanted to resign, but they both knew I was goosed. As sad as I was to hand in my uniform and drive out of the gates, I felt a burden had been lifted from my shoulders. Finally I was making decisions for myself again. I knew there were worse things in life than not becoming a cop. However grateful I was to Nick Brady for renewing my old job, I knew that Vigilance was not the long term answer either. Eventually, I would have to figure out a permanent way back to my life in Ireland.

On another rainy Irish day in December, I had an early Christmas dinner with Karen, Shea, baby Jack and my folks. By the 25th December 2008 I would celebrate my third Christmas in Haiti.

****

2009 in Port au Prince was a period of accelerated change and potential prosperity. Apart from the senate elections in April, the very worst we were witnessing from a security standpoint was the odd protest over wage disputes. By the summer, former American President Bill Clinton was named UN Special Envoy to Haiti. This was a step in the right direction in bringing Haiti to the forefront of international politics. The mass kidnappings of 2006 and 2007 were becoming a thing of the past. Hundreds of criminals and gang members in the capital had been imprisoned. The troubled Caribbean nation was still a rough diamond in blue waters, but the spell of relative calm gave its people the breathing space to at least try and move forward from its troublesome past.

The New Year also saw a period of calm amongst our security ranks. Oliver Tomkins, one of the bodyguards who arrived almost a year before, had been promoted to country manager, replacing Cobus. Oliver had been a copper in the Metropolitan Police for over fifteen years. Lean and with strikingly blonde hair, Ollie looked the part. He was young, tenacious and hungry to do the job.

The team had been downsized and we were in a state of transition having just moved from the Hexagon to the new Digicel Turgeau building near Canape Vert. With new management, a number of changes came in to place. We began to work with a larger number of local bodyguards who had been drafted in. Pavlov became the new sheriff and saw me take over from Iván as team leader. Between the pair of us, we were able to implement a system whereby guys had one day off per week. Watching Pavlov run the sheriff office with his personal Nokia smart phone and a Bluetooth earpiece was like watching a masterpiece being painted before your eyes. Cool and collected, the wacky Slovak could cover a greater number of missions than any of his predecessors (including me) he continued to use the ex-pat bodyguards while at the same time, integrating the new local bodyguards into the ranks. Nobody knew how he did it. But as long as the clients were happy, our management was too. And if the management was happy, then Pavlov and me could run the daily operation between ourselves. Nobody was breathing down our necks.

I could no longer look at Haiti merely as an operational environment. Whether I knew it or I liked it, the little Caribbean nation had become my home. Living there meant exactly that.

For four months, Pavlov and myself ran everything in a smooth, proficient manner. Even the number of client complaints dropped. They had always failed to understand the stresses and strains of the sheriff's job. All they needed to be concerned about was for a car to be waiting for them outside their door. Pavlov changed all that. As long as myself or Ollie kept feeding him Marlboro Lights and cups of coffee, the baldy Slovak kept the cogs turning.

Monday to Saturday, I was down in the office with the morning team. Because of the smaller ex-pat security team, I often stayed until well after six o'clock in the evening. This was something my predecessor never had to do. But it didn't matter. My Saturday nights and Sunday mornings were usually mine to enjoy. I had started dating an American girl who I'd been introduced to through friends. Her name was Rachel and she was working on an aid project in Haiti. With a vivacious passion for life, a gorgeous smile and incredible blonde hair, Rachel became a very positive factor in my new approach to life in Haiti. Early Sunday mornings were spent having breakfast overlooking the city from her terraced apartment in Pacot. I enjoyed every moment that I got to spend with her. When my month of leave came in April, I even managed to share a memorable four week vacation with Rachel traveling in the United States.

Unfortunately, it's true what they say about all good things. By the time I had returned to the team in May, much had changed. After my American vacation, I had returned without Rachel. Her company had assigned her to another project in Washington, which meant her time in Haiti was through. The hardest news to grasp was that Pavlov had been given his 'Spanish Holiday'. Management had let him go. Apparently they thought he had gotten too big for his boots and had developed a poor attitude. My role as team leader had also turned into a farce. I spent all my time out in the cars now unlike the good old days of helping to oversee everything from the office. I didn't mind the missions, but I saw no point in being responsible for a team when I was never actually there to be responsible for them. A rift had developed between management and staff. Missions were becoming more reliant on local bodyguards. The rest of us were designated to senior clients. Piro, the young Hungarian, had also been promoted to a desk job. I was happy for him, but it meant we were another man down on the teams. The 'management versus labor' culture had truly developed and everybody felt the chill.

The system that Pavlov had built in the early part of 2009 was over. Other sheriffs filled his seat but none achieved the same level of efficiency. Even the clients began to complain more, and by God did they know how to do just that. I was reported by a client one morning when I told him to 'stop acting like a fucking baby and get in the car'. He refused to come down from his apartment because we had not sent him an armored vehicle as we had for his neighbor. He was South American and felt he was being ridiculed because of his race. I couldn't believe that a grown man and a father of two small children could act like such a child himself. Later that morning I was pulled aside by management when the emails flowed down from HR.

Not long afterwards, I found myself receiving 'words of advice' from Oliver. One morning, I happened to sleep in and was running late to pick up my client. In all my time in Haiti, I had never slept in. But now, I found myself running ten minutes late. Quick thinking on the part of James, my new Irish roommate, meant that he took my mission as he was ready to leave the house. In turn I took his car to pick up his client, which wasn't for another twenty minutes. James's quick thinking resulted in both clients being picked up on time. As far as we were concerned, the issue was closed. But that was not the case. Oliver had reported me to Dublin about my failing to get out of bed on time. Later that day I received a bollocking on the phone from Nick for my idleness. I failed to understand why Oliver hadn't approached me on this matter himself and why had he run to the Director of the company. Yes, I was in the wrong. But an entire story was being made out of nothing. It was pathetic.

My time with Vigilance was going to be short lived. Whether it was knives in my back from people who I thought were my friends, or whether it was just what the gods had chosen for me. Time was running out. By mid-August I'd finally reached the point where it didn't matter anymore. I had long exceeded my shelf life working as a bodyguard in Haiti.

One evening, I was driving back to the team house with James. It had been one of those shit days and I was in crappy form. From the Digicel building in Turgeau, the commute was proving to be more tedious than in the days of the Hexagon. Traffic moved at a snail's pace and all we could do was stare out the window at life going by in Petion Ville.

'I don't think they'll keep me much longer,' I said to James. 'I can feel it coming.'

James had arrived in Haiti a few months earlier. He had been earmarked for management, but that position was for Indonesia. James had been a corporal in the army. At thirty-two years old, and as well built as Pavlov, he was what you call a 'unit'.

'I wouldn't sweat it, mate,' he said as we made our way into Petion Ville. 'Just don't give them any ammunition to get rid of you.'

'Maybe,' I said. 'Fuck it. We'll see.'

Just as I said this, an old Haitian man stepped out from behind a wall with two gargantuan brown pigs in front of him. He had a thin stick in his hand and was driving the two hogs out onto the road between the traffic. He proceeded to whip the ass off the slower of the two beasts.

'There you go, Paddy,' said James. 'Fucking pig-whipper, mate. Perfect job for ya.'

One day, I was tasked with taking an Irish businessman around Port au Prince for a week. His name was Terry Clune, and he ran a multi-million dollar company dealing with tax rebates. Terry was a tall man, well over six foot. Well dressed and well spoken, he was quite a burly fella who came across as smart, motivated and pleasant.

Terry planned to set up offices in the new Digicel Turgeau building. At the end of his week in the Caribbean, while bringing him down to the airport, I was offered a job as project manager. Terry wanted me to set up his Haiti office. After careful negotiations over the next seven days, I accepted the position. It wasn't without sleepless nights, tons of research, and then considering the idea of stepping into the business world of which, I knew very little about.

One thing I was sure of was that I no longer belonged with Vigilance. Truthfully, I didn't even believe in the mission anymore. I probably hadn't for a long time. Kidnapping was not the big game in Haiti by late 2009 (though it still existed on a smaller level). Public protests (manifestations) were the real potential risk factor for ex-pats. Even that wasn't so bad, providing you didn't drive into the center of an angry mob.

After I handed in my six weeks' notice to Nick, I found myself out of a job effective immediately and out of the team house within twelve hours. He had not taken the news of my parting very well at all. Many of the newer guys were stunned by what was going on, but the senior fellas knew the score, as did I. It was just my time to go. Colin Rawes was all too happy to be the one to drive me off the premises. It felt good not to be beholden to such narcissistic men like him anymore.

I was sad to see things end as they did and I held no ill will towards Nick. He saw my leaving as betrayal. I could appreciate that. Nick had been a friend and thrown me a rope in my hour of need. But that was more than a year before. A year that I spent the majority of in Haiti while he was at home in Ireland living his life. I wanted to go home too. Maybe Terry and his company was the door I needed to open. I had to take the chance.

Chapter Twelve

TAXBACK.COM

TUESDAY, 29TH SEPTEMBER, 2009

KILKENNY, IRELAND

It was a dull, wet afternoon when the train pulled into Kilkenny station. I had made this journey many times as a young soldier. For my last year and a half in the army, I had been posted here with support-company of the 3rd Infantry Battalion. The one good thing about being stationed in Kilkenny was the number of pubs up and down its streets and the fact that these pubs were regularly frequented by energetic and colorful hen parties hailing from as far away as Manchester or Liverpool. I noticed the steeple of the cathedral across the road from the train station. I thought about how I used to run each day, past the cathedral, down through the castle grounds and along the riverside. There was something ironic in how Haiti had brought me back to Kilkenny almost six years to the day I had left. Wearing a shirt and tie, I felt underdressed for the weather. Terry had invited me to visit his office to discuss the Haiti project. Once I got off the train, I flagged a taxi man who was waiting patiently for his next fare.

'Where are you off to?' he asked.

'Eh, the taxback.com office out on the industrial estate,' I said as I got into the cab.

The driver nodded, then drove out of the car park and headed out the Waterford road. When we got there, the building was hard to miss. I looked up to see the red taxback.com logo on the newly built three story business unit. I'd read online that the building belonged to Terry. The first two floors were in use and the third floor would be for their expansion the following year. I made my way upstairs and approached the young receptionist at the front desk. She greeted me with a smile as I said good afternoon.

'Hi. How are you doing? I'm here to see Terry.'

She looked uncertain.

'Okay. What's your name?'

'Paddy. Paddy Doyle.'

'And he's expecting you?' she asked as she picked up the phone.

'Yes.'

We both waited until the call was answered.

'Yeah, hi, Terry. I have a Paddy Doyle here to see you. Mmhmm, right, will do, thanks Terry.'

With that she put the phone back down.

'He's on the way down to you now, Paddy.'

A few minutes later Terry came through a set of double doors. He wore a loosened burgundy tie and a dark, expensive looking suit with a white shirt, just like when I had met him in Haiti. With a broad smile and a warm hand shake, he was one of those positive, larger than life individuals.

'Paddy. How are you? Come on through and I'll show you the setup.'

There must have been about seventy people working behind spacious work stations. The entire operation looked very new. From the desks to the carpeting, everything looked so fresh and new. I still felt out of place in the office environment, but I tried not to let it show.

'Do you want a cup of coffee before I show you around?' he offered.

'Sounds good, Terry. Thanks.'

We walked through to his office. In one corner there was a large mahogany desk with a black leather chair. Behind it, towards the center of the room, a large brown leather couch matched with two leather armchairs gave the place a sense of ease. I hadn't been offered a seat, but I decided to sit in one of the armchairs anyway.

'I bought this new coffee machine the other day,' said Terry. 'It makes espressos too. Which would you prefer?'

'Eh, coffee is fine, Terry,' I answered.

As Terry made the coffees, I was still trying to decide what might be the best way to sit on the leather chair. I sat with one leg crossed over the other to try and look refined and comfortable in the office environment. But after five seconds, my balls hurt so I uncrossed my legs, then re-crossed them at the ankle. By the time Terry came over with the coffees, I was already sweating.

We chatted for a while about my return to Ireland. I'd only been back a few weeks and already I was getting bored. I wanted Terry to know that I was excited about the call center project and I couldn't wait to get started. We discussed the overall end result and where he wanted it to be within six months.

'By all accounts, it will be the first of its kind in Haiti,' he said. 'We'll predominantly be focused on US tax returns for student work visas and so on. Do you think we could have twenty-four people working in it by the end of March next year?'

End of March. That gave me just over six months. Six months away to have twenty-four people under my supervision for a company I had not yet worked for, in a field I had no idea of and in a call center that did not even exist yet. There was work to be done. That much was certain. The project would be a success, whatever the sacrifice. Some common sense, a lot of hard work, and I would prevail. I would see to that.

'Twenty-four. It's definitely achievable Terry. But if you want me to concentrate my efforts on the US tax returns, then I'm going have to learn how that system works. Plus I'm going to need to see how a call center business works.'

'How long do you need?' asked Terry.

'How long where Terry?'

'Bulgaria,' he said. 'I'll send you to Varna. We have a large operation there with over four hundred and fifty staff. That's where the US visa tax returns call center is operating out of at the moment. Just tell me how long you need there before you return to Haiti.'

Simple as that. No bullshit. Down to the brass taxes, so to speak. I liked it.

'Six weeks,' I answered, knowing full well that it was too long, but also knowing that I needed a minimum of three.

Terry frowned slightly.

'Can you do it in less time than six weeks?' he said.

I took a moment to calculate numbers for a task that I still did not fully understand.

'Okay, a month. I can do it in a month, come back to Ireland for a few days, and then be on my way to Haiti.'

He smiled.

'That's great, Paddy. How does Friday suit you to fly out?'

'Yep,' I said. 'That's fine.'

'Good man. But before you fly to Varna I'll need you to visit the Cork office and have a meeting with Janet, our Human Resources lady. Apart from me, she will be working closely with you on this. Would tomorrow be okay to head down?'

'That's not a problem,' I replied.

'And also,' he added. 'Could you visit the Dublin office and meet with Thelma? She is one of the other Directors. I'd like you to have a bit of a meet and greet with her before you leave.'

'Can do,' I answered. My mouth was responding to each request, while my brain was trying to process the one before.

Terry arranged the meetings for Cork and Dublin, and after we finished our coffees he gave me a tour of his Kilkenny offices. There I met the staff of finance and legal, both of which I would be working with over the next six months.

Later that afternoon, he dropped me to the train station in his X5 series BMW. In the back were baby chairs and kids toys. He told me about the summer home he was building for his family on the south east coast and how it was to be an eco-friendly house. I was hard pushed not to be impressed by him. A multi-million dollar international business, beautiful homes and a top of the line car. But behind all that, I was more impressed by his humility and down to earth nature. Terry was a businessman. That was indisputable. But even more so, he was an entrepreneur. A man who followed his instinct. That gut feeling that people have and even fewer people listen to. That same instinct told him back in Haiti that I was the right man for the job, and my instinct told me that right here, with Terry and taxback.com, I had made the right decision. If I was to have a boss who I wanted to impress, who I wanted to show that he had picked the right man for the job, then that boss was Terry.

'Take care, Paddy,' he said as he dropped me off. 'I'll give you a shout before you fly out to Varna.'

With a thank you and a hand shake, I went back into the station coffee shop to wait for my train.

When I arrived back in Waterford, my sister Karen and nephew Jack were there to pick me up at the station. As luck would have it, the sun came out for a while, so

Karen and I took Jack for a short walk along the river walkway, not far from where we grew up. It was amazing to watch him walking and talking. Jack was almost two years old and was already turning into a little boy. His sentences were short but I knew what he wanted to say. Jack wanted to go between his mom and me so that we could hold his hands and give him 'swings' up into the air. He laughed so hard each time that the little mite would gasp for breath with every swing. He loved it and he wanted to do it again and again. Later, we threw stones into the river. I helped him to pick out the best ones that would skim across the surface, just like my dad had done with me when I was small. Jack's face was full of smiles. Wrapped up under the hood of his blue jacket, his rosy red cheeks and his gorgeous blue eyes were beaming with wonderment. Looking at him, I tried to imagine what he was thinking. The river was such a long way from his granny's house. What a wonderful adventure it must have been for him to walk so far, safe in knowing that his mom and uncle were with him.

That night I read Jack a bedtime story about the three bears. It was his favorite. His little eyes soon grew heavy and he was out for the count. I sat with Karen as we watched him sleeping. He was down for the count from his busy day. We talked for a while about Jack, about Karen's life now as a mom and how so much had changed in such a short time. Jack was almost two years old. Two years! Where had the time gone? I had been there for him but had I been there enough? I felt that as his uncle, as his Godfather, I should be doing better. My evening with Jack and Karen had been wonderful, but short. I hugged my younger sister and said goodnight. Tomorrow, I would begin a new chapter.

****

The weeks that followed went quickly. Varna turned out to be a beautiful city but unfortunately my heavy work didn't allow me any time to enjoy it. Upon my arrival, my mind was a blank canvas. Immediately, I began to learn about the various departments I would be dealing with relative to my project and how they operated. IT and Communications. These guys told me what equipment I would need. Phones, computers, servers, data-centers, firewalls, Voice Over IP, how I would link it all up to the company database. I kept notes on everything that they told me, but my head was still spinning with the information.

Next was the US tax refund market for students and how that system worked. That part alone was a mind bender. The system itself was complex to say nothing of the volume of calls that would have to be made on any one shift. I had to master these calls and the system in order to pass on the skills to the first batch of people I would hire.

Then, there was Human Resources Management. Contracts that had to be drawn up. Haiti had different work laws to most European workplaces. I would have to learn how that system worked too.

Legal and finance. These departments had to be constantly up to speed with my progress. Legal would be used a lot more, just before the company was up and running.

Operations, well, that was me. I was pulling these elements together to make it all happen, to build a tax refunds call center.

Then, there would be the endless conference calls to Digicel back in Haiti as I would be working closely with an assigned project manager. His role was to help me implement the planning stages of the project once I returned.

For each department I was dealing with in Ireland and Bulgaria, I would liaise with their equivalent down in

Haiti. Plus, I would have to account for the time difference which meant I could not begin any discussions with Haiti until well after 5pm Bulgarian time.

One day, while I was finalizing some contract details with HR back in Ireland, my mobile rang. It was Terry.

'Janet, I'm going to have to call you back,' I said. 'I've got Terry on the other line.'

She understood straight away. I quickly switched lines before I lost his call.

'Hi, Paddy. How are you getting on over there?'

'Yeah, Terry. All good. A lot going on but all good.'

'I've got some news for you, Paddy,' he explained. 'Clinton announced the arrival of taxback.com in Haiti yesterday evening. I've sent the video link to your inbox.'

The publicity that the project was receiving had increased significantly. The UN Special Envoy for Haiti, President Bill Clinton had announced the arrival of the call center in the Karibe hotel in Port au Prince less than twenty four hours prior.

'It looks like our launch in March may involve Bill Clinton also, Paddy. Do you think you could finish up in Varna this week?' he asked.

I'd only been in Bulgaria a little over two weeks. I thought I'd bought myself a month, but two and a half weeks of training… I thought about it.

'It doesn't give me much time, Terry. But I can speed things up if needs be.'

'Good man, Paddy,' he said. 'Have a look at the link, it's very exciting.'

When he hung up, I opened the email and watched the 42nd President of the United States declare our arrival in Port au Prince. He spoke about our commitment to creating twenty-four jobs by March of the following year. I felt lightheaded as I watched on. It was surreal but Terry was right, it was definitely exciting. I gave every remaining waking hour to my taxback.com indoctrination in Varna. Cut short by a week and a half or not, it was time to make this happen.

Chapter Thirteen

JACK OF ALL

WEDNESDAY, 8ᵀᴴ NOVEMBER, 2009

DIGICEL BUILDING, PORT AU PRINCE

Six weeks had passed since my return to Haiti. Today would be a milestone. The CEO of Digicel, Mr Denis O'Brien, was visiting the new taxback.com call center based on the eleventh floor of his multi-million dollar building in Turgeau.

It felt like we were the pioneers in a grand financial endeavor. Taxback.com had been the first foreign business to set up shop in the tallest and most modern building in the country. We would show other international companies, particularly Irish ones, that Haiti was a land full of potential markets just waiting to be tapped in to. There was more to Haiti than the predicaments of her past. The country that I had flown into almost three years before was changing, and for the better. O'Brien had envisaged that long before. He had been beating the drum side by side with Bill Clinton for more than two years, for the world to invest in the Haitian people. Invest in this country. Do business here.

With each passing day, I came to realize they were right. Since I returned to Haiti, I had managed to put together a call center with twenty-four work stations. Phase one was just about complete with six staff members in place. I had six smart young employees, all eager to work and learn. I had given every waking hour to all departments in Haiti, Ireland and Bulgaria. Though I had only completed the first phase, the taxback.com call center was pretty much running to schedule.

All morning we waited by our work stations for Mr O'Brien. I felt like a young soldier again, waiting for a room inspection by the CO (commanding officer). When he finally arrived, the world-renowned entrepreneur from Ireland spoke with each of my staff, and then with me.

'I wish your company all the very best here in Haiti,' he said warmly. 'It's a bit different from your old job I'd imagine.'

I smiled.

'Yes it is, Mr O'Brien.'

'No Mr O'Briens. Call me Denis.'

'Yes, it is, Denis. But it's a great project and Digicel have been very helpful.'

I briefly explained what our business entailed and why Haiti was the best location. He shook my hand again.

'Well,' he said. 'You have a fine set up here. Taxback is very welcome to Haiti. I look forward to seeing where you are next March.'

His schedule was extremely tight and he had given us more time than I had anticipated. The meeting had been brief but successful. He left with his entourage of managers and directors in tow. I even spotted Colin Rawes standing diligently behind them.

The project was not without its problems. I often found myself seeking mentorship from one of Digicel's operations managers, Jean Marc Le Hir. To be honest, without him, the project could have fallen weeks behind schedule.

Jean Marc was originally from the north west of France. He had arrived in Haiti over a year before. Even back in my security days, the handsome, pleasant Frenchman had always been extremely respectful and polite to the bodyguards. He was a man without an oversized ego and was genuinely concerned about how we were doing or whether we needed anything. Even though I was no longer protecting him as a bodyguard, his generous nature remained resolute.

Jean Marc taught me how to adjust my approach in order to conduct business effectively in Haiti. At first I did not like it as it meant readjusting my expectations of others. If a red ribbon was to be cut by Bill Clinton, Denis O' Brien and Terry Clune the following March, then I wanted everything done yesterday. I was young and eager and driven to prove myself.

'You'll drive yourself crazy,' he said with a smile. 'You will get there, Paddy, but you need to meet this country half way.'

He was right. It wasn't a question of switching myself off to what I was trying to achieve. But I did need to cut myself and others involved in the project a little bit more slack.

'Ask yourself this, Paddy,' he said to me one day on the roof of the Turgeau building. 'You have set up the data center without any IT people coming from Europe. You have gotten servers and modems through customs in a matter of days where it should have taken weeks. You have put together a business in a country that needs investment. But this is Haiti, Paddy. You know this. Everything takes time down here. If you fight it, you will go crazy.'

Jean Marc lit another menthol cigarette as we overlooked the entire city of Port au Prince.

'You will be fine. If you have any problems I will help as much as I can.'

That's what I liked about him. He never appeared stressed and always had something positive to say. I was lucky to have him as a mentor and a friend.

By mid-November, I'd also become aware of the new taxback.com office in Chicago, headed up by a bright young American woman called Sarah. Seeing as how my call center was to deal exclusively with the US market, I made it my business to tip my cap and say hi. As it turned out, Sarah was able to bring me up to speed on other endeavors within her branch. Sarah had recommended that taxback.com should join the Clinton Global Initiative (CGI). This was an organization comprising thousands of internationally renowned companies, spearheaded by Bill Clinton, with the aim of improving the world by investing in the economies of poorer countries. Taxback.com was now a part of that and the potential good that we could do within such an exclusive group drove me to work even harder for Terry and the company. Apart from setting up a business, creating local jobs and making profit, I knew that there was a humanitarian side to my character that remained untapped. The Clintons and O'Briens made me hungry to succeed. I felt I was a part of something exceptional and that I was finally putting myself in a position to help others less well off.

The only downside to all of this was my isolation. From Monday morning to Saturday afternoon, my life was all about the call center. But from Saturday afternoon to Sunday night, I spent most of my time alone. I tried to keep up with my remaining friends in security and even got to meet some them for a beer from time to time.

By November, the only social event I had been to was the Little Brothers and Sisters of Charity Thanksgiving party in their Petion Ville hospital. Gena and Maeve had invited me. I'd never celebrated the American holiday before. Gena's staff and volunteers prepared a delicious feast of turkey, potatoes, veg and an array of Haitian cuisine. There was a girl there too whom I'd never met before. Her name was Erin and she was incredibly beautiful. She had striking good looks with strawberry-blonde hair and freckled fair skin. I could have easily mistaken her for being Irish. I'd managed to grab her attention and chat to her for a while after the dinner. There must have been close to sixty people there, so it was tough to keep her attention. By the end of the night, I hadn't mustered up the courage to ask her out, but I had mustered up the courage to ask Gena for Erin's cell phone number the next day.

My old Hungarian buddy, Piro, had also moved into my apartment block with his girlfriend from home. Piro had been a lot more conservative compared to the rest of the bodyguards. He always managed to bring out the level-headed side of my character, and I valued his friendship for that. The fact that he and his better half were living in the same building certainly helped me to feel a little less alone.

Even with the constant demands of work and the few friends that I kept in contact with, I felt completely cut off. Christmas 2009 was still weeks away and my sense of isolation continued to grow irrepressibly. There seemed to be no stopping it. It concerned me that I was now living for Christmas with my family back in Ireland. Just outside my offices, on the eleventh floor, stood a decorated Christmas tree being used as part of an 'end of year' awards ceremony by Digicel. Every morning when I came to work, and each evening before I left, I would take a moment to look at the tree and let it remind me of all the good in my life that waited for me back home. Jack was now two years old and he was very excited about Santa Claus bringing him fireman stuff. Karen had sent me a recording of him singing 'Jingle Bells' a few days before. Each time I listened to his little voice I could feel all my stress and worries disappear, and when I closed my eyes, I could see nothing but that day we took him to skim stones in the river. All the emotions that I had dismissed throughout the weeks came flooding back in a Christmas Carol sang by a two year old. I thought about my mother and father and how much I missed them. I missed what few friends I had always kept close to me: Mick, Eoghan and Paul. I longed for those Christmas pints in the local and nights out with my best mates. Making it home for my first Christmas in more than three years had become my reward for my efforts in Haiti. I dared not think about the end of those ten days back home.

When my vacation was finally over, I probably would not be returning to Ireland until May or June. Basically, until I could wean my way out of my Haiti position and take up a posting with the company in Ireland. Whatever that job would be, I didn't care. I just wanted to be home and six or seven more months were needed to make that happen.

The ten days back home were exactly as I had imagined. We celebrated Christmas Day with Karen, Shea and little Jack in their home in Wexford. Karen laid on a proper Christmas spread. Roast turkey with all the trimmings. I played with Jack and his fireman toys that Santa Claus had brought him. I tucked him into bed that night and we talked about what a wonderful day he had had and what a good boy he had been for Santa to bring him such lovely toys. My dad had been in great form all day too. I introduced him to the magic of YouTube and how he could watch any singer, sports star or program that he wanted to see, all at the click of a button. I even got my suspended driving license back from the Motor Office. I was so happy to be home and that we were altogether again.

The next night, I met up with Mick and our friend Paul in Waterford. We made our way through all the old haunts. The town was busy that night and we had a ball. The following morning I went to the mountains with my friend Catherine. The Comeragh Mountains were practically on our back door step and I always tried to get up there at least once a year. I didn't feel the best that morning dragging my ass out of bed. The snow covered hills and the fresh icy air soon sorted out my hangover.

My stay in Ireland was extended by three more days. But these were work days. I spoke with Terry on the phone to give him a progress report and told him that I would need a second person to implement the next phase, the VISA First project. I had met the perfect candidate for the job on my visit to Cork in the first week of January. Her name was Elaine and she knew that part of the business inside out and upside down. I had spent a constructive couple of days in Cork working with her. She was excited about the Haiti office and though she was soon to go working for a year in Bulgaria, I was certain that she was the right person to help me with this phase. Once I returned to Haiti, I planned to request that she visit the offices for two weeks to train the next intake of staff.

Wednesday, the sixth of January, was my last full day in Ireland. My flight back to Haiti was departing from Dublin the following morning. About halfway home to Waterford, the weather took a turn for the worst. A massive snow storm hit the south-east of the country and the roads were a white out. What should have been a two hour drive home became almost four hours. Cars crawled as the snow continued to fall. By the time I arrived home, Waterford looked like a winter wonderland.

I had plenty of time to pack before the taxi brought me to the bus station. I left the keys of my father's Passat in the hall and went upstairs to my bedroom to pack. Sitting on the end of my bed, I couldn't bring myself to move. I just sat there looking at my clothes neatly piled by my suitcase. I did not want to leave.

With all of my experiences in life, the army, Lebanon, China, Israel, Denmark, Bosnia, America, the cops and of course, Haiti. I was still a jack of all trades and a master of none. I'd just finally hit the wall. My prolonged shelf life in Haiti had left me with nothing but a profound and empty sadness. I did not want to move. Haiti had been my savior and now my penance. I just could not pack that bag one more time.

'What's wrong, Patrick?' asked my mom standing at the door to my room. She'd heard me come in and go straight up stairs almost a half an hour before. I could not bring myself to look at her. I dropped my head into the palms of my hands and began to weep. I wept like I hadn't wept in years.

I couldn't even remember the last time I'd cried. For me, crying had always been a sign of weakness and the fact that I was doing it now was bizarre.

'I am so alone, mom,' I said. 'I am completely alone in my life and I can't see a way back.'

She sat with me and held me. I was just absolutely miserable and felt so pathetic. I couldn't console myself and continued to weep on her shoulder.

'What do you mean?' she said, wrapping her arm around me. 'You're not alone, Patrick. We're all here for you. We love you.'

Her words just made me feel worse. For a long time I had blocked out such emotion. I dared not to feel anything in Haiti. If I did, I would not last another month there, never mind six or seven. The love of my family and friends was all that I wanted. But I still had half a year before I could get back to all of that love.

'I've fucked up my life so badly, mom. That fucking night, I'm still paying for it. I try to move on, but I'm still paying for that fucking night.'

My mother was a clever woman. She could see that I was venting pressure that I'd been building up for some time.

When I finally gained some composure, we went down stairs, made some tea and talked about things.

Before I left for the bus station, my mother had managed to help me get my bearings for the weeks ahead. Yes, I was getting that bus to Dublin in a couple of hours and I was going back out to Haiti. I would not see any of my family until the summer. To not see them for such a long time scared me. It was too long. In the cold, early hours of that January night, I waved goodbye to my mother as she stood in the doorway. My head was set for going back. This would be the biggest challenge I would ever undertake. And it would be the last of its kind.

Chapter Fourteen

THAT DAY

TUESDAY, 12ᵀᴴ JANUARY, 2010

MORNE CALVAIRE, HAITI

The fan buzzed lazily overhead in the bedroom of my apartment on Morne Calvaire. Daylight broke through the thin lace curtains covering my windows. I lay there staring at a mosquito that had landed on my pillow. Its high pitched whine had woken me a minute before. It was plump with my blood so I clasped him in the palm of my hand and squashed the filthy bugger. The emails had already begun to roll in on my Blackberry. It was only twenty past five in the morning.

I put some fresh coffee in the pot and popped two slices of bread in the toaster. Emmanuel, my driver, would not be here until half past six to pick me up for work so I had plenty of time to work on my emails coming in from Ireland. I was reasonably recharged and fully focused on the work ahead. I knew that by immersing myself back in to the project, I would reacclimatize to life in Port au Prince. Terry informed me that he would be returning to Haiti the following week for the Clinton Global Initiative convention being held in the Karibe Hotel. The word was that Denis O' Brien was bringing a delegation of potential Irish investors with him. Their first port of call would be the Turgeau building and the second, our modest call center on the eleventh floor. This meeting, and Terry's visit, would allow me the opportunity to show him what we had achieved and what we still needed to do in January in order to give the business a more defined function. Bottom line, I was now going to need somebody from the outside to come in and help out. By all means give me the next project. But send the expert in to implement it, even if it was only for three weeks. I still hoped they would send me Anna.

Drinking my coffee on the small terrace of my apartment, I looked out upon the city below. This was my favorite place to sit at night. The view reminded me of my days in team house three with Cerek and Pavlov, when we would sit by the pool at night and have a few beers, or even just lounge on the front steps to the house chatting and drinking coffee. Those days seemed a lifetime ago now.

Emmanuel arrived right on time to bring me to work. As we made our way down Morne Calvaire and through the early morning traffic of Petion Ville, I couldn't help but reminisce over my time here. The craziness of local elections, fuel shortages in the city, carnivals, hurricanes, school collapses, kidnappings, shootings, public protests and all of that colorful atmosphere which came with the vibrant hysteria. How in the hell was I still a part of it all? In comparison to life back in Ireland, it was all so far-fetched.

I arrived at Turgeau at around quarter past seven. My staff arrived just before nine o'clock to begin their second day back to work. Nancy had taken over in my absence. She had come over to taxback.com from Digicel and brought with her a lot of experience. Quiet and polite in temperament, the young Haitian girl was by far the brightest in the group. I had already highlighted her capabilities to Terry and Janet back home.

When the next batch of arrivals began phase two, I wanted Nancy to take the position of supervisor. In fact, I hoped that she might get the opportunity to work and learn more about the company in either Ireland or Bulgaria, for a few months at least. I had no doubt that she had a promising future with the Haitian branch and I wanted her to absorb as much as she could in the short time I could give her.

Later that morning, I met Maeve outside the Digicel building. I had not seen her since the Thanksgiving party at the Little Brother and Sisters of Charity hospital in November. During the Christmas holidays, Maeve's sister had been to Waterford and had left a sum of money that she wanted me to give to her sister. I didn't expect to see Maeve so soon and I was glad to hand it over to her in a timely manner.

Irish meeting Irish in Haiti was becoming an increasingly rare thing. There was something really special about it. There weren't many of us left and yet those that were here came from so many different backgrounds; medicine, business, security, accountancy, humanitarian and education. Here we all were, less than twenty of us. Some had been in Haiti for a few months, while others had been here for years.

I spoke to Maeve until it was time for me to get back up on the eleventh floor and continue on with the day's work.

Once lunchtime had passed, I knew that I would need to stay late into the evening. I rang Emmanuel to tell him that I would be delayed for some time and asked if he could give me a call back at around seven o'clock to arrange pick up. I spent much of the day with my staff in the call center, and all my personal work outside of that was building up gradually throughout the morning and early afternoon.

At four o'clock, I took a quick break. Normally I would head up to the roof of the building, but for some reason, today, I decided to go down stairs to the car park on the lower floor. Since I returned on Friday, I hadn't seen any of the security boys that I kept contact with, so I thought I'd pop down to the basement floor for a smoke and a coffee.

I always felt a little self-conscious showing my face down there as I knew that security management still saw me as some kind of 'Judas Iscariot.' This didn't really bother me too much anymore, but still, I didn't want to be an ass about it.

When I stepped off of the elevator, Mac was there with a coffee and a smoke in hand. I hadn't seen him since before Christmas so a firm handshake was definitely due.

'Jaysus, Paddy,' he said. 'Good to see you boy. Happy new year to you. When did you get back?'

'Many happy returns, Mac,' I said with a grin. 'Got in late on Friday. I meant to give you a call but my phone wasn't working until yesterday.'

We talked some more about Haiti and the changes the country was going through. Mac, for as long as I had known him, had always seemed tired of Haiti. But at the same time, after almost five years here, he had more Haitian friends than Irish. His life was Haiti now. Chatting with Mac was like standing with a farmer or a builder back home. Plenty of chat full of colorful anecdotes. All that was ever missing was a quiet country pub and a few pints. Soon another familiar face joined us.

'Anybody got a light?' asked Jean Marc.

Cars were rolling in and out of the basement parking. We carefully moved away from their path to continue our chat.

'Hey, Jean Marc,' I said. 'So what's the news, mate? How was Christmas? When did you get back?'

He smiled.

'Yeah, Christmas was great. I was in Martinique with my family. We had an incredible time.'

Jean Marc took a pull on his menthol cigarette and then continued to tell me his more recent news.

'So, have you heard?' he asked.

'Heard what?'

'My contract is finished', he told me. 'I am expired here with Digicel. Maybe you can give me a job in your call center.'

'What the hell Jean Marc?' I replied. 'Finished with Digicel, you never said.'

He had been a friend and an adviser to me for some time now. I was surprised that he had not told me about finishing with Digicel sooner. Even Mac raised an eyebrow at the news. I was also surprised that Jean Marc wasn't too phased by it either.

'Yes. But it's okay,' he added. 'I want to stay here in Haiti. I am happier here than I have been in a long time. Now I just need to find a job to stay.'

Jean Marc was definitely recharged from his holidays. I was delighted to hear that he was staying.

As he and I talked about work, Mac stubbed out his smoke and headed away. He didn't talk shop with clients.

'Do you know that there are a dozen or so Irish investors flying in next week with your former boss from Ireland?' I said. 'My boss is flying in too. Why don't you come down to the meeting? It's on next Wednesday in the Karibe. I reckon it would be a great opportunity for you. Not that you will need it, but it wouldn't do any harm.'

Jean Marc seemed enthused.

'Okay, yeah, that's great, Paddy. Just let me know if you find out any more. But it sounds good.'

Looking to my watch, I saw the time had just gone half past four. I had been downstairs for almost a half hour and I still had work to do.

'Jean Marc, I have to go,' I said, heading towards the elevators. 'I'll talk to you tomorrow about the investor thing.'

The elevator doors opened. I stepped in and pressed the button for the eleventh floor. I needed to meet with the staff before they finished work at half past five. I also needed to see Nancy for a progress report on the guys.

When I got to the office, everybody was busy working. I asked Nancy to call into my office next door. She followed me in and sat down opposite me at my desk.

'Nancy, my apologies for being late getting back to you. How is everybody getting on inside?'

She began to go through some progress reports. The time was now 4:48pm. We were both immersed in our talk. Since she had started working with me, the young Haitian wife and mother had impressed me with her attitude and intelligence. I wanted to see her get that supervisor role before the end of the month.

Suddenly, a thunderous noise reverberated thought the air. Like a constant, menacing rumble. At the same time, the ground began to shake beneath my feet. I don't know why but I looked at my watch. The time was 4:53pm.

The office was moving. I looked at Nancy who was staring directly back at me. She had a look of surprise and concern etched on her face as I probably did. My mind fought to rationalize what was happening. There was a loud groan rolling up through the building as the floor and the walls began to move. At first I thought it was a malfunction in the air-conditioning units on the roof. They had been acting up all week, causing odd vibrations to run down through the walls. That was the only explanation I could muster.

Then BAM!! BAM! BAM! BAM!

Not only my floor, but the entire Digicel building was now shaking violently. The movement was out of this world. The sheer colossal power relentlessly hammering the building was like a giant trying to rip the entire structure from its foundation. Nancy curled herself into a ball on the chair on the other side of my desk.

'MOVE!! MOVE!! MOVE!!'

I was screaming at the top of my lungs but I could barely even hear my own voice over the moans of the moving walls. I ran around to the other side of my desk. It felt as if time was running very, very slowly. Like one of those dreams where you can't get your legs to move fast enough. I was convinced that the roof was about to collapse on top of us or my office walls would peel away from the inner structure any second.

I grabbed Nancy's petite frame by the back of her blouse, then we quickly moved towards the door. All I could concentrate on were the persistent waves of the tiles on the floor, moving beneath my feet. To my right, about twenty-five meters to the next doorway, was the secondary stairwell. I didn't this exit as I was positive this side of the building would certainly peel away in moments. I held on tightly to Nancy. Clasping the back of her blouse, I ran her out to the central part of the floor, driving her forward with my right forearm. The entire eleventh floor looked like it was falling apart. Ceiling tiles and air vents were collapsing all around us. I was convinced that the Digicel building would not last much longer. If we were to die here and now, then, in a manner of speaking, we were already dead. Deep down inside me, I could not accept this. I wanted to live. I wanted Nancy to live and I didn't care if we had to run, crawl or climb to make it happen. We were doing it right now.

'RUN, Nancy!! RUN! RUN! RUN!'

The building was shaking furiously and swaying from side to side. I could see nothing at this point, except blurred images of left and right turns in doorways. What should have been a forty second walk to the elevators and the main stairwell felt like an age.

At some point I lost my grip on Nancy's blouse. I looked over my shoulder and saw her lying on the ground. I thought this was strange as I couldn't even remember losing grip of her. The floor was now moving in more irregular and violent waves. I was sure we only have seconds left before the central column collapsed and we would descend with it. I ran back for Nancy and pulled her to her feet. Her shoes had heels that were strapped to her ankles. Once she was back on her feet, we continued running. There were other people joining us, all heading in the direction of the stairs. I wanted to look at their faces and see who they were, but I couldn't afford to take my eyes off of the ground. Though I did notice one man drop to his knees and pray to Jesus for help, for mercy. CRACK! Something fell and hit me on the right of my forehead. It might have been a piece of metal but I wasn't sure. It didn't matter.

'FUCK!!Nancy!!COME ON!!COME ON!!'

One more time I lost my grip of her. The situation was out of control. I grabbed her, much more firmly this time, until we finally made it to the main stairwell. From here I could see Port au Prince, all the way down to the docks from my left field of vision. The city was ablaze with sporadic explosions and surging fireballs. In a split second view, it looked like a city under siege. As if invisible bombers were carpeting the capital with high explosive ordnance.

The shaking continued as we struggled to move quickly down the stairwell. Floor by floor, I just could not descend fast enough. Tenth floor, ninth floor. More and more people were joining us. I felt more vulnerable here than I did on eleven. This was the make or break stage. My heart pounded rapidly. I could not see Nancy. I couldn't remember where she was, but I knew she was somewhere in front of me. I dared not look back at anybody behind me for fear of slowing down or losing my step. Eighth floor, seventh floor, sixth floor. Alarms continued wailing throughout the building. The descending flow of people was constant, yet nobody pushed. It was clear that everybody had that impending sense that the building was going to give way and that we had been lucky to make it this far. Every soul was running for their life. It was surreal, like a very bad dream or a scene from a Hollywood disaster movie. Everybody was touching the back of the person in front to move faster. Fifth floor, fourth floor, third floor. So close. So close.

I jumped step after step after step. The alarms grew louder and louder. Some people ran back up the stairs. One man ran past me saying, 'My Blackberry, my laptop.' He was in a daze. I wasn't sure if he knew what he was doing. The levels were pitch black now. There were some flashing lights which only added to the confusion. I looked down to see the daylight shining inwards on the second last floor. A few seconds later I exited the main door.

'Move, move, move,' I whispered to myself.

The daylight hit my face as I ran away from the Digicel tower. There was dust everywhere and it was difficult to make anything out in the clouds of dust. The roars of thousands of people could be heard for miles around. I made my way from the outside parking area onto the main road the Digicel gates.

I felt as though my life had been spared. I was still alive, and I was deeply grateful.

Hillside chaos. Fallen homes on one of the many mountainous residential areas in the capital city

(Courtesy of Bright Harbour Productions)

The earthquake proof Digicel building stands tall, surrounded by dust and fire. This shot was taken less than ten minutes after the initial quake
(Courtesy of A. Snellig)

Another series of damaged homes on the hills in Petion
Ville

(Courtesy of Bright Harbour Productions)

A sight typical of many of the streets in Port au Prince
after the quake (Courtesy of Bright Harbour Productions)

Even the rich suffer. An affluent residence in Pacot is left
in a pile of rubble

(Courtesy of Bright Harbour Productions)

"Father, why have you forsaken me?" (Courtesy of BHP)

A Navy Seahawk drops off Airborne troops on the front lawn of the collapsed Presidential Palace

(Courtesy of Associated Press ®)

The nights that followed saw piles of bodies build on the streets (Courtesy of Bright Harbour Productions)

Military aircraft buzz over the skies of Port au Prince

(Courtesy of Bright Harbour Productions)

Remains of the dead. The bodies of those killed, left in a
pile to be buried in mass graves outside the capital

(Courtesy of Bright Harbour Productions)

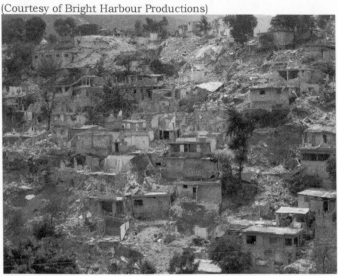

The leftover remains of a hillside housing area one week
after the quake.

(Courtesy of Bright Harbour Productions)

Chapter Fifteen

THE ROAD

TUESDAY, 12TH JANUARY, 2010

RUE DE CANAPE VERT, PORT AU PRINCE, 17:01HRS

When I stepped out onto the main road, I realized how fast my heart was beating. It felt as if it was going to burst out of my already heaving chest.

It was an earthquake and I was still alive? And yet I was acutely aware that this was just the beginning of something very bad. Of that much I was sure.

Dust rose from all around, blocking my view of the adjoining roads. Car alarms wailed while panic stricken people ran about the street in all directions. Some were crying hysterically. Others appeared to be injured. Blood pumped from various open wounds. Most of the injuries appear to be superficial at first glance. It was the hysteria that added to the chaos.

My forehead was thumping. I checked my reflection in the wing mirror of an abandoned Honda Civic. There was no blood, just a mark. I took a closer look at what was happening around me. The roadway and surrounding routes were in complete disorder. Dozens and dozens of abandoned cars were choking up the sidewalks and roads.

I couldn't stop coughing with the undulating dust. The sky was grey with powdered concrete and my eyes were itching. More people arrived in the area. The screams of traumatized Haitians filled the air. Many were screaming for their God. Some cried out in Creole and some yelled in French. 'Why, God? Why?' They were covered in blood and grey powder from the concrete.

I looked around, absorbing the scene. Surrounding buildings had fallen. Some obliterated, and others only partially collapsed. The three story Canape Vert hospital to my left had buckled into itself like a badly controlled demolition. I wondered how many people were in there: patients, nurses and doctors.

More and more people arrived from further up the street. More bloody faces and injured bodies. Only these look a hell of a lot more serious. I began to realize that it must be really bad up there. They had come here for treatment. But there was no hospital.

The ground shook with the first aftershock. It only lasted a few seconds but the magnitude was fierce. More dust rose into the air. The roars of helpless people reverberated throughout the city. Shock and distress increased amidst the helpless and scared. Somebody roared that the end of the world was upon us. Crazy as it sounded, I hadn't ruled that possibility out. I knew I couldn't stay there. But where the hell were the lads? I couldn't make out one familiar face among the hundreds. Nobody seemed to know what to do as the confusion mounted. I knew that I had to leave, but I wasn't sure where to go.

The one object to the forefront of my vision was the intimidating sight of the eleven story Digicel building that could yet come hurtling down. Less than ten minutes ago I ran out of there with my life. If it collapsed, nobody would be able to outrun the wave of bricks and mortar that would follow. I simply could not stay there.

The megastore building to the front was badly damaged. The megastore was a large, red, two story commercial building that had an uncanny resemblance to a fire station. It was standing, but just barely.

I looked at my watch. It was almost a quarter after five. Night would fall within forty minutes and I was wasting time. I took one long, last look for a familiar face, but I couldn't see anyone. I had to figure out what I was going to do. Then it hit me, my next move: a two kilometer trek uphill from where I was on Rue Jean Paul II to the Canape Vert apartment complex.

My sense of self-preservation ordered me to clear out of the area but my conscience insisted that I locate some of my staff before I left. Even if it was only one of them.

Finally, I recognized a colleague.

'Nancy! Nancy!' I roared.

She could neither hear nor see me amidst the pandemonium. I noticed her fumbling with her cell phone. I walked towards her, cautious of my surroundings as I paid heed to the badly damaged walls of neighboring structures.

'Nancy,' I said, tapping her on the shoulder.

With an expression of relief she raised her head from her Blackberry. Grateful to see a friend but still fraught with panic. We were both captive to the unfamiliar terror that was unfolding around us.

'Paddy, I cannot get through to my husband. What about my son? My husband is supposed to pick him up from school.'

'I know, Nancy, I know. The network is probably down. It's the earthquake. Have you seen any of the guys? Did you see Claude, or Lisa, or anybody?'

'No, Paddy. I'm sorry. I haven't.'

Her breathing was short and rapid. I was still jacked up, switched on and trembling inside. I didn't know what I was feeling exactly, but I did know that there was a part of me that was happy. Happy to be in one piece.

'We have to go, Nancy. It's not safe here.'

Her attention was divided between me and her phone. Her slender fingers struggled to punch digits while she glanced up at me and our hellish setting.

'There's no network, Paddy. Oh please, Jesus. My family.'

Another aftershock hit. It was big. The ground rumbled and the city screamed. That was it for me. Time was up.

'Let's go, Nancy. I know a place not too far from here. We'll contact your family soon. But we have to go now.'

Empty promises? I didn't know. The utter hopelessness of our situation left no room to question such thoughts. Despondent and afraid, she put her phone in her left palm, while clasping my left arm with the other. In my mind, she was my responsibility to get off the eleventh floor. She was still my responsibility.

I didn't know where my other five staff members were, but I was positive that they must have made it out of the call center by now. They must have been clear of the Digicel building. I could only hope that they were okay.

Somewhere above the blanket of grey dust the sun was setting. What we did in the next hour was important. It was the difference between hooking up with familiar faces or seeking shelter on the darkened, unpredictable streets of a terrified city. Options were simple and clear in my mind. Canape Vert apartments was my only viable possibility. They were home to many of the Digicel ex-pat staff and their kin. Beside the apartment buildings was a large open spaced garden. If the apartments *had* collapsed, it would not have affected the garden area which was free from any solid constructions. The security boys would reach it eventually. Hook up and re-org. Safety in numbers. To get there was normally four minutes by vehicle. I'd never had to walk it before. Never thought I would have to, and certainly not in these conditions. I took a quick breath, stared at the route ahead and began to move.

My peripheral vision took in what lay to my left and to my right. Material debris and traumatized victims dominated the scene. Tumbledown houses had buckled under the pressure. Collapsed walls claimed possession of the road, combined with steel rebar jutting out from columns at oblong and hazardous angles. It was as if they have been randomly planted there like some bizarre array of Vietnamese punji sticks, just waiting to be treaded upon. These menacing hurdles shadowed our every move.

'Watch your step, Nancy. Watch the bricks and metal.'

She had her phone out again and was desperate to make contact with her loved ones. Casually, I took it from her and placed it in my pocket. I needed her to focus on where we were in that moment. It was a shitty situation, but her family would have to wait for a while.

'There's no network right now,' I told her. She looked frightened. 'You've got to watch where you're stepping and just keep moving forward. Okay?'

She nodded, and then looked to the road under her feet.

By now my throat was burning from inhaled particles of dust. I breathed heavily as we needed to keep a steady pace upwards. I wanted to get away from the crowds and the concentration of larger buildings. The deeper my breathing, the more chalky dust I inhaled.

Nancy looked to be struggling and was coughing heavily. We past more concrete debris and stepped over more rebar.

'We'll contact your family when we're safe,' I added, trying to reassure her but my voice was drowned out amongst the aggravated roars of those running down the street in the opposite direction.

With each careful step, the howling cries of the badly injured increased in pitch and volume.

'Just look down at where you're stepping, Nancy,' I yelled. 'Don't worry about anything else.'

I'm not sure if she was listening to me. Her hand was struggling to stay grasped in mine as she stared ahead. Her palm was drenched in sweat as I increased the pace of our upward march.

'Maidais! S'il vous plait! Maidais!'

I stopped momentarily to see who was calling. To my right I noticed a woman in her late forties, lying half buried under the fallen front wall of a house. I could see her legs were trapped beneath the rubble, but they no longer appeared to be a part of her. The only thing connecting her upper body to them was a sliver of flesh on her right hip and lower back. Her innards streamed down from her abdominal region. Blood seeped steadily from this lady's helpless, distended figure. Her life was streaming away in equal measure. The blend of light grey concrete particles and blood added to the shear horror of her hellish ending in this world. I imagined this house was her home. Home to her family. Less than a half hour ago she was probably preparing dinner in the kitchen, while waiting for her kids to come home from school and her husband to return from a day's work. Now she lay on the side of a road. Her body ripped in two. Her life slipping away. Dying alone in a scene of carnage and mayhem.

'I'm so sorry,' I whispered. 'I cannot stay. I have to go. There's nothing I can do. I'm so sorry. What can I do? There's nothing I have that can help you.'

Her cries dwindled as we pushed on up the road. Cries that were replaced by more. Many more.

Men cradled badly maimed or even dead children in their arms. The alarming high pitched screams of little kids pleading for a dead mother or father to wake up added to the insanity. Cries, screams, pain and anguish filled the road. Perpetual suffering on only one of a thousand streets throughout Port au Prince tonight.

Collapsed homes lay behind capsized perimeter walls. Small fires burned furiously from the exposed gas mains of a demolished kitchen. I thought of the people who must have been trapped beneath it all. They probably never had a chance. Those of us who are alive were just lucky.

I recognized one house that belonged to a Digicel colleague, Claude Berechet. Though his house looked bad, I knew that he was not in there. I was, however, aware that he had house staff and a girlfriend with a baby. It crossed my mind to stop, but I continued onwards regardless, mindful that I could have stopped to check Claude's house for signs of life.

The top of the road was in sight now.

'Not too far to go, Nancy,' I said. 'Two hundred meters and we'll be at the T- junction.'

She was exhausted and wanted to stop for a moment. I was out of breath myself, yet I was also relieved to have escaped the carnage. My lungs were heaving and I promised myself that I would quit smoking, but not today.

'We're almost there, Nancy. Okay?'

She nodded, barely glancing at me. Too breathless and shell-shocked for words. I am mindful that I am taking her away from the direction she had wanted to take, but now was not the time to go wandering down through the streets of Port au Prince. Darkness was coming and God only knew what else.

Finally we reached the T-Junction. It marked the end of the tarmacked section of the road, which then broke left and right onto smaller, more derelict dirt tracks.

Our turn was to the left. It was a dirt road that stretched for more than five hundred meters, leading down towards a small residential area and then finally onto the back gates of the Canape Vert apartments. We quickly rounded the turn. It was clear of people, bodies and chaos. Unfortunately, this didn't last long. I was conscious of the thirty foot wall running along to our right. I must have driven by this same structure a hundred times over the years, but never have I been so aware of its height and bulk as I was at that moment. I tried to push this thought to the back of my mind and we continued on as swiftly as we could.

We were completely alone for about two hundred meters. I prayed to God that another aftershock would not strike within the next sixty seconds, burying me and Nancy in bricks and mortar as we attempted to pass the looming edifice. We round the final turn only to see more debris of fallen homes. The remaining section of the road ahead couldn't have been more than four meters in width. It was more of a concreted dirt track than anything else. The entire path was covered in heavy rubble. Twenty-five minutes ago, this was a small neighborhood of about twelve neatly built houses. But now, those homes were left to nothing. God only knew about the occupants. The rooftops and the rear walls had toppled onto the center of the road. I noticed a rusted bath tub and a water tank that hang warily to the rear of the road. Electrical cables had fallen close to battered concrete pillars and jutting rebar. The whole scene looked as if some foreign army had been dropping mortar rounds on it all evening. We simply couldn't turn back now. We had come too far to return to the madness below. There was no choice but to plough forward as quickly and cautiously as possible.

Behind the fallen homes I got my first glance of Port au Prince. A large white/grey cloud of smoke and dust hung over the entire valley. It was tough to imagine the death toll at that moment. Displaced fires still burned throughout the hundreds of streets below. I was grateful to be so far above it.

The green gates to the apartment complex were within sight now. I tried not to get too excited as I didn't know what waited for us on the other side. I just hoped that all the people inside were okay. I was getting very frustrated, fighting to negotiate a safe path across the rubble. I looked over at Nancy who was struggling in her heeled shoes behind me.

'That's it, Nancy,' I say. 'Take your time. Keep moving.'

I was anxious now. Anxious of another large aftershock or second earthquake to follow. Anxious to hook up with some of my old security buddies. Anxious to know that all my friends are alive and well. But mostly, I was anxious to just get through those blasted gates as quick as we can.

Amidst these thoughts, my concentration suddenly returned to my footing. All along I'd been standing on hard, jagged pieces of concrete. But in an instant the ground had become surprisingly soft.

'That's weird,' I thought as I looked down. Then it hits me in a sort of fuzzy, dreamlike fashion. Beneath the sole of my shoe was somebody's face.

A human head. A grey powder covered head whose body was submerged beneath layers of strewn rubble. It was an adult face, but I can't make out if it was male or female. There was no shock or surprise. I simply thought about how soft it felt on the bottom of my shoe.

Unlike the perimeter of the Digicel building, there were no terrifying roars to be heard here. Just an eerie, peaceful, deathlike silence. Nobody dug through the rubble in search of loved ones. I turned my back and my mind on where we'd just come from. Almost two kilometers of bloodshed and havoc. Nothing waited for us back there. Just the dead.

Chapter Sixteen

THE GARDEN

TUESDAY, 12ᵀᴴ JANUARY, 2010

CANAPE VERT APARTMENTS, 17:35HRS

'Ouvert! Ouvert s'il vous plait!' I yelled as we stood waiting outside the gates. I didn't want to knock too loudly as I was sure the security guard was nervous enough already. It would be a shame to survive an earthquake and get shot in the chest with a Remington twelve gauge forty minutes later. Soon enough, the guard arrived.

'Oui,' said a solemn voice on the other side of the large metal barrier.

'Oui,' I responded calmly. 'Je suis un client avec Digicel. Ouvert les barrières pour moi s'il vous plait.'

The guard opened the gate. My mind buzzed in anticipation of what I might see within the apartment complex. Both of the large three story apartment buildings were still standing. I did however notice significant fractures running up through the first structure. It looked bad but was still intact. We walked a little further until the main garden came into view. The open spaced lawn was free of any damage. About twenty people; women, children and some men, were sitting there on the grass. These were the wives and children of the Digicel ex-pat staff. Most of them were the Lebanese wives, a few South American spouses there as well. A couple of the women sobbed uncontrollably as they clasped their babies tightly. I was relieved to see they were all okay. I had not seen any of these people for five months. Some of them I knew on a mutual first name basis.

One of the Lebanese men, Hakim, was sitting on the green with his wife and two babies. He was calm and collected. Hakim was probably a year or two older than I. Athletic in build with short jet black hair, he calmly stood up and approached me.

'Hi, Paddy,' he said coolly as we shook hands.

'Hey, Hakim,' I answered. 'How are you man? How's your family?'

'They are okay. They are really shaken up.'

He paused.

'What's it like down there?' he asked.

I didn't know where to begin.

'It's bad, really bad my friend. I think everybody made it out of Digicel. It's still standing anyways.'

'It's still there, thank God,' said Hakim.

'Yes, mate,' I said. 'It's still there, but I didn't see any familiar faces on the street when I got outside. I waited for ten minutes but the crowds down there are in the hundreds, maybe thousands. I couldn't see anybody.'

As we spoke, I glanced at the people on the lawn. Babies were crying while their mothers nursed them by singing soft lullabies. Only a half hour before, they had run from their apartments for fear of being killed. They too had probably been preparing dinner, while their children and babies were watching cartoons or napping. By now the time was just after five forty. Night would soon be upon us and nobody was prepared for that.

Hakim's wife, Rashida, was sitting on the grass holding their two babies. They were twins, a boy and a girl. I had always liked Hakim and his young family. They made me think about the more important things in life. Whatever the case, Hakim, his family and the half dozen other families were going to need supplies.

'Paddy, can you help me get some things from my apartment for the children?' he asked.

Going back into any building was the last thing to do. But his kids were in need of supplies.

'Yeah, Hakim,' I said. 'Are you still in the same apartment?'

Nancy sat down with Rashida while myself and Hakim went over to his apartment.

The structure was only three stories high and his place was on the top floor. We quickly moved up the flights of stairs. There were cracks and gaps in the walls and on the floor tiling. It didn't matter. Just get to the apartment, grab what we needed, and get the hell out.

Once inside, Hakim's place looked as though a herd of elephants had just ran through it. All the crockery and cutlery, cans of food, cereal boxes, toaster, TVs, everything had fallen from where it once stood or sat. Even the couches had been bounced around.

I gathered whatever I could. Food, water, powdered milk, baby bottles. I even spotted a pacifier and put it in my pocket.

We made three more runs to take out blankets, cots, diapers, torches and any other essentials. We just grabbed it all.

It was gone six o'clock when I noticed Alexi and Roberto arrive through the gates of the apartment complex. Tall and well-built like most of the Slovak boys, Alexi was one of the old-time bodyguards. He had arrived in Haiti not long before me in 2006. Roberto was the Chilean residential security team leader. The security of the compound fell onto his experienced fifty year old shoulders.

Alexi and Roberto approached Hakim at the bottom of the garden. They spoke quietly, away from the group. I noticed a look of concern emerge on Hakim's face.

Alexi looked at me as I approached him and Hakim. I hadn't spoken to him since my return to Haiti in October. We shook hands. I was eager to hear the news of what was going on down below since I'd left.

'Oliver Tomkins wants everybody to come back to Turgeau,' he informed me.

Now I knew why Hakim had such a grave look of concern on his face.

'You cannot be fucking serious, Alexi. Please tell me you are joking.'

He was puzzled by my statement.

'That's why he sent me here,' he explained. 'To take everybody down to Turgeau and count them.'

I glanced back at the distraught families on the grass, trying to gather my thoughts and figure out what kind of decisions were being made at Turgeau. I thought about the road I had just walked less than an hour before. These people did not need to be subjected to the destruction and mayhem down there. Ollie would not make a decision like that if he had all the facts. In fairness, the guy was probably under so much pressure to make all the right calls based on limited information. He probably didn't even know how bad the neighboring streets were at that point. Many people would be looking to him now. The safety and security of almost a hundred and fifty people were his responsibility. It was a tough position to be in.

'Listen, Alexi,' I said. 'You cannot bring these people out onto the streets. There must be an alternative.'

Hakim nodded in agreement. Alexi looked uncertain. I knew he had his instructions and who the hell was I to countermand that?

'But this is what Oliver Tomkins said,' he answered.

'Can you get him for me on the radio?' I asked.

He made a few attempts to raise Ollie on his Motorola set. Eventually he got him and passed the radio to me.

'Ollie. It's Paddy. Message, over.'

'Send, Paddy.'

The signal was strong but there was a hell of a lot of noise in the background.

'Roger, Ollie. Listen mate, I'm up here with Alexi in the Canape Vert apartments. He has informed me he is to escort these people to your location. Confirm, over?'

I knew at this stage that Ollie did not have to entertain me. We hadn't really talked much since I returned.

'Yes, Paddy. That is correct. I need to confirm that we still have everybody. Over.'

'Understood, Ollie. I do not advise that you take these people to your location, mate. They are all pretty distraught here and the road is covered in bodies and rubble all the way down to you. Give me figures five and I can get back to you with a head count. Please advise. Over.'

There was a moment of pause as he processed my proposal.

'Yep, roger that, Paddy. Get back to me as soon as possible with those figures mate please.'

'Will do, Ollie. Wait out.'

I quickly tallied who I had and if there were any other families missing from the complex. Perhaps somebody had been out shopping. I had to be sure before I reported back.

Soon enough I was back on the radio giving him the figures. Ollie was happy with the names I called out. He could now tick them from his list. I told him that I would stay at the Canape Vert location and keep an eye on everyone present. He left Roberto there with me while Alexi was pulled back to Turgeau for another tasking.

About ten minutes before the sun finally set, another familiar face arrived through the gates. It was one of the Digicel managers, Meredith. I had only just had a meeting with her earlier that morning on the tenth floor. Instinctively, she too had decided to come to the garden. None of the other women recognized Meredith except for Nancy, who immediately ran to her. They were hugging when I walked over. Meredith was fraught with panic.

'Paddy, I have to go,' she cried.

I hugged her and told her to stay. It would be dark soon and it would be better to wait until morning before going back out.

'I have to go. I have to find my children and my husband. I cannot get through to him or anyone.'

'I will come with you,' said Nancy.

'No no, Nancy,' said Meredith through her tears. 'Please stay here.'

'You should too, Meredith,' I added. 'Please will you stay here with us and wait until morning? The power grids are probably down. You will be out there in the darkness. It will be safer to stay put until first light.'

For a moment, I thought I had persuaded her. But family is family no matter what. She had to go. I knew that if it were me, I would do exactly the same.

I watched Meredith walk down the garden, past the trees, then lost sight of her as she went back out the gates of the complex. She had not been gone long when another aftershock hit. It lasted a few seconds. The ferocious moans from the earth were enough to make everybody panic. The roars of two million people rang through the twilight sky. Adrenaline began pumping through my veins. The anticipation of the unknown. It was impossible to relax.

I lit a cigarette that Hakim had given me and drank a can of soda from the batch we had taken from the apartment. In the dwindling twilight I pulled the smoke deep into my lungs and savored the sensation.

The night finally fell and Port au Prince was a complete blackout. Another aftershock trembled through the earth far below our feet. Tonight, the 12th January 2010, Haiti was cut off from the rest of the world.

The aftershocks were unrelenting. Their forceful tremors pushed our nerves to the limit. There was nothing any of us could do but sit there and wait. Wait for more quakes. Wait for the world to hear what was happening. We hoped and prayed for the sun to come up, so we could see again, and orientate ourselves to the new city.

As I sat beside Nancy on the grass, I noticed a small group of people walk through the gates. With their heavy footsteps and beams from their flashlights, I knew it was some of the bodyguards. They had escorted some of the ex-pat clients back to reunite with their families. I smiled when I heard a unique voice among the group. It was James. I hadn't seen James in more than a year. I had heard through the grapevine that he was back from his Indonesian gig while he waited to get his work visa arranged. I carefully walked through the darkness towards the lights.

'James,' I said. 'Is that you man?'

'Who's that?' he answered.

'It's the pig-whipper, mate.'

'Paddy! What the fuck are you doing here?'

We shook hands. James had kept in regular contact with me since he had left Haiti. To see him here like this was absurd and fantastic all at once. The small talk and beers would unfortunately have to wait.

'What's it like down there now, James?' I asked.

'It's still fairly fucked up, mate' he said, trying to catch his breath. He had marched his way up through the two kilometers of rubble and bodies in the dark. The sweat dripped from his forehead when he switched on his Petzl (head torch) for extra light.

'We managed to get into Claude Berechet's house. The whole thing had pancaked. I tried to get his housemaid out of there but I couldn't fucking get to her. I did everything, Paddy, I swear mate. If I'd crawled into her I'd have never gotten back out.'

James was one of the hardiest men I knew. An ex-Para of the British Army, he had soldiered from Bosnia to Kosovo, and Iraq to Afghanistan. For as long as I'd known him, he always maintained a level of composure in times of crisis. Yet standing with him in the middle of the night, I could hear the hurt in his voice. I really wanted to talk with him and help sort out whatever he was thinking. When all of this was over, and we were someplace else, like a pub, we'd drink and talk, and drink some more. James fell quiet.

'Has everyone been accounted for?' I asked.

He continued to catch his breath as he answered.

'We're still fucking missing Jean Marc Le Hir. Is he definitely not up here with you guys?'

'He couldn't be missing, James. I was with him in the basement car park less than twenty minutes before this shit started. He has to be down in the Turgeau area mate. Or maybe he ran someplace nearby in the panic.'

The building hadn't collapsed. Jean Marc was probably taking shelter somewhere. The time was now ten o'clock. James and the boys had been on the go for five hours.

'Hang on here a second,' I said as I ran back to the garden.

I grabbed a couple of sodas and a pack of cigarettes from the carton.

'Here, mate,' I said, placing them in his hand. 'Give the drinks to the boys.'

It was nothing for me. But it was a small morale booster of sugar and nicotine for those that wanted or needed it.

'I fuckin gave these things up after Christmas,' laughed James as he took a drag on his smoke.

'Fuck it, Jimbo,' I said as I lit one too. 'No point worrying about it right now.'

The big man practically drank an entire can in one go. When he was finished, he wiped his mouth, and put the can on the ground.

'Listen, Paddy,' he said. 'Is Antonio here? You remember the Digicel engineer? They're looking for him down below. They want to get the network back up and running as soon as possible.'

'Yeah, he's over there by that tree, with his wife and kid,' I answered, pointing in the general direction of James's torchlight.

'Thanks mate,' he said, stubbing out his smoke. 'I'll talk to you in a bit.'

I could just make out the muttering of a conversation as James told the South American client that he was to return with them down the road and back to Turgeau. Very soon the conversation flared up.

'No way! No! No! No! I am not going!'

The guy looked stereotypical of a man who worked in an office. Well dressed, skinny with a little protruding belly, neatly combed hair and glasses. He had been in Haiti for a few years but I'd never really had many dealings with him.

James tried to calm him down as he stepped away and contacted Ollie Tomkins on the radio. The radio was handed over to Antonio's boss, who basically ordered him to get his ass down to the Turgeau building. The problem was that the switch at the back of the Turgeau building had been damaged. The north wall had collapsed, and though most of the servers were still intact, they were overheating and shutting down due to no air-con. Unknown numbers of other, smaller switches were down also. The Digicel network was offline and it needed to be remedied ASAP. Communications was paramount.

Antonio hugged his wife and baby daughter as he packed a small bag and joined the group of bodyguards leaving Canape Vert. I felt sorry for the guy leaving his wife and kids there. It couldn't have been easy. As the group walked away, I felt I should have been heading out there with them. The difference between me and the boys was that they had the right clothing, footwear and gear. Weapons, flashlights and shoot 'n' scoot packs loaded with water, emergency rations, spare ammo, wet gear, medical kits, money and personal I.D. (we used to call them 'break for the border' bags, in case everything went pear shaped in Haiti, and we each had to make our way to the Dominican border).

Because the number of people taking refuge on the garden had increased significantly, the Captain, Joseph, had been ordered to stay with the group. Here was another Slovak whom I had not seen in months. Joseph shook my hand as wholeheartedly as I shook his.

Almost in that instant, another aftershock hit. People screamed and cried again. Pure terror.

'Jesus! These things aren't going to stop,' I said, finding a place to sit on the lawn.

'This is crazy, Paddy. This is all just so crazy you know. You know what I mean?'

'Yeah I know, Captain. It's crazy buddy.'

I wasn't sure if it was the Captain being his usual highly strung self, or if he had been genuinely affected. It was hard to tell. The Captain was a nice fella, but an intense man at the best of times.

I sat talking with him well into the night. The aftershocks seemed to hit every hour or so. In the darkness, it was almost dreamlike. Everything was real but not real. My imagination ran riot. Each time the aftershocks hit, I was sure that the ground was going to open up right beneath my feet.

We liaised with the owner of the apartment complex and his wife. Dave and Jenny Williamson were both Americans but had been living in Haiti with their twenty year old son, Mike, for fifteen years. As luck would have it, Dave, a gentleman in his mid-fifties, had direct contact via sat-phone with the American Embassy down by the airport. With so many American citizens living and working here, the world would begin to hear about the predicament that Haiti now found itself in. Help would come. It was obvious that any American involvement would prioritize their own citizens before anybody or anything else. It was nice to know that somebody was aware of the country's plight, but it brought little by way of reassurance to the millions of Haitians who would continue to suffer on the streets below.

I tried to get some sleep during the night, but I could not switch off my mind. The anticipation of the next aftershock, or even a larger earthquake, was too great to allow any of us to rest. Also, even though we had a beautiful star filled sky above us, the air was extremely cold due to zero cloud cover. I had nothing with me but the shirt on my back and a bed sheet that I'd borrowed to keep from getting bit by insects in the grass. In the garden, people held their cell phones above their heads in the hope of picking up a signal. I cursed myself for not bringing mine with me. It had been on my desk charging when the earthquake hit and I just never thought about it in the rush to get out of the building.

The Captain had been trying to get a signal for quite some time. Even if the network was up, it would be inundated with millions of calls from both Haiti and the rest of the world. His chances of getting through to home were slim.

'I have it!' he said with a smile on his face. 'Fuck! I have a signal.'

The Captain managed to get through to his mother back in Slovakia. Though I didn't understand the language, I knew that the sense of relief he must be bringing to his family was beyond words. Secretly, I hoped that he would give me the opportunity to do the same. When he eventually finished his call, I asked him as nicely as I could if I could borrow his phone and make a thirty second call to my family to tell them I was alive.

'Okay,' he said. 'But be quick. I don't have many units left.'

I bit my tongue and humbly accepted the phone.

It was close to early morning back in Ireland when I dialled my sister's number. I just needed half a minute, even less. I just needed them to know I was okay. The phone rang, and rang, and rang until I got voicemail. I left a brief message but that still wasn't good enough. The Captain was busy taking a leak somewhere in a bush, so I dialled a second number. I was certain this one would pick up. I still had a good signal. The phone was ringing.

'Hello?' said a quiet and sleepy voice on the other end.

'Mick. Mick, its Paddy. Can you hear me?'

'Paddy, I can barely hear you. I saw the news. What's the story?'

'The story is bad down here, Mick. But don't worry about that. Can you just call my folks in the morning and let them know that I'm okay. I'm not injured. I'm okay.'

'Yeah, no bother, lad. Will do. Mind yourself and get home.'

'I will do, brother. I have to go. Talk to you soon. Thanks.'

As often as Mick has been there for me down through the years, that short, simple phone call is the one I thank him for the most.

Once the Captain came back from his latrine detail, we lit a couple of cigarettes and talked well into the night.

Word eventually arrived from Turgeau that Jean Marc had finally been found. It wasn't good. The bodyguards, Mac, Ollie, and Piro, along with Friedrich (a German bodyguard) had found him. That was all we had been told. Our hearts sank at the news. I kept waiting to snap out of it. If I wasn't to wake from this nightmare, then at least let the sun come up.

The aftershocks continued into the night. Songs of prayer could be heard throughout the night sky. Almost like choirs of angels were singing down from above. We were a city in darkness, blanketed by a sky of bright shining stars, pounded by powerful and unrelenting aftershocks. I closed my eyes and listened to thousands of voices all singing to God as one. Chanting hymns with great belief and conviction in their maker. They were praying that he would come to help them. I've never been a big man for religion, but I took solace in those harmonic sounds. No phones, no loudspeakers, no technology. Just the human spirit expressing its fear, love and hope as one.

Chapter Seventeen

FIRST LIGHT

WEDNESDAY, 13TH JANUARY, 2010

CANAPE VERT, 05:30HRS

The black sky of night gave way to the dawn. Shadowy figures sleeping on the lawn gradually took on colors and dimensions. As the brightness grew, the fear and apprehension that had been with me throughout the dark hours subsided.

We were still far from safe, but at least the red glow of morning signified the end to that first hellish night. To get to my apartment in Morne Calvaire, I had about two hours of walking to do. Hundreds of thousands of people, Haitian and foreign alike, would spend the morning knee deep in rubble searching for friends and loved ones buried under collapsed buildings. Thousands more would battle to stay alive. Their torn and beaten bodies were submerged beneath incalculable amounts of concrete. Holding on to life and drawing precious air into their lungs, waiting to be rescued. They were out there in places I couldn't possibly imagine.

The sun peered over the horizon in minutes. Some of the garden party had already begun to move. I noticed a

South American woman feeding her young baby in the middle of the lawn. The infant lay protected in its mothers arms, utterly content and oblivious as it sucked formula from a bottle. Behind me, a Haitian family snuggled up together on an assortment of blankets. The children had been traumatized all through the night. The last aftershock happened more than an hour ago. In the quietness, fear was replaced with exhaustion.

Nancy was still sleeping. Her petite frame looked peaceful as she lay there curled up on a small blanket. I thought about how her day would differ from mine. She had tried desperately all night to get through to her husband and parents, but without success. Soon, her eyes would open to daylight. Maybe for a moment she would forget about what had happened. Crouching down beside her, I gently tapped her shoulder.

'Hi, Nancy.'

She slowly sat up and looked around the garden.

'Paddy, hi,' she said, wiping the sleep from her eyes. I told her that I was setting out to get back to my apartment. As necessary as it was for me to leave the garden, I felt that I was abandoning her. Yesterday had been pretty emotional and I had felt a strong sense of responsibility towards Nancy, right from the moment that we ran from the eleventh floor. She needed to find her family, but I had convinced her to wait until morning. Now it was time for us to go our separate paths. I was unsure as to when I would see her again, and how or where she might find her family. Nancy knew that her husband had been down town collecting their son from school when the earthquake hit. But the school was situated in a part of town with a high concentration of buildings.

'Be safe, Nancy,' I said. 'I hope that you find your family okay.'

She masked her fear with a weak smile and a thank you. We hugged, then said goodbye.

I told Roberto, the Chilean security guard, that I was leaving the compound and making my way towards Petion Ville. Vigilance was under no obligation to prevent me from leaving or provide me with protection. Apart from getting some gear together and finding my passport and money, I had no idea what my next move would be. I was alone, and there was a terrific sense of freedom in that.

I stepped from the relative safety of the garden and made my way towards the top gate. This was a short cut which would bring me onto the Canape Vert road. It would cut a half an hour from my journey. I had walked less than two hundred meters and I was already sweating.

Once again, I found myself negotiating a path over fallen rubble. Though this road wasn't as bad as the one from the previous evening. But still, damage, destruction and decay were evident. On one particular section, a mudslide had occurred, bringing tons of red clay down onto the main road.

Surprisingly, I didn't feel much apprehension as I walked down towards the main Canape Vert road. Usually, this area was awash with markets, but this morning it was quiet. Traffic was sparse. My estimation had been correct. In my head I was amused. Not at the level of destruction. Certainly not. But rather, how random and fucked up the situation was. Nobody could have imagined this.

The hard part of my slog back to Morne Calvaire began at the foot of the market area across the street from the Canape Vert police station. It was all uphill from here. Six miles of twists and turns along a tarmacked road. Already, some crowds had gathered. What was once a market was more like a triage center for the injured who had arrived during the night. One old lady sat by the side of the road with two children beside her. The older looking child had a large white bandage wrapped around his lower leg. It appeared to be a piece of clothing rather than a surgical dressing. Everybody was making do with whatever they could find.

The first mile of the hill was the steepest climb. Between the morning heat and rising humidity, every couple of steps demanded further exertion from my legs and lungs. My shirt was drenched in sweat by the time I reached half way. Hundreds of people were walking up and down the same stretch of road as me. Those who worked in Petion Ville were most likely making their way home downtown. They had probably waited out the night in Petion Ville until it was safe to move. Looking back over the city from where I now stood, I could see buildings smoldering from the night before. Grey plumes of smoke stemmed up from burning gas stations into the blue morning sky. The drone of distant helicopters moaned overhead. They didn't sound like the usual UN military choppers.

The sense of freedom I had set out with that morning was prudently being replaced by an air of caution. It was going to be difficult to avoid areas of risk in a city that had been beaten to the ground.

'Hi, Paddy,' cried a voice behind me.

A large, stocky Haitian man approached from the Petion Ville side. It was Evens. He was a member of the Digicel staff. He had helped with the installation of our computers in the call center. He was also Nancy's cousin.

'Evens, good to see you,' I said. 'Where are you going'?

He looked distressed.

'I am on the way to my uncle's house. He has died. Some of my cousins also.'

I didn't know what to say. Not much can be said in such circumstances. My attention was briefly caught by a bright red chopper that flew directly overhead in the direction of Montagne Noir. We were both stunned by how low it was flying. I looked at Evens.

'Nancy is safe. She was with me and the Digicel people in Canape Vert last night. I know that she is headed down town to find her husband and son.'

He looked relieved to hear this.

'Well, mind yourself, Evens,' I said. 'And best of luck to you.'

'Thank you, Paddy. God bless you.'

I walked the last mile into Petion Ville as quick as I could. To the right, up in the hills, was where the poorer Haitians lived. These homes were so jam packed together that when the earthquake hit, each brought the next one down like a game of dominoes. No doubt there were a lot of people hurting up there. Some folks wandered aimlessly up and down the street, coming from various laneways and smaller interconnecting roads. Apart from those who were adamant to get downtown, nobody else was moving with any real urgency.

The sun was high in the sky when I walked onto the first streets in Petion Ville. There didn't seem to be any major damage to the area I was in. I walked by the Dominican Consulate on Rue Rigaud. Around the corner from there, was a small Sicilian restaurant called 'Il Vigneto'. As a bodyguard, I had often come here both while taking care of clients and in my free time with friends. All the buildings on that street were intact. Fabrizzio, the owner of Il Vigneto, saw me walking in front of the restaurant, and waved from the doorway, gesturing for me to enter.

Fabrizzio, with his plump belly, sallow, sweaty skin, and short sleeved white summer shirt was a welcome sight. The circumstances of my being there may have changed, but his hospitable, homely manner was the same as ever.

'It is good to see you, Patrick,' he said as he poured me a glass of water from an ice cold metal jug. His voice was always low and he moved at his own unhurried pace.

'Good to see you too, Fabrizzio,' I said. The walk had taken me just under an hour. I hadn't eaten anything since the morning before, and I was incredibly thirsty from lack of proper fluids. With a short supply of rations in the Canape Vert apartment complex, I had made do with a few cans of coke and a lot of cigarettes. Not exactly sustaining. The ice cold water was blissful.

'The power is out throughout Petion Ville,' said Fabrizzio. This was nothing uncommon for Port au Prince or for Haiti. Power was always cutting out. Many establishments such as restaurants and other businesses often had their own generators at the ready just in case. Luckily, Il Vigneto was no different. From the small generator out back, Fabrizzio was able to power the TV up over the counter of the small bar. On it was CNN News. The report was in Spanish (it was coming from the Dominican Republic) but the images were enough to explain the main topic of the day.

'We are all over the world today, my friend,' he added. 'This earthquake report has been on TV all morning.'

I wiped my mouth after guzzling my third glass of water. 'Are they saying how many are dead?' I asked.

Fabrizzio continued to stare at the screen.

'No exact figures yet, but they estimate more than ten thousand', he answered. This figure was nonsense. The destructive power of the earthquake and the poor infrastructure of Port au Prince would leave a hell of a lot more than ten thousand dead.

Camera footage taken from helicopters high above the city was being televised. I recognized many of the downtown areas from the remains of their structures. One of the most shocking images was the Presidential Palace, which now lay in ruins. The center piece had dropped straight down into itself leaving both connecting wings barely intact. Seeing it all on the screen made it all the more surreal and yet all the more real.

'So what about you, Patrick?' the plump Sicilian enquired. 'What will you do? Are you staying here or heading for the airport?'

'I don't know yet, Fabrizzio,' I said as I continued to look at the images. 'I'll have to wait until I get to my apartment and see what I can find. I don't know.'

I had not thought that far ahead. I didn't see how heading for the airport would help. Surely, with the unpredictability of the aftershocks, no aircraft would be able to land or take off. Maybe the airport was in as bad a condition as the Palace. After all, that too was downtown and, judging by the aerial news footage, downtown appeared to be the worst affected area.

I thanked Fabrizzio for the water and his hospitality and continued on my way to Morne Calvaire. Out on the street, I walked by a group of men sitting around a television set on the side of the street. The television was covered with a blanket to shield the screen from the glaring sun. On the screen it showed a map of the epicenter of the quake. It appeared to be running directly beneath Port au Prince. The images changed to a US Naval aircraft carrier with dozens of helicopters on its deck. It looked like the marines were coming after all.

Once I turned onto Rue Clerveaux, I saw the 'Little Brothers and Sisters of Charity' Land Rover parked outside a house. It had to be Gena! A young Haitian man sat drowsily behind the wheel.

'Excuse moi, chef,' I said, tapping on his window. The skinny local was startled from his slumber. He rolled down the driver side window.

'Hello,' I said. 'Is Madame Gena here?'

The young man was reluctant at first to tell me until I explained that I too was Irish and that she was a friend of mine. He pointed in the direction of the house that his car was parked outside.

As I opened the gate, a large, black guard dog began barking and snapping in my direction. Gena soon arrived from the kitchen and ordered the brute to stop.

'You have a good guard dog there, Gena,' I smiled as we embraced in a warm hug

'God, Paddy. Where are you coming from? When did you get back?'

'Got in last Friday.'

'Gena. I'm so happy you are okay. Where is Maeve? Is she okay too?'

'She's fine, Paddy. Maeve is up in Kenscoff with the children. I'm heading back up there later.'

Gena brought me through to the kitchen. In Fabrizzio's, I had only sat by the doorway. I was concerned about my chances of a speedy escape should another earthquake hit. I noticed a fruit bowl full of bright orange mandarins sitting on the kitchen top counter. Gena offered me a few and I heartily accepted.

'I'd offer you a cup of tea but the power is out,' she said.

I ate the mandarin like it was nobody's business.

'What about Erin?' I asked. 'Is she up at the orphanage as well?'

I had chatted to Erin on the phone the Friday evening that I got back. I was supposed to meet up with her later in the week.

'She's in the hospital , Paddy. We found her just a few hours ago. We are waiting on people from the American Embassy to come and evacuate her to Miami. This is my friend's house – I am here to use the internet to send info out to everyone.'

'What do you mean?' I said. 'Found her where?'

'At the hospital,' she explained. 'It has completely collapsed. We think she was there with Molly when the earthquake hit. But we can't find Molly. Erin's brother

Ryan was there too and we can't find him either. He'd only just flown in on holidays for a week.'

Molly Hightower was a student and one of Erin's closest friends in Haiti. Molly was from Port Orchard, in Washington, and had come to Haiti as a volunteer. I'd gotten to know her from my visits to the orphanage in Kenscoff over the years. She was a beautiful young lady with nothing but dedication and love in her heart, for the orphans under Gena's care.

'Where was Erin, when ye found her?' I asked.

Gena paused.

'She was badly injured in the earthquake, Paddy. Her body was under immense pressure from all those floors of concrete. We didn't find her until early this morning. We've done everything we can for her with what we have here. We're just waiting to hear from the Embassy now.'

My mind raced as Gena explained all of this. Molly, like Erin, was an American volunteer. She had come to work in Haiti the year before between and I had met her in the orphanage many times. She was amazing, giving up her time and working so selflessly with the kids. Everybody loved her. Now she could not be found and Erin was fighting for her life in the hospital just up the street. None of it was fair.

I wanted to see her but I was afraid to ask Gena. I couldn't imagine what she had experienced and how terrible an ordeal it must have been for her to find her friend, and colleague, in that condition. Like a coward, I just ate another mandarin.

'What's your plan then?' asked Gena. 'Will you be staying?'

'I don't know,' I said. 'My project will definitely be on hold for now. So, I'm not sure yet.'

'Is everybody okay down in Digicel?' she asked.

The situation was desperate. I was only adding to the despairing news when I explained to her about Jean Marc.

I still wanted to see Erin but I couldn't muster the bravery to ask Gena.

'Is she sleeping?' I asked.

Gena stood by the kitchen countertop with her arms folded.

'We gave her what we could for the pain,' she explained. 'It's best just to leave her sleep now.'

I nodded. Gena had been on the go all night and her day had not yet even begun. She had an orphanage of four hundred children to take care of, as well as her injured and missing colleagues. She loved this country very dearly. For all my time put into Haiti, none of it counted in that moment. I felt like a spoilt outsider. I threw my mandarin peels in the bin and politely took my leave.

'Mind yourself, Paddy,' said Gena as I gave her a hug. 'If you go back to Ireland, you have to tell them that we need their help.'

Gena looked at me with her gentle, warm regard as I walked out the gate and back onto the street.

'I will, Gena. I promise you I will.'

Chapter Eighteen

THE APARTMENT

WEDNESDAY, 13ᵀᴴ JANUARY, 2010

MORNE CALVAIRE, 10:30HRS

The morning was passing much faster than I had anticipated. I still had to put a 'bail out' bag together and figure out what my next move would be. The fastest route for me to reach Place St. Pierre, before going to Morne Calvaire, was to pass by the old Hexagon building.

There didn't seem to be a whole lot of damage to the buildings I saw in lower Petion Ville. Certainly nothing like what was down in Canape Vert. Most of the damage here looked to be large, deep fissures running through walls. The one constant reminder of what had happened was the white sheets laid out along the footpaths on every street. Under the sheets lay the remains of those who had not made it through the earthquake and those who had died during the night.

The Hexagon building looked like it had received a wallop from the fist of a disgruntled giant. Though the building had not collapsed, there was significant damage to the four exterior walls. Between each window of the nine story building, an 'X' shaped crack ran across, each one adjacent to the next.

I was no more than a hundred meters away from the next crossroads, when I spotted a familiar face. There he was, directing traffic away from the Hexagon, Graham, the old Canadian son of a bitch. He stood there in his khaki shirt and combats, same as always, with a cigarette pursed in his lips and a broad smile. He spotted me as I walked in his direction.

'Well well well,' he said. 'Nice clothes. Are you a businessman now or what?'

I laughed.

'What the hell are you doing back here?' I asked.

'I could ask the same of you, man,' he said. 'I'm managing the Blue Force security contract here in the Hexagon. Just like old times, eh. What about you? I thought you were in the cops?'

It had been almost two years since I'd last seen Graham. He was still as cool and composed as I had remembered him.

'Long fucking story, mate,' I said. 'I'm back as a project manager setting up a call center business in the new Digicel building. Well, at least I was until this shit happened.'

Graham laughed as he offered me a cigarette.

'For Christ sake,' he said. 'Talk about bad timing to be down here. I just got back yesterday from Montreal.'

I leaned towards him as he offered a light.

'Now that is just bad fucking timing, man,' I said. 'But it is great to see you.'

'Old times,' he said. 'How is Mac? Is he okay?'

'I haven't seen him yet, but I heard he is fine.'

We chatted for the time that it took us to smoke our lucifers.

'What's it like further up?' I asked.

'I'm not sure,' he said. 'I hear it's the downtown that took the worst of this.'

'Graham, buddy, I have to get going. Hopefully my apartment is still fucking standing.'

Seeing Graham standing outside the Hexagon brought back a lot of old memories. I couldn't help but think about the guys from the old crew. The Hexagon and Petion Ville of 06/07. It was our part of town only a few years before. And now, here I was, on foot and alone.

The remainder of the walk was on a stretch of Rue Kenscoff, until finally I reached Morne Calvaire and my apartment block.

'Alo! Overt les barriers si'l vous plait!' I yelled as I tapped on the main gate.

The security guards opened the long, rusted, red gate, slowly revealing that the four story mountainside apartment block was still standing. I didn't have my keys to the front door so I removed a small panel of glass from the kitchen window, reached my hand inside and slipped open the lock on the other side.

I glanced around the kitchen. Everything I had purchased to make it more homely had fallen from its place. Plates and cups lay broken on the tiled floors. All smashed into a thousand pieces. I carefully made my way into the bedroom. A massive crack ran from the wall on my left and all the way down through the floor. The front half of the bedroom dipped slightly downwards. Luckily, I did not have to step out too far to gather my things.

I grabbed my back pack. It had been lying at the back of the wardrobe and I had completely forgotten its existence. The last thing I wanted to do was to roll a suitcase back down the road to Turgeau or onwards to the Dominican Republic. Next I found my passport, my bank cards and my wallet with $400 US inside. I was still conscious of another aftershock hitting, but I needed to change out of my clothes. Jeans, a light khaki shirt and a pair of suede slip on shoes was the most practical wear I had available.

Next, I grabbed a couple of pairs of socks, jocks, another shirt, t-shirts, a North Face arctic fleece, a flashlight, beanie cap, gloves, toothbrush and toothpaste, deodorant, 2 liters of water from the fridge, some soft drinks and a pack of Marlboro Lights from on top of the fridge. The only object to stay in its place as it turned out. The fleece took up a lot of space in the bag. But I knew it would be worth it for the cold nights ahead.

There were five cans of Presidente beer also in the fridge. I took one and gave the remaining four to the two security guards. They were more than happy to take them. A number of aftershocks had hit that morning and judging by the precarious angle of the apartment complex, and the overhanging twenty foot wall on the opposite side of the road, I was quite surprised that the guards hadn't abandoned their post.

As I was organizing my backpack outside my apartment, a car pulled up outside and beeped its horn. One of the guards put down his can and opened the gate on its sliding rails. A white Nissan Patrol drove through with Piroslav and one of the Vigilance drivers inside. I hadn't seen Piro since Monday.

'Hey man,' he said. 'How's your morning so far?'

Piro always had a suave, sort of chivalrous manner about him. His 'Three Musketeers' type goatee and wild fawn hair just added to his persona.

'Have you been here long?' he asked.

'Not long. Just came up to get a few things together. What about you? What are you up to?'

'Something similar,' he said. 'Do you want to come down for a drink?'

His apartment was three floors below mine. Not the most ideal place to be caught if another earthquake was to strike. We walked down the flights of stairs, and I waited out on the terrace with Celestin, his driver. Piro soon came back with three soft drinks. We sat out in the shade of his small veranda watching a half dozen or so helicopters fly above the city. Buzzing above the carnage like mechanical mosquitoes. The fires still plumed smoke from far away.

'I'm going to take a shower,' said Piro as he placed his can down on the sill.

'Are you fucking serious?' I said. 'What if another....ah bollocks, I'm gonna grab one too.'

I ran back up the three flights of stairs and went directly into my bathroom where I quickly stripped naked before jumping into the shower. A quick splash of water, shower gel on, rinse, then out. When I was dressing, I realized that I hadn't taken a crap for almost a day. So I dealt with that as well.

Piro was just coming out of the shower by the time I was back on his veranda finishing my drink and sparking up a cigarette. I had smoked more than twenty five in less than twenty four hours. I couldn't have cared less.

Another aftershock hit. It was bigger than any of the others. The city rumbled and the apartment building moved. We all stared at each other with dumb, smiling, blank faces. The thought of this building giving way was too much. We'd pushed our luck by even being there for as long as we had been.

'Time to go,' muttered Piro as he picked up his backpack.

We ran up the three flights of stairs and stepped out into the small car park.

'What are you doing now?' asked Piro, throwing his gear in the back of his Nissan. 'Wanna come with us? We're gonna take a quick tour of Petion Ville on the way back to Turgeau. Interested?'

As tempting as the Dominican border sounded, it would be days before I got there by foot. The real challenge was to stay. See what happened. Help out if I could. Roll the dice. At least I'd be with friends.

'Fuck it,' I said. 'Let's go.'

When we drove out of the apartment gates, it was already midday. I felt better to be out in the open spaces, wearing clothes that made sense to me and having a bag with everything that I needed.

'Petion Ville didn't look that bad on the walk up,' I said.

'I know,' answered Piro. 'But the word is that it's pretty bad down toward the Caribbean market side. In fact I've heard that the Caribbean market collapsed last night.'

The Caribbean market was based on Route Delmas. It was the most popular and prestigious supermarket in the city and was constantly busy with Haitian people, UN and ex-pats. If that supermarket had collapsed, hundreds would have been trapped and killed inside.

'It gets worse. The Presidential Palace has collapsed.'

'Yeah, I saw that earlier on CNN,' I answered.

'I think the UN Headquarters has also fallen,' he continued. 'And the Hotel Montana is completely gone.'

The scale of the disaster was only just coming to light. The entire situation was like some sort of Armageddon. Who knew what might be next?

Having passed through Place St Pierre, Celestin drove us down towards the market area on Rue Gregoire. The place looked as though a rebel army had swept through the area, killing everyone and destroying everything in sight. We drove slowly, taking it all in from the confines of our car. Damaged and collapsed buildings, sporadic fires, young and old, men and women, boys and girls. Some lay caught between pancaked houses. Their legs and arms were strewn between the crushed layers of concrete. Others lay down small alley ways or in gaps between houses, small piles of stacked human beings. All covered in white powder from the dry, chalky cement and sodden in blood. To think that they had been alive less than twenty four hours before, living their lives like they'd always done, oblivious to anything like a natural disaster such as this. All I could do was stare.

As we moved nearer to the turn onto Delmas, the stacks grew higher. Many more dead bodies lay on the footpaths streets. A few times, Celestin had to swerve to avoid driving over the corpses. There was no way of rationalizing the sights we saw. Flexibility and acceptance were the keys to functioning effectively in this madness.

We drove past the Caribbean market. The streets were awash with both the dead and the living. Celestin turned left, bringing us back towards Petion Ville. Delmas was completely closed off by the swarms of people on the streets. We would have to find an alternate route.

Eventually we found ourselves back on the Canape Vert road heading down to the Turgeau building on Rue Jean Paul II. A mass exodus from the hills was underway. The entire route was jammed up with traffic as far as the eye could see. All we could do was sit there.

'They've packed their suitcases and are off to the airport,' said Piro in the front of the Nissan.

He was right. Anybody with enough money was headed to the airport and off of the island of Hispaniola. Miami, Jamaica, Cuba, it probably didn't matter to them. Just flash the cash and get the hell out. For those without funds, well, today wasn't that much of a different story for them. Though the earthquake had inflicted misery upon the country, millions of Haitians were already used to surviving. The earthquake just brought with it a different, deeper form of despair. To leave Haiti was not just incomprehensible to them. It was impossible.

As Celestin, Piro and I sat in the stagnant flow of traffic, another aftershock hit. I couldn't really feel it due to the suspension on the Nissan, but the roars of panic crying upwards from the city below me was enough to rattle my senses.

Piro and I got out and walked our way down through the river of traffic. Car horns honked. Panic and frustration was all around. Nobody was going anywhere fast. Just then, a voice called out from about ten cars back. I couldn't discern the language but I definitely recognized the voice. It was Sándor. He got out of his jeep and walked down to greet us. Piro held on for him. I walked on slowly as I knew the lads were good friends and would need a quick catch up. The two boys spoke in Hungarian for a while before they eventually caught up with me. Sandie looked surprised to see me.

'Oh, Peggy!' he roared with his thick Hungarian vocals. 'Big shit, huh.'

I took that as more of a statement than a question.

'Fucking very big, Sandie,' I said with a smile. 'What's the news your side?'

'My side is not so bad. I took the client to the airport this morning but no planes are flying. So I just take him to the home now.'

I noticed a car making its way uphill in the opposite direction. It was a red SUV and its lights were flashing erratically. The driver seemed to be looking for my attention. It was four of the women from the tenth floor of Digicel. I walked over to where they were pulled in off the road.

'Paddy, thank God you are okay,' said one of the ladies. 'Your company in Ireland have contacted us to check if you are okay. Oliver Tomkins told us that you were with the security guys.'

'Yes, ladies, thank you. Thank you for that. I'm fine.'

The driver was a Haitian lady called Veronica. I had sat down to a couple of meetings with her and had always found her to be cold and standoffish. The fact that she was smiling and asking how I was from the window of an SUV confused the hell out of me. We exchanged a few more kind words before they continued their journey into Petion Ville.

Piro looked at me from underneath his shades.

'Looks like you have some fans there.'

'Oho, Peggy!' roared Sandie. 'You have girlfriend local now!'

We kept walking until we reached the Canape Vert police station. The traffic was less congested there so we parted ways with Sandie and got back in our respective cars. The only downside was that we were headed back into the concrete jungle of Port au Prince. As Celestin zipped through the side streets, we came face to face with more bodies and more collapsed and distorted buildings.

After a few minutes, we reached the Digicel building. I wondered if I'd made the right decision in returning to Turgeau.

'So, Paddy,' said Piro as we rounded our last turn. 'Are you ready to come back to work?'

Chapter Nineteen

NAZON

WEDNESDAY 13TH JANUARY,

DIGICEL BUILDING, TURGEAU, 13:40HRS

It was a peculiar feeling to be back at the Digicel building. Less than twenty four hours before, I had run out of this same place for fear of dying. The crowds had since dispersed and a couple of vehicles were abandoned on both sides of the road. Celestin drove us down to the main entrance leading to the underground parking. Many of the security vehicles were parked out on the main road while others were parked just inside of the main gates.

When I dismounted the vehicle with Piro, I grabbed my bag from the rear and went over to speak with Ollie. There had been times in the past where we failed to see eye to eye on things, but I still considered him a friend. I hoped that he took my presence here as one of solidarity. He was chatting to Mac by the back of a green Prado.

'Welcome back, Pad,' he said. 'Thanks for yesterday.'

'Not a problem, Ollie. Just glad to see you in one piece, and you, ya bollocks,' I said, looking at Mac.

'Jaysus, Paddy,' said Mac. 'I was fuckin delighted to hear your voice over that bloody radio yesterday evening.

I wasn't sure if you made it out or not. Fucking good to see ya, mate.'

'So what's your plan now?' interrupted Ollie. 'Are you staying here or breaking for the border?'

'Well I can stay here if you boys will have me. I reckon you need every experienced bod you can get your hands on right now. I don't know how long I'll be here but I can certainly help out until the cavalry arrive.'

They both looked chuffed with my response. It was an uncertain time, and as much as I had been excluded from the ranks, these lads were still my friends. I needed to do something that I knew well and I knew I could help.

Ollie sorted me out with a pistol and a radio. I slipped the pistol between my belt and right hip, covering it with my shirt. The Motorola I clipped onto my left hand side. I'd never worked as a bodyguard in a pair of jeans before. The lads weren't long slating me about it.

'What the fuck is this?' remarked Viktor.

He and Jaroslav, another Polish bodyguard, were two old school ex-legionnaires. Between them, they had fifty years of soldiering experience. Both were standing at the rear of an armored car, eating rice covered in copious amounts of Tabasco sauce.

'I thought you were a businessman now?' said Viktor. 'Why aren't you in your office making money?'

'Well, I heard all you legionnaires were crying your little eyes out, all scared by the big bad earthquake so they asked me to come back and sort you out.'

I took a paper plate and helped myself to some rice.

'Where did this shit come from?' I asked.

'The United Nations,' answered Jaro, with a grin on his rough face. Jaro stood at five foot eight. Short, stocky and with a character full of mischief.

'I am sorry we didn't get the caviar for you,' said Viktor. 'They never told us that a VIP was coming.'

I poured some Tabasco onto my plate of plain rice.

'Fucking handouts from the blue helmets these days, is that it?'

Jaro pointed at my attire with a fork in his hand.

'What is this shit? You wear what you like? This is not a fashion parade here. I know you like to be gay but today is a very serious day.'

'Yeah, well,' I muttered as I ate my rice. 'I suppose it's better to be gay than old and Polish.'

Jaro smiled with a mouthful of rice.

'So, Vik my old pal,' I said. 'How was your two year holiday in Indonesia? Are you still single or have you fallen in love yet?'

'Fuck off, you Irish gypsy,' he answered.

I'd only just finished eating my rice when another powerful aftershock hit, sending everybody scattering back out onto the street. I stared up at the eleventh floor, waiting anxiously for something to give way. I dreaded the thought of ever being up there again. Even though she had withstood the magnitude of the earthquake and the dozens of tormenting aftershocks that followed, nobody knew the solidity of the building at that time. As far as any God fearing soul in that car park was concerned, it could still come crashing down at any moment. Viktor looked up at the eleventh floor and then back at me.

'Is that where you were yesterday evening?' he asked.

'Yep,' I said.

'Eleven, eh. We have a winner.'

Mac came over to me as we walked back inside the gates.

'It's fuckin crazy, Paddy,' he said, handing me a smoke.

I leaned forward for him to light it and asked, 'Were you still downstairs when it happened? Was Jean Marc still there?'

Mac lowered his head slightly and took a puff from his cigarette.

'It was just chance, Paddy, a fluke. When it hit, I ran for the exit as fast as I fuckin could. I mean I fuckin ran, bud. The bloody pillars were exploding either side of me as I tried to get out of there. It was like something out of a fuckin film. I swear.'

'Jesus, Mac,' I answered as I tried to imagine his story. 'That's some seriously crazy shit alright.'

Mac took another pull from his cigarette.

'Jean Marc just ran the wrong way. He ran down into the back of the car park. There was no way out down there. There was just no time for anything. Everybody reacted in their own way.'

I'd seen similar reactions from others up on the eleventh floor and on the stairwell.

'I know, Mac. I hear you, brother.'

I was beyond gutted by Jean Marc's passing. It still hadn't sunk in. There was just too much going on around us to contemplate any one death. None of us were out of the woods by any stretch.

'Paddy! Mac!' Ollie Tomkins called out.

We stubbed out the cigarettes and made our way down to him.

'Alright, boys,' he said. 'I've got a job that needs doing. A two vehicle convoy needs sending to the switch down by the airport. We need to get some fuel from the reserve down there and bring it back here for the cars and generators.'

'Yeah, no bother,' I said. 'What vehicle do you want me to take?'

'Mac, you can take Ralph with the Toyota pick-up. And Pad, can you go with Tommy in one of the Land Cruisers?'

'Tommy?'

'Yeah, mate. That's him there with standing by the silver Prado. He's a new lad, got in a few weeks ago. A lot of drivers are still missing so he'll be your driver. You still know the way to the airport switch? The one that's part of the warehousing facility.'

'Yeah, I remember. No worries, Ollie,' I replied. 'So the switch and straight back then, yeah?'

'Yes, mate. Any dramas, just give us a bell on the radio.'

With that, we dispersed and went to our vehicles. I introduced myself to Tommy explaining who I was. The buff looking Brit seemed a bit doubtful as to my presence. So with brief introductions out of the way, we pulled out of the Digicel grounds, turned right and made our way onto Martin Luther King Avenue.

'Have you been down this way since yesterday, Tommy?' I asked, all the while looking at the collapsed buildings either side of the road. Tommy looked straight ahead concentrating on the long line of traffic in front. He paid particular attention to the traumatized locals stepping out onto the road between cars. Mac remained one or two cars behind us.

'No, I've been up near Canape Vert and Debussy most of the day,' he answered. 'We've been checking in on clients and making sure they're okay.'

Traffic was moving incredibly slowly once again.

'When did you get down to Haiti then?'

'About two weeks ago. You've been down here a while, I've heard. You're running a call center, the lads were saying.'

'Yeah, I was trying to anyway. And now I'm back sitting in an air-conned B6 headed to the airport switch.'

'Yeah, that's pretty mental alright. Jesus! Look at that.'

Tommy pointed to a three story building that had pancaked. Strewn throughout the sandwiched floors of concrete were at least twenty bodies. None of them had any definite form, just remains of what once were people. The more we moved along the road, the more disheartening the scenes became. Traffic moved at a snail's pace due to sections of the road being inaccessible with debris. Hundreds of Haitians climbed through the rubble, removing bodies and laying their remains on the street.

Another aftershock hit the city sending people every which way for shelter. But seeking shelter was one of the reasons why so many people were still being killed.

Was it not enough that these people had to search through fallen wreckage for their loved ones? They also had to contend with the ordeal of continuous tremors. What we all know now, but didn't know then, was that this was normal after a shift in the tectonic plates and that aftershocks were actually a good thing. They relieved any remaining pressure below the earth's crust and allowed the two rifting plates to fall back into alignment. That's all well and good in the comfort of a geology lecture, but out here on the streets, it was nothing short of torment. As far as people were concerned, another earthquake was imminent. Every tremble was a reminder of that prospect. Many of us believed it was inevitable. Mother Nature's pounding wrath pushed our sanity to the brink, if not beyond. Nobody was exempt from the madness. Hell was all around us.

Tommy negotiated his way through the maze of parked and abandoned cars, rubble and dead people, eventually arriving in the Nazon district. Traffic was now at a standstill. Policemen with white handkerchiefs tied around their mouths supervised the movement of diggers and dump trucks. There was nothing we could do but sit and watch what was happening outside our vehicle.

The bucket of the two yellow diggers were loaded with people. Body piled on top of body were scooped from organized mounds and poured into the back of old American dump trucks. Tommy and I watched as the digger spilled its morbid cargo on top of the mass of corpses already inside. Every nook and cranny in every back street contained mounds of human flesh and bone. Women, men, babies, little boys and girls. The earthquake had not been prejudiced.

I felt cold and disconnected from what I saw in Nazon and the neighboring communities. Not by way of denial as to the severity of the situation. But detached from the misery of it all. The dead, mutilated baby being cradled by its dead mother. Not my problem. Move on. The disfigured old man entombed beneath a fallen slab of concrete. That's not my concern. Move on. The ghostly stacks of dead over there on that street, all covered in white, chalky cement and seeping dark red blood like a fucked up Christmas cake. It had nothing to do with me. Get to the switch, pick up fuel, avoid tumbling debris and get back. That was my job now. That was my mission. That was my way of coping. For now.

The dump trucks were destined for mass grave sites outside the city. Once the street was somewhat clear, we made our way out of Nazon and into the downtown area. Once the Prado was clear of the crowds, we made a push for the airport switch. Surprisingly, many of the buildings in the warehousing compound remained undamaged. For a while, everything felt normal again. The sun shone down on the soccer pitches, giving their dusty grass a golden glow.

After a quick cup of coffee and a smoke with Mac, we loaded the pick-up with the four large fuel drums and made our way back to Turgeau.

It had been a long drive down and it would be a long drive back. But once we all stuck together, it would be okay. I was with friends now.

As odd as it may sound, I felt safe.

Chapter Twenty

FLYING DOLPHINS

WEDNESDAY, 13ᵀᴴ JANUARY, 2010

DIGICEL BUILDING, TURGEAU, 16:50HRS

The two car convoy pulled back into the Digicel yard with its cargo secure. As Tommy parked up the Land Cruiser, I could see James in the distance instructing some of the drivers to move a couple of the Nissans to another parking area. James was acting as operations manager prior to the earthquake. I always knew him to be a funny, high-spirited and light hearted kind of fella. He was of the 'work hard, play hard' breed of soldier, and right now, he was working fervently to keep everything flowing operationally. Many of the clients and their families were running low on water and food supplies. The fleet of cars needed more fuel, as did the generators to power the emergency flood lights put in place by the bodyguards. Security operations had taken on an entirely new role. The guys were now responsible for the safety and the wellbeing of almost a hundred and fifty ex-pats.

More Digicel staff had gathered at the Turgeau building. Senior technicians roamed the grounds; some of the night duty drivers also appeared for work, as well as the local bodyguards. Their commitment to their job was commendable. I thought of how difficult it must have been for them to leave their families behind and report for duty.

After we unloaded the fuel from the Toyota pick-up, Ollie informed me that I could head back to Canape Vert if I wanted.

'We won't need you for a while, Paddy. You might as well go see if you can get some food and rest.'

'Are you sure? I'm good to go as I am,' I insisted.

'It's fine, Pad. Honestly. I'd prefer to have a few extra bods up there if I could. We've moved a number of clients from Debussy to Canape Vert today, so a little extra security is definitely needed. DOB (Denis O'Brien) has chartered an Air Jamaica 737 to start evacuating clients. I'll probably need you with the lads in the morning to start getting clients down to the airport. Go get some rest for now, mate. I'll talk to you later.'

'Well, if anything comes up, Ollie, you know where I am.'

'Yes, mate. No worries. I'll see you up there later.'

Throwing my bag on my back, I walked out the Digicel gates and made my way on foot once again to the Canape Vert apartment complex. This would be my second time making this ascent. Some of the bodies had been removed from the streets. The only indication of their passing through to the next life was the broken, hard rubble and stones still stained with thick coats of blood.

I took solace in the fact that at least this time I wasn't running from the mayhem and anarchy like the evening before. With my backpack weighing me down, I had an opportunity to take a more detailed look at the street and my surroundings. On closer inspection, the carnage had been as bad as I had remembered. The community college to my right had pretty much collapsed entirely. Both high rise structures had been demolished. For the students inside, there would have been little hope of escape.

The situation in Haiti was beyond dire. Apart from a number of Dominican diggers working down by Route National One, there was still no sign of outside assistance. US Coast Guard Dolphins continued to show a presence in the skies above the city. The bright orange helicopters had been the first sign of any presence from the outside world. Help was coming, but when it would finally have a positive impact on the thousands of victims on the ground was anybody's guess.

As I neared the T- junction to the apartment complex, I spotted my friend Ernesto sitting on a rock under some shade by the side of the road. It had been hot and humid all day and we had all probably been exposed to more sunshine than usual. The burly Chilean smiled as he saw me humping my pack up hill. I had been keeping a steady pace and was sweating profusely in the ninety two degree heat.

I walked over to him, dropped my bag and sat straight on top of it while catching my breath. Ernesto was sitting on a jagged rock with his left boot off. His foot was bleeding.

'What the fuck, man?' I said, still slightly panting for air and wiping sweat from my brow.

'It's nothing. I just messed it up a little. I had to jump out of a window during the earthquake and landed straight down on some of that damn metal in the ground. Hurts like a bitch, man.'

Ernesto sported an immensely thick black goatee which made him look like Sylvester Stallone from the movie 'Get Carter.' A former Blackwater operative in Iraq, he was always cheerful and professional. Even now, with a busted foot, he had a calm manner as dozens of locals moved steadily up and down the road in front of us.

We smoked a cigarette and talked about the chaos throughout Port au Prince. With a Marlboro hanging from his mouth, Ernesto continued to nurse his injured foot.

'Mate, you need to get that foot checked out. It's going to get infected.'

'Yeah,' he said. 'It's fucking killing me.'

The blood had hardened to create a blackened crust around the exposed region.

'Seriously, Ernesto. In this climate it's going turn septic pretty quickly. Then you'll really have a problem, my friend.'

He gently poked at the wound.

'I gotta check with the medic and see if he has anything. I'll sort it out then. What about you? When are you getting out of here?'

'No idea, man,' I answered. 'I'm stuck here now like you. I still work for a company that I haven't been able to contact yet.'

I stubbed out my smoke under the sole of my shoe, got up and wrestled with the straps of my pack that weren't sitting correctly on my shoulders.

'Take care of that foot, brother. And stay safe.'

Ernesto continued to self-diagnose his foot.

'Will do, Paddy. You too.'

It seemed wonderfully absurd to meet friends in the most random of locations. Our dilemma was not as drastic as that of the local populace. But be that as it may, one way or another, we were all in this together. Unless we were medevac'd or flown out, there was no escape. Right now, Ireland was only a daydream to me. It was a place that lay thousands of miles away in Western Europe. By keeping busy all day, I had put any thoughts of family and home to the back of my mind.

Once I was back within the secure confines of the apartment complex, I dropped my back pack on the lawn and joined the line for food. The owners of the Canape Vert complex, the Williamson family, had been kind enough to cook up a Christmas turkey which had remained in their freezer. Turkey and rice complemented by a can of warm coke to wash it all down. It was heaven.

More clients now sat out on the lawn. Sun beds adorned with yellow mattresses spread haphazardly across the garden. A lot of people's belongings had been salvaged from the two apartment buildings. Up at the Williamson residence, folks had placed about a dozen or so deck chairs and sun beds on the front porch. Some of the clients lay there sleeping in the warmth of the late evening sun. As tempting as it looked, I was still wary of the aftershocks and feared the possibility of a second earthquake. I continued to take my chances on the grass out front of the old colonial residence.

The darkness soon set in as I found myself once again in Canape Vert. The stars appeared brighter tonight. I noticed the satellites buzzing past at an incredible rate. The rotor blades of helicopters still echoed in the pitch black sky. I could see their red and green lights blinking intermittently, like tiny bright dots above the city. I envied the people aboard and wondered what they must be thinking about all of us down below.

Thankfully, the rain was still holding off. It was a small blessing for the hundreds of thousands still sleeping outside on the streets and in parks and gardens. On the Friday before, the day of my return, it had rained heavily for an hour that night. One hour of rain here would be enough to increase the death toll, cause more injuries and heighten the risk of disease. We were lucky for now.

By about nine o'clock, Piro arrived. I flashed my torch over my head so as he could see me. The amiable Hungarian came over and sat down. The tiredness in him was showing.

'Any news?' I asked.

Piro sighed as he tried to make himself more comfortable on the grass.

'Not good, man. Not good. The United Nations have lost their Head Quarters at the Christopher Hotel. They've lost maybe up to two hundred of their staff. The Hotel Montana is definitely gone. They say about four hundred guests were in there. Also, MINUSTAH had a meeting in the conference hall. They've lost a couple of hundred too. It's some pretty bad shit down there.'

I didn't really know what to say. We just sat there in the darkness and waited out the unending rumbling of the aftershocks. Many people sobbed with the frustration and ordeal of it all. We were into a second night and sleep was severely lacking. Some people tried to put their heads down on duvets and blankets, but with each horrific aftershock they were abruptly awoken and filled with fear.

Once again, the night was extremely cold. I was so happy to have found my North Face fleece and beanie hat to keep me warm. I never would have brought them to Haiti if it hadn't been for the bitterly cold journey to Dublin airport the week before.

I managed to doze off for about twenty minutes before the next aftershock hit. My reaction was the same every time. In a second, I would pounce to my feet, but keep my upper body as low as I could. Then I would listen for any sound of trees or earth giving way. As quickly as it had begun, the trembling would cease. Once my adrenaline levels dropped, I checked my watch. It was only one o'clock in the morning. Not even twenty minutes since the last pounding had hit. I lit a cigarette to calm my nerves. Young children were sobbing somewhere behind me. If my resolve was being pushed to the limit, those poor tots must have been in a really bad way. But in the bigger picture of things, the siblings of the ex-pats were the lucky ones. A second night in the city would see thousands of children, hundreds of them now orphaned and alone, trying to seek refuge from the impending dangers.

I thought about Gena and the news she had told me earlier that morning. She had probably made her way back to the orphanage in Kenscoff by now. Her children would need her. I wondered if Erin had been evacuated in time to save her life. And what about Molly? Had she been found yet? And if so, what condition was she in? I thought about Jean Marc and how happy he had been less than half an hour before the quake. I thought about the futility of it all.

Above all else, I desperately wanted to get through to my family and tell them that I was alright and that I would be home to them as soon as I could. I wanted to hold Jack in my arms and take him on more walks with his mom to the river. In the darkness of the night and with nothing but my thoughts, I longed for all of these things. Sitting there on the cold, damp grass, without knowing it, I'd made up my mind. My time in Haiti was over. I would stay and help for as long as I was of some use. But when that time came to an end, I was going home. If Taxback didn't understand that, then screw them. If people wanted to view me as a coward, screw them too. I wasn't getting paid a remunerative salary like many others to risk my neck. And even if I had been, so what? Fuck the money. I was trying to build a call center, and for what? To prove I was worth something and get offered a job back home. I had spent the best part of my life proving myself. Where was any of it getting me? Farther and farther away from all that I truly loved.

As I waited for the next aftershock to hit, I knew that if I survived all this mayhem and carnage, I would start living my life exactly as I wanted. But for now, I just tried to stay warm until another day started.

Chapter Twenty One

SHOELACES

THURSDAY 14ᵀᴴ JANUARY,

CANAPE VERT APARTMENTS, 05:00HRS

I awoke to the rattling of the rear gates to the apartment complex. Checking my watch, I realized that I must have slept for about twenty minutes. Twenty minutes of uninterrupted sleep. I almost felt refreshed. Random beams of torches shone out towards us. The distant muffling of male voices could be heard as I wiped the sleep from my eyes. I noticed the outline of Piro's silhouette when he stood up. I watched as he made his way over to the newly arrived group of men.

One of the shadowy figures appeared to be laden down with a large backpack on his back and smaller pack cradled on his chest. The full load made him look like a paratrooper in the darkness. They moved away from the garden area where everybody was trying to sleep and headed over to the nearest apartment building on the far side of the bushes. Curiosity got the better of me so I got to my feet and walked over to see what was going on.

As I got closer, I could hear them speaking in English. One of the men spoke with a British accent and the other, with the heavy load of bags on his person, sounded Irish. Both were anxious to know more about the exact situation in the country. They bounced as many questions as they could off of Piro. The amenable Hungarian did his best to answer, but there was very little in the way of 'big picture' analysis he could give.

'We are taking care of security for the Digicel staff,' explained Piro. 'I am not sure as to what the exact plan is for today, but hopefully we can begin evacuating people by the afternoon.'

The Irishman with the bags noticed me standing on the side-line of their small gathering.

'And what about you?' asked the Irishman, looking at me. 'Are you security also?'

For the sake of simplicity, I answered, 'Yes.'

'You're Irish?' asked the bag man.

'Yep, from Waterford. What about you? What are you doing out here?'

'I'm with an NGO. I'm spearheading our response here on the ground. Have you been out in the city at all? What's it like?'

'Yeah, em, it's not great. But you'll see it for yourself soon enough.'

I don't think he liked my brief and blasé response. I could appreciate that the bag man was playing catch up, and in fairness to him, I was impressed that an aid worker from Ireland was on the ground already. Yet whatever his business was here, it was nothing to do with me. The British guy who arrived with him was a bit more unruffled and reserved. He was dark skinned with thick long black hair. I guessed he was of Indian descent. He told me that he was a reporter for the BBC and had managed to get into Haiti via the Dominican Republic. Both men were keen to get out on the streets and see what was going on. For the rest of us there that morning, all we wanted was another hour of sleep with no aftershocks.

'Do you want to go down to the Digicel building?' asked Piro.

Both men nodded. I decided I might as well join the group, so I dumped my fleece in my back pack up on the terrace of the main house.

Light was beginning to show as Piro, me, Dan Slater (a Digicel technician) and our two new arrivals made our way back down the road to the Digicel building. Once again, we had to negotiate a safe passage over the jagged rubble just outside the back gates of the apartments. Everybody moved carefully so as not to get injured. Once clear of the mounds of debris, Piro and I waited for the others to catch up. Having no bag on my back, I helped the Irish aid worker carry one of his. In the darkness, I hadn't realized how many bags he'd brought with him. He also had a gym bag thrown over his shoulder. Tall, thin, pale skinned and speaking with an educated voice, the bag man struck me as more of an administrator than an operator.

Dan, an ex-Navy man from New York, had outside priorities that he needed to consider. I'd known him for a number of years and to hear him speak so boisterously was something new to me.

'They have to start getting people out of here soon, he said. 'I mean, this is just fucking crazy right now.'

'I'm sure they will,' said Piro.

'They'll definitely detach an Expeditionary Unit for this,' added Dan.

'Do you think so?' I asked.

Dan looked a little calmer and confident.

'Most definitely. Imagine how many US citizens are down here. They gotta get them out. Who the hell knows what is gonna happen down here now? This thing could get messy. They'll send the marines in for sure.'

Dan was right. We'd long since passed the first twenty four hour shock factor. If the world did not soon respond, thousands of people would become hungry, thirsty, restless and angry, creating an entirely new security situation.

Once the two newcomers caught up with us, we continued to make our descent to the Digicel building. Dawn was on the way. Before we'd even moved more than twenty meters, the Irish aid worker had to stop. Some straps on his backpack were catching, digging into his shoulder. Piro helped him free up the snag. Just before we walked away, he looked at me with a 'lost sheep' kind of look on his face.

'Can you do me a favor?' he asked me as Piro stepped away.

'Yeah,' I said. 'What's up?'

'Can you tie my shoe lace?'

The last shoe lace I had tied for another person was for my two year old nephew. I bit my lip, said nothing and dropped a knee to tie his open lace. I could feel Piro's eyes staring down on me in amusement, but I dared not look up for fear of laughing my ass off.

With this critical task completed, we continued on our way.

'How long have you lived down here, Paddy?' he asked.

'A while,' I said. 'A few years now, on and off.'

'So you know Port au Prince pretty well?'

'Pretty well, I suppose.'

'Do you speak French?'

'A little. Yeah.'

'Do you want to be my interpreter for the day?'

I could hear Piro snigger behind me. I wasn't sure if this guy wanted a babysitter or a boyfriend.

'Not really, buddy,' I said. 'I got a lot on today. You're bound to find somebody though. I wouldn't worry about it.'

James, Mac and some of the lads were already there as we walked through the side entrance to the building.

Everybody appeared to be living on a diet of nicotine and caffeine with mugs of steaming coffee and a plentiful supply of cigarettes.

'Alright, Paddy. Who's yer men?' quizzed Mac.

'An Irish aid worker and a fella from the BBC. Can I bum a smoke off of ya, Mac?'

He reached into his shirt pocket and pulled out a pack of Marlboro Reds.

'Course ya can, here,' he said, handing me a smoke. 'There should be some coffee left over in a flask in the back of that Nissan.'

I'd just about smoked the last oxygen cell out of my lungs, but I was too tired to give a shit. Plus the smell of cigarette smoke was much more welcoming than the stench of decay which was beginning to waft heavily in the stuffy, polluted air.

I gave James a nod as he dealt with the two new arrivals. Thankfully, 'the bag man' was no longer my concern. He could go and blaze his own trail out in the city.

'Have you heard the latest?' asked Mac.

'No, mate,' I said. What's the news?'

'The marines have landed. The airport is buzzing down there today apparently. Looks like the world is starting to respond.'

The Americans were finally arriving down at the airport. Word had it that units from the US Air Force Special Operations Command were now running the show. This was both good and bad. It meant that any chartered flights coming in from Jamaica to get Digicel people out could be turned away, giving precedence to more vital aircraft carrying aid workers or medical/food supplies. Security would start sending airport missions with evacuees but their leaving the country still remained to be seen.

After an hour, a convoy of six vehicles pulled out of the car park. They were headed to Debussy and Canape

Vert to pick up families and escort them to the airport. Dust rose wildly from the ground as the assortment of Land Cruisers, Prados and Nissans headed for their respective locations. The word was that an Air Jamaica flight, compliments of DOB, was due to leave Jamaica and touch down in Port au Prince at around half past ten. Even though that gave security about four hours to be on site, they would need that time due to the uncertainty of available routes down to the airport.

I found myself working with Tommy again. The ex-British Army soldier was a cool and easygoing fella to work with. We had been tasked with taking two technicians down to the Acieri switch next to the airport. Since the earthquake, the airport switch had become a secondary base of operations. It was imperative that the network be back up and operational. Thousands of people around the world were struggling to contact missing loved ones. Not only that, hundreds of people still remained trapped under the fallen rubble. There was a strong possibility that many of those victims had a cell phone on their person. Digicel technicians had struggled all night to reboot the telecoms systems in the partially collapsed Turgeau switch (the three story building at the back of the Digicel tower). Communications was everything right now. It was critical. All available technicians were working around the clock to get the network back up. I was happy to play a part in getting those men where they needed to be.

In the rear of our vehicle sat two of those technicians. Emmet, the senior of the two, had been here since the Hexagon days of 2007. Smart, polite and unpretentious, he was a true gent. The other man was new and I did not know him. He was Hispanic and had a bodybuilder physique. We were probably no more than fifteen minutes into our commute when the first aftershock of the morning struck. And it struck hard, shaking the life from our world for all of about five seconds. Hundreds of people ran out onto the middle of the street. Buildings moved once again and rubble slipped further out onto the roads. No sooner had it happened than it was all over. Five seconds. Enough time to keep our minds tormented by the uncertainty of it all. Tommy looked unfazed. However, the Hispanic muscleman panicked immediately.

'This is crazy,' he said, almost crying. 'Why is my door locked?'

'It's locked so that nobody can open it from the outside,' I answered.

'And what happens if a wall falls on me? How do I get out then?'

I considered that concept for a second.

'You'll be fine, sir. Just stay calm and we'll get you there safely.'

My words did little to sooth his woes.

'This place is crazy. I'm only a contractor,' he said, peering out at the road.

He wasn't far wrong. More bodies lay wrapped under more white sheets by the roadsides. I had to switch the air-con system off as the stench of decaying bodies seeped into the car.

The drive down onto Route National One was much faster than the day before. In the distance, I could see a half dozen or so US Navy Sea Hawks taking off from the far side of the airport runway. This was a clear indicator that there must have been a helicopter carrying vessel either in, or on the way to Haitian waters. Also, a number of US Coast Guard Jay Hawks buzzed gracefully high above us. Finally, some real help was on the way.

When we were safely inside the Aciérie switch compound, I had only just stepped out of the vehicle when an American C-130 Hercules flew in on approach directly above our position. Her massive engines left us deafened as we stared up at the grey beast. Her pilot pulled some seriously aggressive landing maneuvers before she finally disappeared below the tree line. True to their form, the

Americans had arrived with their inimitable noise and spectacle. Personally, I was glad that they were here.

Most of the day ran pretty much the same. Tommy and I conducted shuttle runs up and down to the switch throughout the morning and afternoon. On our second run back down, I noticed the BBC man whom I had met earlier on in Canape Vert. He spotted me immediately and gave a salute as I walked over to him.

'Alright, mate,' he said. 'How are you doing then?'

'Yeah, not too bad. Just been doing runs up and down to here all day,' I answered.

'So how long have you been working security for Digicel then?'

'I don't. I'm just helping out.'

'What?' he said, surprised.

'I used to work with them for a few years, but I'm actually out here on my own setting up a call center for an Irish firm.'

'Are you serious? So what are you doing down here then? Why don't you go to the airport and head home?'

'I'd just prefer to be with the people that I know. Some of these guys are old friends and I'd rather be of some use to them than sitting outside the airport looking for a ride home.'

'Fair play to ya, mate. This place is proper mental in fairness. I've been around a few disasters before but I haven't ever seen anything quite like this.'

'Yeah,' I said. 'It's mental alright. Is there much news about it on the papers back in the UK?'

'On the papers! Are you kidding? This is the biggest piece of news right now in the entire world, mate. It's on every news channel in every single country.'

'Really?'

'Yes! Absolutely!'

He looked at me as though I was completely out of touch.

'Sorry, is there any chance I could ask you a favor?' I said.

'Sure.'

'Would it be possible for me to borrow that sat-phone from you for a minute? It's just, I haven't made any proper contact with my family and I'd really like to let them know that I'm okay.'

'You seriously haven't talked to them yet?'

'No. The network is up and down and my phone is still somewhere in my office. I haven't gone up there yet because of the aftershocks.'

The BBC man gave me his satellite phone without any hesitation. He hastily showed me what buttons to hit then left me to work away.

'You take as long as you need, pal,' he said.

I tried to find a more private location away from any of the other bodyguards or clients that were hanging about outside the main building. At the same time I battled to get a few signal bars on the phone. Knowing my sister's number off by heart, I punched in the country code and her digits. The signal was weak, but her phone rang out.

'Hello,' said the crackly, distant voice of my sister.

'Karen! Hello! Can you hear me?' I called out.

'Hello? Patrick? Hello?'

'Karen, it's me. I can hear you. Can you hear me?'

'Hello. Patrick, I can't hear you but I know it's you. I can't hear you but I just want you to listen to me, okay? We all love you and we are just so worried for you. But we know that you are alive. Mick called mom yesterday morning. I've arranged an emergency passport for you. It's in the Spanish Consulate in the Dominican Republic. If you can get there, it's waiting for you.'

By now my sister's words were just too much. I could feel my own emotional barriers gradually crumble. I turned away from those who could see me as tears ran down my face. I fought hard not to let them get the better of me as I listened to my sister's voice.

'We are all here waiting for you, Patrick. Terry has been ringing mom and dad. He's waiting to hear from you. We all love you, Patrick. Just stay alive and get home to us. Jack is waiting for you to take him to Woodstown again.'

'Karen! Can you hear me? I'm going to get out of here and come home. I promise!'

Before I could say any more, the line broke. No bars. She probably wouldn't have heard me anyway. But even still, I felt so happy to hear my sister's voice.

I walked away into the dusty air by the perimeter fence. I just needed a moment to get myself together before I could return and face the boys.

Chapter Twenty Two

THE LIVING AND THE DEAD

THURSDAY 14TH JANUARY,

ROUTE DELMAS, 19:20HRS

Nightfall had set in by the time Piro and myself dropped three technicians back to their houses for some well-earned sleep. They had been working around the clock to get the network back up. Not an easy feat given the circumstances. Tiredness was becoming an issue, even for the bodyguards. The boys had been working for more than forty eight hours straight. Though they had done so with no complaints, I knew most of them long enough to see the tiredness showing. Some of them slept sitting upright in their car seats. Even if it was just a quick ten minute nap.

When Piro drove the white Nissan back out onto Route Delmas, we found ourselves back amidst the bedlam. To the right of us was the collapsed Caribbean supermarket. UN forces from the Nepalese contingent attempted to secure a perimeter around the debris. However, these efforts were proving all too late. After two days of little or no food, people had become desperate enough to climb in amongst the rubble, scrounging for any food that might be within reach. Others were also most likely trying to find loved ones deep below the mounds of concrete. With our limited vision from the half lights on the Nissan, the only prominent color among the hubbub was the luminescent glare emanating from the white bed sheets covering the dead on both sides of the road.

US military Humvees were also parked up on the street corners. Some of them were green in color while more looked like they had driven all the way from Kabul or Baghdad with their khaki paint for desert terrain. I could only imagine what could be going through the mind of a young army private or specialist experiencing Haiti for the first time. Haiti was not a warzone, and yet, with the fires burning, most of the capital city left in ruins, and thousands of bodies still left rotting on the streets, it certainly had the appearance of one. It could have been Rwanda thrown in with about fifty sorties of carpet bombings. I could appreciate that these soldiers were probably anxious with what they now found themselves a part of.

Before we made our return trip to the Aciérie switch, Piro decided to take a quick detour to the Karibe hotel. If the Montana had collapsed, then there was a possibility the Karibe had too. When we arrived, the area was deathly quiet. The main structure was still in one piece. Because we were under pressure to report back, there was no time to park the vehicle and take a closer examination of the recently built hotel. Through the looming darkness, I pointed my torch towards the hotel lobby. No lights were on. No people present. The only signs of life were the stray dogs roaming the street outside.

'Okay,' said Piro, still peering in at the main entrance. 'We better get back.'

The return drive to the switch went much faster. Though it was still relatively early in the evening, many thousands of Haitians were already trying to sleep. Aftershocks were still occurring so people were too scared to go indoors. The only available space for most people to sleep was on the streets. This was also the most logical, as it allowed survivors to keep a fairly safe distance from nearby houses and buildings. It also meant that when we passed by in the Patrol, we could not distinguish between the living and the dead. Everybody was covered in white sheets. Even for the living, their heads were shrouded so as to protect them from rats and wandering animals scavenging for food. It was all anybody could do to rest their exhausted bodies.

More and more military vehicles were heading in the opposite direction as we continued to make our way back down towards Route National One. The US Army had also begun to set up road checkpoints along the way. Rumor had it downtown was rife with looters. I hadn't witnessed much of it myself (aside from two grown men fighting over a pack of Doritos earlier that day) but word had spread that all was not well on the security front.

In any disaster, opportunists will slither to the surface and endeavor to stake a claim. No catastrophe would be complete without its looters. Haiti's was no different. Unfortunately, this activity was likely to attract the wrong sort of news coverage. Adding to the despair, we had also received news that the main prison in Port au Prince had collapsed, releasing up to four thousand prisoners back out onto the dilapidated streets of the nation's capital. It was bad news for the ordinary Haitians who were waiting patiently for outside help to mobilize on the ground. It was even more bad news for the United Nations troops struggling to maintain some sort of mandate. It was bad news for everybody all round.

US Navy Sea Hawks continued their humanitarian flights in and out of the national airport well into the dark hours of the early night. In relation to the airport, the Digicel switch really was not that far away. From where we stood in the compound yard, we saw the night sky lit up with military aircraft. The skies of Port au Prince had never been so occupied.

'So what's the news from up town?' asked Mac as I dismounted the Patrol.

'Still the same. More Yanks on the streets. That's all.'

I decided to get a coffee inside the security accommodation block of the switch. Some of the lads were sitting in one of the bedrooms watching CNN on the TV as I came in and pulled up a chair. I was deeply conscious of the fact that if another earthquake hit, we would not make it out of this particular part of the building in time. A large chunk of one of the walls in the security office had already fallen away from the main structure. I was so tired that I had begun to not even care.

CNN was already dominating the news coverage on the ground. Their lead news reporter, Anderson Cooper, was already covering the disaster from inside Port au Prince and the surrounding areas. I sat on a small wooden stool, drinking my coffee and watching updated scenes of bloodshed and misfortune as the earthquake stories continued to unfold. I wondered how many Americans were sitting at home in the comfort of their own living rooms, watching these scenes play out on their screens. What were people thinking, seeing all this loss of life? I even thought about what kind of news coverage my own country had on the disaster at this point. This really was a disaster. It had to be covered. Then the news became even more personal for me. A picture of Molly Hightower, with her name at the bottom of the screen, was being televised. The news reporter said that Molly was still on the missing list. I felt a rush of incredible doubt and despair watching her image. Molly was this tremendous girl who had chosen the noblest of reasons to work and live in Haiti. At twenty-two years old, she was already putting her beliefs into practice, working with the orphans. My thoughts then drifted to Erin. Had she made it stateside and was she still alive? I thought about Jean Marc, poor Jean Marc, how he should be here with us now, drinking his coffee and smoking his Menthols. And I thought about Gena and how she was fighting tooth and nail to protect all those little orphans up in Kenscoff.

'It's messed up out there,' said Ollie, standing by the door.

I hadn't noticed him at first.

'Yeah,' I answered.

'I've just been on the phone to Nick. He is in New York tonight with Martin and Colin Rawes. They'll be in Santo Domingo by the morning to make their way in here by road. When I told him that you were with us, Nick said 'Yeah, no problem. Take care of him.' I had to explain to him that you were actually working with us.'

'What did he say to that?'

'He seemed a bit flabbergasted to be honest. But I reckon it's fair to say that you've done enough with us. Maybe you should try and get on a flight out of here. Possibly even on that inbound chartered flight coming from Jamaica in the morning. Tonight's was turned away by the Air Force. Too many medical and supply transports coming in.'

Part of me was gutted at the thought of leaving all of this behind me. Particularly the idea of parting ways with the boys. As absurd as the circumstances of my re-joining (temporary as it was) the ranks had been, I could not have imagined myself being anywhere else. But Ollie was right. My responsibilities lay elsewhere. I suppose I just needed reminding.

'Mac will be back down in an hour or so with James and Piro. Piro will be taking that car back up to Canape Vert for the night. You should go with him.'

'Well, Ollie,' I said. 'Odds are I will be out of here tomorrow my friend. Let me pull stag in Turgeau. Give whoever is on up there tonight a chance to get some shut eye.'

Ollie smiled and gave me a slight nod, then headed back out the door to his desk.

I was outside chatting to some of the bodyguards and a few technicians when Piro, James and Mac pulled up in the Prado. James slammed the passenger door behind him and stormed over to where we were standing.

'Hey!' he yelled. 'You bunch of Jack bastards. Are you gonna help him change that fucking tire or just stand around yapping like a bunch of fucking old women?'

We hadn't noticed one of the drivers struggling to change a car tire a few meters behind us. Or maybe we had noticed him, but we were just too tired to give a fuck. It had been another long day and people were beginning to miss the little things that were happening around us. Myself and Alexi turned to give the struggling driver a hand.

'Anybody seen Ollie Tomkins?' shouted James.

'He's upstairs, Jim,' I yelled back. He then threw the door open and went inside.

'Is he alright, Mac?' I asked as he came over to where we were fixing the tire.

'Yeah. He's alright. Ya know yourself.'

Just then, one of the technicians muttered something about being hungry.

'Dominos was open, mate,' Mac remarked. 'We got pizzas in the car for ya.'

'Yeah!' answered the tech with a smile. 'Fantastic!'

Mac looked at him with a disbelieving grin as he sparked up a cigarette. The technician was not impressed. I couldn't help but smile..

'Any news down here, Paddy?' asked Mac.

'Nah, mate. I'm heading back up to Canape Vert with Piro as soon as he is ready. Some of these fellas are coming with us,' I said, gesturing towards the technicians.

Mac seemed to be quieter than usual. He pulled heavily on his cigarette.

'You alright, mate?' I asked as we stood there in the darkness of another late night.

'Yeah, grand. We just took care of Jean Marc. We were told that some French authorities were supposed to come today and see that he was repatriated home. But that never fuckin happened so we took care of it ourselves.'

Eventually Piro and I got into another Patrol and made the journey back to Turgeau. Jaro was already on guard duty when we pulled into the car park.

'Did you feel that aftershock?' asked Jaro. A colossal shuddering had hit just a few minutes before we arrived.

'I don't know if I'm feeling them anymore or imagining the fucking things.'

Jaro looked exhausted. The poor son of a bitch had eight more hours of stag to pull before sunrise. When I told him to go home with Piro and the technicians for some sleep, he was too tired to be grateful. He simply got into the car and closed the door behind him. I didn't really care. In twenty four hours, I'd probably be in Jamaica. I could manage one more night of staying awake.

I watched as Piro, Jaro and the couple of technicians pulled out of the Turgeau car park and headed for Canape Vert. I stayed behind with a radio, a pistol and three local bodyguards to secure the compound and prevent any loitering or trespassing. Staring up to the eleventh floor, with a starry sky as the backdrop far above, I played with the notion of running up to my office to see if I could find my laptop and phone.

After an hour or so of wrestling with the idea, I ran in the back entrance and leaped onto the first flight of stairs. With nothing but a small flashlight and a heaving set of lungs, I ran as fast as I could. Floor by floor I ran and I ran. There was nothing to guide me but the beam from my torch. I just wanted to get up onto eleven, grab whatever was worth grabbing, and get the fuck out. It seemed like forever and an eternity, but eventually I stepped out onto the eleventh floor. I ran into the call center and checked all work stations to see that nobody was in there. All the computers and phones had crashed to the floor. The pictures on the walls had fallen. Even the pot plants by the door had tipped over. In the darkness, the place had an eerie feel. My own office was in disarray too. My laptop lay smashed to pieces beside my desk. Everything was covered in chalky white dust and, for the life of me, I could not find my phone. I searched in every corner with my torch. Still nothing. Then another aftershock hit. The tremors ran up through the eleven stories, causing the building to rock slightly. Through leaps and bounds and unadulterated fear, I ran the stairwell and all its steps as fast as my legs could move. When I stepped outside, my body was shaking like jelly. I cursed myself for taking such a risk. The local bodyguards looked at me sheepishly as they wondered why in the hell I had gone inside in the first place. I spoke with them into the early hours of the morning. They were good guys; young Haitian men who were left with a terrible emptiness by what had happened. Thankfully, their families had survived. Even still, everybody knew of somebody who hadn't made it. Their questions to me were full of fear, disappointment and disillusionment. I empathized with their troubles. How could a city so big suffer so much?

'I think it is our destiny in this life to suffer,' said one of the men.

'What do you mean by that?' I asked.

'We always have something happen here. Hurricanes almost every year.   Now this. Why us every time?'

Some helicopters flew overhead. They flew so low that I could hear their engines whining and their blades rapping loudly in the star filled sky. A volley of gun shots rang out in the distance somewhere near Pacot.

'Maybe this is the price you have had to pay,' I said.

They were confused.

'Maybe this is what had to happen for the world to know that Haiti exists. I know that it has been such a terrible cost. But you can build from this. You can show the world that you are here. That Haiti is real. Maybe this is where it all changes.'

I could see that they wanted to believe my words. I wanted to believe them myself. During those early morning hours of Friday the 15th, those young security men had no idea what the future of their country might be. I just hoped that my words would prove to be right.

Chapter Twenty Three

AIRPORT APOCALYPSE

FRIDAY 15TH JANUARY,

TURGEAU BUILDING, 05:40HRS

The prickly heat of the morning brought with it a stench like no other. My eyes strained in the morning light. The night had been long and generally uneventful. In the solitude I daydreamed about home. My belly rumbled with hunger as I waited for the morning relief to arrive. The word from the night before had been that a chartered flight was arriving in for half past ten. That meant early morning pick-ups of clients and their families. I still needed to get back up to Canape Vert apartments and grab my bag.

It was about ten past six when some of the bodyguards arrived in two Nissan Patrols.

James and Jaro were in the front white Patrol while Viktor drove the second. As the boys hopped out of the front car, I could see that the morning was going to be far from laid back. Jaro immediately began refueling his car. James spotted me standing by the main gate.

'Alright, Paddy,' he said, walking towards me. 'Were you on down here last night?'

'I was, yeah,' I answered.

'What's the deal with you? Are you staying on for the morning?'

'Sorry, James, no. I'm gonna try and grab this flight this morning. In fact, I was hoping you might be able to let me take one of these cars for ten minutes to grab my gear.'

'Where's your gear?'

'Canape Vert.'

'Ah, mate, I fuckin need these cars to pick up clients from Debussy in fifteen minutes.'

James was under pressure, but no way was I walking up that road again and then marching all the way to Debussy. Besides, this morning's exercise was most likely going to end with the old army proverb of 'hurry up and wait.' We had time.

'Look, dude,' he said. 'Go with Vik right now, get your bag and go back with him to the team house. But ten fuckin minutes, Paddy. That's all I can afford.'

I didn't need convincing. I simply nodded and left.

'What the fuck do you want?' said Viktor as I got into the passenger seat of his Nissan.

'Canape Vert, Vik. I need to grab my bag and then straight back to the team house with you.'

The grumpy Polish bastard grunted something under his breath as he started the engine and pulled out of the gates of Turgeau. I didn't even look over my shoulder for fear of James beckoning the car back.

'So a bag then, yeah?' Vik said as he put the foot down making a fast run up Rue Jean Paul II.

'Yes sir. In and out. No gay shit of hanging around touching arses.'

He laughed, a slight and wiry grin. As good a reaction as I could expect from the old salt at that hour of the morning.

The vehicle went as far as it could to the T-Junction, and I was on foot from there on.

'Don't fuck around, you Irish idiot!' he yelled as I jumped out.

'Four minutes!' I shouted back as I quickly rounded the corner and went out of sight.

The contrast of being bored silly less than five minutes before and now grappling my way over the all too familiar rubble to get to the back gates of Canape Vert made me feel a little excited. I didn't want to injure myself, but I just couldn't get to the green gates fast enough.

The security guard peered through the small hatch and allowed me in. If he hadn't known me from the old days, he certainly did since Tuesday evening. I kept a steady jogging pace as I ran past the garden and up onto the steps of the Williamson residence to pick up my bag. Most people were still trying to sleep even though it was already daybreak. I spotted the Haitian family from Tuesday night. They were all huddled together, asleep on their blanket. For most by now, it wasn't difficult to sleep. Sheer exhaustion had finally set in. Two wives of Digicel technicians sat upright on the grass feeding their babies.

My backpack was stacked under a pile of about twenty other bags on the front porch of the house. Next to the pile, four ex-pat clients lay fast asleep on deck chairs. I pulled the top strap of my bag as hard as I could and managed to knock over four other backpacks and a suitcase in the process. The client sleeping next to the pile slowly opened his eyes and looked at me. I didn't give him the opportunity to ask me what I was up to. I simply threw my bag over my shoulder and made a dash across the cracks of the cobbled driveway and back towards the gates. I really did not want to converse with those who were awake. Firstly, I did not want to tell them about an inbound chartered flight. I didn't know the manifest and it was not my place to create a shit storm if their names were not on it. Secondly, even if I didn't mention the flight to them, they would surely be full of questions as to where I was off to. Even though I was moving suspiciously fast for such an early hour, I was certain that my eyes, rather than my legs, would give me away.

The security guard looked at me inquisitively as I quickly walked out and thanked him for opening the gate. I climbed my way back over the long stretch of rubble and smiled to myself. I started to think more and more about getting out and returning to Ireland to be with my family again. I couldn't help but feel good about that.

I threw my pack in the back door of the car, slamming it against the rear of the passenger seat. Viktor had already turned the vehicle around and was drumming his fingers on the wheel.

'Four and a half minutes,' he said, flashing his watch. 'Shit time.'

'Screw you. Now let's get moving.'

The Nissan Patrol ripped up loose chippings and stones behind its wheels as we made haste for the team house in the nearby residential area of Pacot.

Pacot was where many foreign diplomats and their families lived. It was also home to various international consulates. Or, at any rate, it used to be. Driving through the winding back roads, I caught my first glimpse of houses in the area. Most of them had collapsed in the same manner; pancaked due to heavy roofing and poor column support. The sun was well and truly up now. And though the neighborhood sported colorful shrubbery and lush, green vegetation complementing the blue morning sky, the entire area was awash with a pungent stench of rotting flesh.

'It's unbelievable,' I muttered, staring out at the passing homes.

'Yeah,' said Viktor. 'It is what it is.'

When we arrived at the gates to the team house, he dropped me off and then left for Debussy. From the way he was driving, he'd probably be there with minutes to spare.

The security guard opened the gate and let me in. This was my first time seeing the new team house. The front garden was like a scene from an outdoor music festival. Some of the clients had been brought here from Debussy the night before. Husbands, wives and children sat around on chairs and blankets just outside the front door. Some of the bodyguards lay sleeping in half open tents which had been constructed on the far side of the garden, away from the house. One of the Slovak bodyguards had even engineered his own hammock with an overhanging mosquito net. I went upstairs to see if I could find Piro. There were two large couches outside on the upstairs terrace. Piro was asleep on one of them. I decided to leave him be and went back downstairs.

'Howya, Paddy,' said Mac. He was standing by the kitchen doorway with a mug of tea in his hand.

'Do ya want a brew?'

'I'd fuckin murder one Mac. Thanks.'

We stood in the kitchen waiting for the kettle to boil over an old metal gas stove. I told Mac that I was planning to leave Haiti on the ten thirty flight. I was concerned as to how my friend would react to the news.

'Paddy. You're better off, buddy, and ya know it. Listen, you helped us out here when ya didn't have to, but at the end of the day, you should go while you can. You have a boss back home that you still need to make comms with. Get the fuck outta here while there are flights.'

After Mac gave me a quick guided tour of the new team house, we headed back outside to the front garden. I spent the rest of my time chatting to some of the clients and the Chilean residential bodyguards. I was one of those who didn't want to tempt fate by staying indoors when it wasn't absolutely necessary to do so. I was standing near the main gate with Mac when a woman's voice called out from a window on the second floor. It was Brenda, the security company's accounts manager.

'Well, Paddy,' she hollered.

'Hiya, Brenda,' I called up, shielding my eyes from the sunshine.

She stood looking at us from the window for a few seconds.

'I'll come down,' she said, then went out of view.

'When did she get back?' I asked Mac.

'She never left, Paddy.'

A moment later, she came out to greet me. Brenda told me that she had been in the team house when the earthquake struck and hadn't left since.

'So are you getting on this plane this morning?' she asked.

'I hope so. Women and children first and all that. But if there is space, I'm definitely getting on. Are you packed?'

Brenda looked puzzled.

'Packed? Eh, no. Sure there probably won't be any room on this plane. And besides, no one asked me.'

'What? So what are you gonna do? Stay here?'

'Do you think I should pack?'

'Brenda, there's a convoy leaving this location in the next twenty minutes. Nobody knows what state of affairs this city- this entire country- is going to be in by the end of the week. From what we've seen, food and water is not getting in fast enough. Nobody knows what's going to happen next. Pack a bag, Brenda, while you still have the time.'

She went back inside and I turned to Mac.

'Does she have any idea what's happened here at all?'

Mac just shrugged.

I had been right about the 'hurry up and wait' of our convoy to the airport. By the time the entourage of five vehicles was finally ready to leave, it was already half past eight. I rode shotgun with Viktor in his white Nissan Patrol. We were the rear vehicle in the convoy. All cars were packed with evacuees and baggage. And there was a lot of baggage. The temperature was sweltering as we drove along the winding roads of Pacot and on towards the airport. At first, we moved with relative ease. There weren't as many people on the streets as the mornings prior. A lot of the dead bodies had also been removed. After Nazon, the traffic began to slow down, nearly to a halt. It was more than the usual traffic pile up. There wasn't much that could be done other than stay in line and wait.

When we arrived at the outer perimeter of Toussaint Louverture Airport, we were met by large crowds of people trying to enter onto the grounds. Surprisingly, our small convoy of ex-pats cleared through without difficulty. But the more we bridged the final gap to the main entrance, the worse the scene became. It was like a mass triage center that had grown horribly out of control. Hundreds of injured Haitians lay stretchered on the ground. There were so many casualties, hundreds lay badly wounded with multiple injuries. Those on their feet looked to us as we pulled up in our small convoy, shouting in Creole, signaling for help. It was another desperate scene of injured people seeking medical aid and evacuation. It was a struggle to get the vehicles through the last one hundred meters. I could hear Viktor cursing profusely under his breath at the chaos surrounding us.

Eventually we had to park up and get everybody to dismount the cars, grab their gear and start walking with the security staff to the departures doorway. A lot of the clients were scared and confused by the scenes they were witnessing. It was as if all the dying and badly wounded had been abandoned on every stretch of open ground. We had to wade carefully towards the departures area so as not to step on any of the injured. Many of the victims were wailing to Jesus to ease their suffering. Family members lay by their sides trying to bring them some comfort. The only thing more dispiriting than the cries for help was the diabolically putrid stench of death and rotting flesh that filled the air. I really felt deeply troubled for what I saw before me. It was all just so far beyond my immediate calling. I stepped out of the Nissan Patrol and held back for a moment. I waited until everybody else from our convoy was escorted by the guys to the main entrance.

'So this is how we go our separate ways then, Viktor.'

The cantankerous ex-legionnaire looked at me. I noticed a slight smile on his face, but he said nothing.

I removed the magazine from my pistol and cleared the chamber, placed the two magazines and my Motorola into Vik's small day sack now on the passenger chair. The Digicel clients were already hurrying to the departures door. Mac and Ollie approached the armed US Air Force and Army personnel standing guard. They would have to make this a speedy process to get inside. Hundreds of Haitians were already showing signs of anger and hostility at not being allowed to enter the terminal while dozens of ex-pats were about to be ushered through. And who could blame them. I closed the zip on Vik's bag, leaving it on the chair.

'Do we hug now or shake hands now or what?' I said smiling.

'Fuck off, Irish. Don't crash your plane.'

'Take care of yourself, you grumpy Polak fuck.'

Vik smiled. That was it. I ran to join the evacuee party already making their way in through the main entrance. Even though I had my passport in hand, nobody was checking them. We were briskly ushered through by military personnel into the main building. Another passageway had been set up where soldiers and airmen continued to send us through. There were no metal detectors or security checks. We just walked down through unfamiliar corridors, eventually stepping outside at the back of the airport.

My new surroundings were in stark contrast to where I had just come from. Things were still busy, but not as chaotic as it had been out front. I moved further along the tarmac to where Mac, Ollie and some of the other security boys stood waiting with the twenty five or so ex-pats. We were a small party in comparison to the hundreds of French, American and other nationalities who stood parallel to us. All lined up in formations of fifty, just waiting to be instructed as to which plane to go to.

Out on the runway, US Navy Sea Hawks came and went like work bees to a hive. Every fifteen minutes, a Hercules C-130 or a C-17 Globe Master would touch down and drop off hundreds of troops and hardware. Much of the gear being unloaded on an area to my left appeared to be live ordnance.

To the right, incoming civilian aircraft parked up, and military liaison staff from France, Canada or America escorted groups of evacuees to their respective flights. US military Humvees ripped up and down the surrounding areas. Platoons of the US Army's 82nd Airborne formed neat lines in front of their platoon commanders and sergeants, all waiting for orders to deploy on the streets of Port au Prince. In a remote area of the field, a team of US Air Force special operations soldiers organized some of their equipment onto the back of a bunch of dirt bikes and quads. With their shades on and weapons slung across their backs, the small group of men in their tiger striped camouflaged uniforms appeared to be getting ready to head out onto the streets.

The entire ensemble could have been mistaken for a military invasion if it wasn't for the hordes of rescue teams arriving in on civilian flights. They were men and women of all nationalities. United Kingdom, China, France, United States, Germany. All adorned with yellow, red, orange and navy jackets and jumpsuits. Some of them had rescue dogs on leashes. The entire scene was beyond impressive. It was intoxicating.

So too was the smell of aviation fuel that wafted through the heat of the late morning. It was a more welcoming scent than the rotting flesh that many of us had been enduring for a number of days now.

After an hour and a half of waiting, our group was escorted to the vicinity of the Air Jamaica flight which had just landed a few minutes before. I stood with the others as Jamaican Defense Force personnel and a number of civilians walked down onto the tarmac. The overpowering heat of the morning didn't help our standing around. Some of the women in the group were trying to prevent their babies and children from coming down with heat exhaustion. I helped Ben Smyth's wife, Rita, with her four young children over to a more sheltered spot. Ben was now a senior body with the company and was staying behind to re-establish the Digicel network. All we could do was continue to wait for somebody to tell us when to board our plane.

As I finished helping Rita settle her babies into their buggies, I spotted a friend of mine step off of the Air Jamaica plane. It was Sheila Flanagan. The last time I had seen her was the night she loaned me her laptop in the Karibe hotel to try and arrange a flight home almost six months before. I knew that she was still working with one of the Irish charities, and was now based out of their New York office. I walked over to greet her. The tall blonde from Cork looked at me and smiled. It was as if she had seen a ghost. Given the fact that I hadn't showered, slept or changed my clothes for a few days, I probably did look like some sort of ghoul.

'God, Paddy! How are you?' she said, giving me a hug. 'How's everybody doing? Are ye okay?'

I didn't really know how to answer her question so I just said, 'We're okay.'

A reporter from home stood to my left with a cameraman and a soundman beside him. I recognized his face instantly. It was Charlie Bird. The black-haired Dubliner was the US Correspondent in Washington DC, for Irish television. I had met him many years before when

I was a twelve year old kid playing the snare drum for my school pipe band. He stood there in a khaki shirt and khaki pants. The guy certainly looked the part.

'Sorry, Charlie,' said Sheila. 'This is a friend of mine from Ireland who lives here in Port au Prince.'

Mr Bird turned his attention to us.

'Charlie, this is Paddy Doyle. Paddy, this is Charlie Bird from RTE.'

Over the roar of the turbines, Charlie shouted, 'Paddy, we're trying to get to the epicenter of this disaster. We need to get to ground zero.'

'Ground zero?'

'Yes. We've been told that it's in the Carrefour area. That it's the worst hit part of the city. How do we get there?'

'To be honest, Charlie, you won't need to go far for what I think you might be looking for. You'll see the bodies once you are clear of the airport.'

He frowned. I wasn't sure if he really knew what waited for him out in the city. If it was dramatic images he wanted, there would be plenty to go around for him and all the rest.

'Look. Do you see those men over there?' I said, pointing at Ollie and Mac. They'll be able to help you better than I can. You'll be safe with those boys.'

Charlie wandered off our part of the tarmac and over to where they stood. Sheila looked at me with a cheeky smile and shrugged.

'You missed your six o'clock news interview there, Paddy.'

'Yeah, I probably did. So how long are you staying?'

'Not sure yet. I'm waiting for our main body to arrive from Ireland in the next few days. Is it as bad out there as they say?'

'A lot of the bodies have been cleared off of the streets. But it's still pretty bad.'

Soon the Digicel evacuees began boarding the plane. I wanted to be the last evacuee to board the flight. I knew it was kind of corny but I wanted to keep my feet on Haitian soil for as long as I could. I felt I'd earned that right. As I said goodbye to Sheila, I watched six Jamaican soldiers carry a metallic casket over to the rear cargo hold of our plane. It was then I realized that Jean Marc was coming with us. My mind drifted back to the last moment I had shared with him. I thought about what he had told me about his Christmas with his son and father. I thought about how much had changed in a couple of days. How I'd probably changed too.

With all of the activity, I'd almost forgotten to grab my bag and say goodbye to Mac. He was standing there waiting for me as I ran over to say my farewells.

'You take it easy, mate,' he said as I picked up my bag.

'You too, Mac. Mind yourself, man, and stay safe.'

He gave me a hearty hug. Not something us Irish are used to. Mac had been a rock throughout. Because of men like him, Jean Marc was going back to his final resting place in France. The unassuming, easy going Galway man had always been a true and loyal friend, and I would miss him.

The other security guys were out of sight as I turned around and headed back out onto the tarmac to the awaiting plane.

I climbed the silver metal stairs up to the main cabin door. As clichéd as it was, I turned to take one last look at the country that had played a monstrously significant role in my life since 2006. It was never how I imagined leaving it all behind. Way off in the distance, I could see Sheila chatting with the reporter and Mac walking back inside the main terminal. There was nobody else out there that I recognized. Far off in the distance was Montagne Noir. Many of my warmest memories remained in those hills. Beneath it all now was an unrecognizable city. I turned and entered the cabin where two air hostesses were preparing drinks. In all the hustle and bustle of the morning I had forgotten to drink any water. It was now pushing on one o'clock. I was dog tired and completely dehydrated from the ninety five degree heat outside.

'Excuse me. Is it okay if I take one of these cups of water?' I asked a young Jamaican air hostess.

She stared at me as if I was some sort of ragged gypsy, but she still managed a courteous smile. I must have knocked back four cups full of water before I finally felt satisfied. Staring down the center aisle, I could see an abundance of seats. Seeing as this was a unique flight, I sat up front. It was the first comfortable seat I'd been in for a while. Even in the peace and quiet of the cabin, with my body so desperate for rest, it was difficult to switch my mind off.

'Mind if I sit in here?' said a voice over my right shoulder.

I looked up to see Brenda. I thought that she had boarded long before me. I really just wanted to be left alone. The people I really wanted to be with were still outside this airplane, and yet I had my family and Taxback waiting for me back home. I was tired. Bone tired. I really did not want to converse with anybody.

'Sit down if you like,' I answered, standing up to let her take the window seat.

I tried to close my eyes again and sleep. Each time I did, my mind drifted off to a bizarre array of dreams. I was spinning a thousand images a second and still I could hear Brenda chattering in my ear.

Just as I thought she had finally figured out that I wasn't interested in talking, Digicel's Madame Khedy, boarded the plane and started to count how many people were on board.

The middle aged woman had just counted the two evacuees opposite me, when she stopped and gave me the most disdainful and piercing stare. I knew what she was thinking. Why was I on this flight? I was security. What kind of audacity did I have to be leaving? In all my time in Haiti, I had never had direct dealings with her. Yet I had watched her from the side-lines and was never her biggest fan.

'Madame Khedy,' I said in a low and tired voice. 'I know what you are thinking. I am not security. I was just helping out. I work on the eleventh floor.'

'Great,' she said loudly. 'My security is leaving me. That's great.'

With that, she continued to walk down through the plane and count the remaining passengers.

I could feel Brenda looking at me with bemusement, as though I had just been chewed out by my old school teacher. I began to feel deflated in spirit, unappreciated and yet completely enraged and resentful at the same time. Had she any idea how many people had died? Did she have any clue how many people were still out there suffering? And yet, above all that, I had been the immediate focus of her attention.

When she finally returned, I stood up and tapped her on the shoulder.

'Excuse me, Khedy,' I said. 'You've made a mistake. I am not your security. I just helped out your lads. I'm working for an Irish company on the eleventh floor.'

She looked at me and gave a nervous smile.

'Oh. Sorry.'

I wanted to shout at her, but I didn't.

Her attitude towards me had answered any doubts I had about leaving Haiti. Getting on that plane was the right thing to do. Thousands of people were dead and everything else paled into insignificance. I'd done my bit with the boys and I'd loved every minute that I'd spent with them. It was how it was meant to finish.

That young, naïve twenty six year old lad who arrived in Haiti three years before had learned more here than some men could learn in a lifetime. He had seen the best of people in the worst of times and forged friendships that would last for a lifetime. Now he was going home with mixed feelings for a country that he had come to know so well.

As the engines roared and the Air Jamaica 737 thundered down the runway, I took one last look at Port au Prince. Fires burned all around the city. For the first time, I saw the collapsed Presidential Palace and the ruins of the Hotel Montana. Where was Haiti's future now? There was no doubt that the tables had turned and everything had changed. But what that change would mean remained to be seen.

Sitting back in my chair, I could feel the soft, cool air blowing from the air-con system onto my face. I could no longer fight the urge to close my eyes. I nestled my head into the headrest of the chair and drifted off into a deep and disturbing sleep.

Afterword:

When the chartered flight landed in Kingston, we were warmly met by Digicel senior executives HR staff, ushered onto buses and brought to a hotel in the city. I remember how people looked at us. We were different, somehow. Everyone who approached us had empathic words to share. I remember feeling very much detached from it all. I even felt distant from the others I had been evacuated with. After everybody had eaten, most of the evacuees went to their hotel rooms to get some well-deserved rest. I went to mine, took a shower and changed my clothes. I lay on the bed, switched on the TV, and stayed there for no more than a few minutes. I could not sit still. It was impossible. I was jacked up from everything that had happened. There was still so much that I needed to do.

After calling home and speaking to my family for an hour or so, I went to the hotel bar to have a beer. I ordered a Heineken and was handed a cold longneck bottle. I felt like Lawrence of Arabia having walked into the officers mess after he crossed the desert and arrived back in Cairo. As I took my first sip of cool beer I spied a familiar face walk into the bar. It was Niall Merry. A Dublin man who was a senior manager for Digicel. Niall had worked in Haiti for years and was one of the more colorful characters I had gotten to know. He always bore a cheeky smile and had a sharpish wit to boot. It was good to see him.

Niall insisted that I go and stay with him and his family until I flew home. After a few more beers and a couple of meetings with other people at the hotel, I grabbed my backpack and left. The next three days and nights passed hazily. I could not sleep more than an hour at a time. After I made contact with my Haitian staff and confirmed their whereabouts, I contacted Terry back home. He was relieved to know that I was okay. I also called friends and family again, spoke to the Irish national radio stations over the phone and at night, I soothed my thoughts with a few more beers.

When I eventually flew out of Jamaica, I was again puzzled with doubts as to whether I was doing the right thing. Either way, I was relieved to be sitting on the British Airways flight bound for London. From London I had to spend most of the day in Gatwick Airport. It was frustrating to be so close to home and stuck in the UK. I tried to explain to the lad at the Aer Lingus check in desk where I had just come from and if they could get me home on an earlier flight. He was none too bothered.

I arrived into Dublin on a miserably wet and dreary Monday night. It was late so I booked into a hotel not too far away. The next morning was fresh and sunny as I made my way through Dublin city center to the taxback.com offices on College Green. All the way down Grafton Street there were people wearing yellow bibs and holding white buckets in an emergency appeal for the Haiti disaster relief. I couldn't believe the response I was seeing in my nation's capital. I felt extremely proud to call myself Irish.

I stayed in Dublin for another three nights as I had to report to work, check in with my staff in Haiti again and bring Terry up to speed on everything that had happened and what we needed to do next. Everybody at the taxback.com offices were supportive. On the Thursday evening, one of the company directors even offered to drive me home to Waterford. I remember my mother opening the door to see me there. It is still one of the most memorable moments of my life. I hugged her so hard; I could feel her tears land on my neck in our embrace. She was so relieved and joyful, as was I. I was home in one piece.

The following week I arrived into Beauvais airport just outside Paris. I spent the rest of that day travelling to Brittany in the northwest to attend the funeral service of my friend Jean Marc Le Hir. The next morning was cold and overcast with grey clouds. It remained that way throughout. I was chilled to the bone and couldn't get any heat back into my body for the remainder of the day. It was tough to meet Jean Marc's parents, but I was glad I did. He was well loved by so many and his service reflected that.

A couple of weeks later I returned to Haiti. I still had responsibilities to take care of. It wasn't easy to go back. In fact, it felt completely wrong. I stayed for two weeks and did my best to see if we could get the call center up and running again. It was an impossible task, and to be there by myself was utterly depressing, especially with the continuous aftershocks. It felt like I had never left.

The hero's welcome home a few weeks prior had long since disappeared. I didn't know how to rebuild a business in a post natural disaster environment. Almost 200,000 houses were badly damaged and 100,000 were destroyed. 1.5 million people were now homeless. A quarter of civil servants in Port au Prince had died. 60% of government and administrative buildings were destroyed or badly damaged. What people didn't understand back home was that Port au Prince needed to be rebuilt from the ground up. Even the very concept of such a notion was beyond many. I would have served much more effectively as an aid worker than a single businessman.

I met some great people who had come to help. Most had never been to Haiti before and they were teeming with motivation and inspirational ideas. I was a man in the wrong job. I couldn't share their enthusiasm. Their naivety pissed me off and I was being far too critical for somebody of my nature. In a way it was like a changing of the guard. My time in Haiti was well and truly up.

There comes a time when we each must face our demons. I did my level best to run from mine until I could no longer escape them.

To be honest, I felt ashamed of myself. Ashamed that I hadn't reacted to the earthquake and the aftermath the way I thought I would have. It would be months later when I'd come to have these thoughts. And it would take a lot longer to overcome them and finally put them to rest. Nonetheless, I am hopeful for Haiti's future. I have been to many countries in my years and I am certain that one day, I will return. When that time comes, it will be for *my own* reasons.

SURVIVOR STORIES

A COLLECTION OF STORIES FROM FELLOW SURVIVORS

Ambroise Pinchinat (Digicel)

For me, January 12th started out as any other day. At Digicel, I was handling logistics and logging inventory as a team leader for the facilities department. Today was a particularly busy day for me as my supervisor was still on vacation. If he had been back, I would have left work at a quarter to five as I was taking an evening class at the Universite d'Haiti. On this particular evening I wouldn't be leaving until after five as there were deliveries to register into the database. My work was based on the ninth floor. This was one of the busiest floors in the building. Just before 4:53pm, I started to gather my stuff and shutdown my computer. I was really looking forward to going to my class.

As I began walking towards the back door everything started to shake. I was still trying to figure out what was happening when suddenly the shaking became more and more violent. I ran for the stairway like so many other people. As the rumbling worsened I reached out to grab the handle of a door so I could keep standing. My legs were slipping from under me really badly. I couldn't help myself as I fell to the ground. I struggled to my feet and each time I did this, I would fall again. This happened three times. Each time, I got up, I was pushed back down by the force of the quake. Eventually I made it to the stairs. Even though there were no lights on as I made my way downwards, I could still see cracks race along the side of the structure of the building. I kept on running!

In my mind, I thought that the building was sinking into the ground. I didn't know what was happening exactly. We had never learned about earthquakes in school. When I got out of the building I could see that it was still standing. By then, I began to understand what was happening.

I thanked God and called out to Jesus. I was so happy and grateful to still be alive. As I looked out toward the downtown area, I saw white dust coming up from the gas station. There were loud explosions and fireballs bursting into the sky. I truly believed that a lot of people must have died down there.

After a while of standing in the streets and being somewhat unsure as to what to do next, I began to walk up to Petion Ville to find my sister, Lisène, who was working at the Philips Electronics store. I took the road through Canape Vert going to Petion Ville. The streets were blocked with cars and rubble. There were soars of people on the streets. Many of them were in a panicked state. When I finally reached Petion Ville I noticed the amount of damage to the buildings. When I found my sister, I was so relieved to see that she was okay. I loved her so much and I couldn't imagine finding her under rubble. I hugged her so tightly and afterwards I told her to go home and wait for me there. I realized then that I had to go back to the Digicel building and help.

So, I started to help the team evacuate people, especially those in shock who were too afraid to move and did not want to leave the building. I started looking for people in the darkness. I found some people who were still in their offices or at a desk. I escorted them to see my superiors who would then advise them on what to do next. My managers helped to calm them, trying to help them through the emotional shock and to muster enough courage to leave the building. Everybody had reacted in different ways.

When we finally evacuated everyone, we gathered together to figure out who was or wasn't present. Then, I began to worry about my team at Aciérie, Digicel's storage facility by the international airport. I had 22 men there doing some maintenance work. Then, I happened to cross paths with René Vitalem, a maintenance technician, who was assigned to be at Aciérie that day.

'Rene, where are the guys?' I said.

'They're still alive.'

I was so relieved. Once I knew my team was ok, I went home. I was really tired but I didn't care. That was only a small problem compared to what was happening to my city. I walked back to Delmas 72 and met up with my sister. We were in a closed complex with eight houses. It was only then that I realized that our house was gone. It had collapsed into itself. I was shocked. There was one other house nearby that was severely damaged. The other six houses had major cracks in them. Fortunately, no one was home and nobody was hurt. Throughout the night our neighbors and I stayed out in the court yard. None of us slept. We talked and supported each other through all the aftershocks that shook the ground all night long. We were too afraid to enter our houses. When the sun finally came up, I went back to the Digicel building.

It was there that I saw Maarten, the boss of Digicel in Haiti. He was pouring diesel into the generators all by himself. Rene and I went to help him. The first time we tried to start the generator there were several major sparks flying. The electrical wires were busted. We fixed them and then tried starting up the generator again. It worked! We continued to check the electric system to make sure that there were no other issues and then we had the technicians go to Aciérie to check on the electric system there. With the electricity working again, senior management wanted to get the entire network going and to start with getting customer service prepared to respond to client's needs. Thousands of people were depending on us. A group of us started fixing the desks and equipment. Once the room was ready, I went to the storage where there was food. We started to distribute noodles, cornflakes, milk, juice, water, peanut butter, tuna, and spam and sausages to the employees. By 3pm, more than 60 employees were set up at their desks to start working and by then the communication system was somewhat back on line.

By the time I got home that night my neighbors had gathered together. They were in the main yard and preparing a big meal for more than thirty people. Rice and beans with some sauce was my first hot meal since the earthquake. Again, no one really slept that night. We just prayed to God for help and kept each other company through those dark hours.

The next day I went back to Digicel at 7am, I started to log the employees who arrived and collected information on them about their family situation. I was so tired but I had to do my work. It was important to me.

The three main departments working in the building at the time was management, technicians and customer service. On this day, we went to check each floor and room to make sure that there were no electrical problems. We needed to ensure that the lights were working.

That afternoon, I saw a group of five people arriving with food, toiletries, clothing, sleeping bags, tents, stretchers, etc. It was Digicel Jamaica coming in with support. Then, Digicel Guadeloupe arrived. I particularly appreciated the assistance from Digicel Jamaica. They had called me from their customer service in Kingston to see if I was alright and to share words of comfort. I was so proud to be a Digicel employee and I felt that we were working together and that we were all human. I had always thought that Digicel was a company that if you couldn't work under pressure, then it might not be the place for you. Yet since the earthquake had hit, I realized that those of us who were strong willed took care of those who were finding all of this extremely difficult. The days and weeks to follow were some of the most difficult of my life. But I feel proud of who I am and where I am from. I never lost hope and I still believe in my country so very much.

Julio Reischoffer (United Nations Officer)

I remember that I was at the gym Fitzone in Petion Ville. I had just finished a weights session and was heading to my car in the underground car park of the gym. First thing I recall was how everything around me began to shake so violently. Suddenly someone shouted "EARTHQUAKE!" Everybody on that basement floor sprinted from the underground parking out onto the road. As I ran, one of my sneakers fell off. I had to run back to grab it. It was like Indiana Jones running back for his hat.

At the parking lot of the gym I saw people screaming and crying. Some were quite disorientated. I knew that I had to get out of Petion Ville and go find my colleagues. I needed to know that they were okay. First, I took a ride with a friend of mine to the corner of the Big Star Market. As I was walking, I could see a lot of people crying and panic stricken. I heard someone say that a building had collapsed nearby. I didn't know which building they were talking about. I only hoped that it wasn't the Apollo Market. It was a four story apartment building and my home was on the top floor. Many of my friends and colleagues lived in the same building. I just couldn't bear to imagine friends and team members living in the Apollo Market having suffered, or even worse. When we arrived, I was relieved to see the building was still standing. I ran up the stairs to check on my apartment. It was there that one of my colleagues, a Canadian guy called Ollie, came running and shouting my name.

'Julio! We've been trying to call you, dude,' he said. 'We couldn't get through to you on your cell phone and we didn't know if you made it or not.'

Ollie was a big guy and worked out in the gym with me often.

'Good to see you're in one piece. I suggest you gear up bro. Radio traffic has been heavy on the net. Word is that the Hotel Christopher has collapsed.'

I was shocked at what Ollie was telling me. Two of the UN delegates I was responsible for protecting were in that same building for a meeting with the Chinese delegation. We didn't know if they were alive or not. We didn't know who was alive!

After throwing some supplies into my patrol pack, I quickly checked my weapons. I had food, water and ammunition. I had grabbed as many bottles of water as I could from my apartment. I had a feeling that we would need them. I departed with five other colleagues by car to the Hotel Christopher. We heard many incomplete messages on the radio, but we could understand a few of them. Unsurprisingly, many of the roads were blocked with abandoned vehicles, debris of collapsed buildings and cracked roads. A route that would normally take us twenty minutes to commute by car was now going to stretch out over three hours. We had to negotiate a new path to the hotel and with the current state of affairs, this wasn't easy. I felt like I was in some kind of screwed up maze. Along the way I realized how bad it really was. I saw many desperate looking people lingering outside collapsed buildings. It was also incredible how many cars were abandoned on the sides of streets.

Hotel Christopher was where the MINUSTAH Headquarters was based. It lay at the end of a one-way street. Even as we arrived in the darkness, I had an uneasy feeling in my stomach. We still didn't know what the exact integrity of the building was. I prayed that the reports on the radio had been wrong. As we drove closer my mind battled to fathom what my eyes were seeing. What had once been a six story hotel lay completely obliterated. Shattered and to the ground. I couldn't even see the last two floors of the hotel. It was really dark by now. I could hear generators cranking in the distance. Soon, powerful floodlights were shining down onto the collapsed site. What was once a magnificent building was now nothing short of a mess of debris. I was deeply affected by seeing colleagues injured and crying. There was a kind of triage area set up where so many badly injured people were being gathered. Those who were uninjured struggled to dig through rubble to get to others who were trapped.

I had two friends of mine working with the UN at the time. Both of them were married and very much in love. Though my colleague was out of the country, his wife was still working in Haiti. I needed to know her whereabouts as she was pregnant. I asked where they were concentrating the people that were alive. I was told it was near to the lower parking lot. I went there to see if she was alive and who else might be there. When I arrived there I immediately spotted her. I was thankful to say the least. So too was she as she tried to stand up while nestling her plump belly with her right hand. We spoke for a while, but she was really tired and needed to try and sleep. Their baby was going to see the world and would grow up. Thank God for miracles.

After I had checked in on her I returned to the main point of the rescue efforts. It was here that I overheard the voice traffic on some of the other UN bodyguards' radios.

I turned my own radio volume up and that's when I heard the voice of Gary, one of my Close Protection team members. I couldn't believe it. We thought that he had died in the quake. He was calling out on his Motorola radio for help.

'I'm alive. I need to get out from here. Can anybody hear me?!!'

It was incredible to hear Gary's voice. Even though we were grateful that he was alive, we knew that he was still in a lot of trouble. Gary had been in our office on the fourth floor when the quake hit. It was a miracle that he had somehow managed to survive. It still meant that there were two other floors right on top of him. We wanted to get down to him and try to find his exact position. But with the amount of concrete and metal, that was an impossible task. The UN Fire Marshall did not want us to stand directly on the fallen hotel as we could have disturbed what concrete was under our feet. Also, our own lives would be in danger as the aftershocks were hitting us at an incredibly frequent rate. The Marshall didn't want to risk losing anymore UN staff. Everybody there knew we had already lost hundreds of people only a few hours before. Be that as it may, we convinced the Marshall to let us work in finding Gary and any others who might still be alive.

I was one of the four guys that were allowed to climb the debris as I have a good sense of orientation. I went straight to the place where I guessed our office might have been. I had told Gary on the radio to tell me when he heard footsteps overhead. He told me that he couldn't hear any footsteps but he could see lights shining through the cracks in the debris.

'I see the lights Julio. I'm not sure but I think they are shining from the south.'

Gary wasn't certain. He was completely disorientated and was doing his best to figure out his bearings. He could still see the lights coming from up top. I did my best to match up his description from where I was standing.

I searched for anything that might be familiar to me. After a few minutes I could see the outside corridor of the floor where my office was. As I began to walk on it another aftershock hit.

The Fire Marshall shouted, 'Get out of there!'

I stood completely still as the aftershock came and went. I was sure I would die but I saw no point in panicking. I needed to stay sharp for my friends, my team and my family back home in my country. When I realized that everything was okay, I continued working my way to the area of my office.

'Hey, I hear steps above me,' shouted Gary over the radio. 'It's far away but I can hear it. Keep walking.'
I answered Gary and did as he asked. As I stepped over the area where I thought my office was, Gary said that the steps were much louder. My sense of direction was right. We were exactly where we needed to be.

I crawled down into the cracks of the debris. I fought with myself as I went further and further down. With my flashlight, I could make out the little window to our office. It was smashed. As I shone my light, I could make out the shape and body of a colleague of mine. He had been crushed badly in the earthquake. He had been the duty officer that day. The only way I could recognize him was from the pistol in its holster on his hip and his boots. I had given him a pair of desert boots that Christmas as a gift. He had been one of my best Close Protection officers. I found it hard to accept that this was all that was left of him. A column of concrete had fallen on him and killed him instantly. I will never forget that image.

Just then another aftershock hit. This one was much stronger than any of the ones prior. I could hear the Marshall shouting once again for me to get out of there. We were all afraid. The aftershock had lasted for more than ten seconds. An eternity from where I was. We were far from a safe location and we still found ourselves compelled and obligated to search for our missing colleagues.

The hours were ticking by and we still hadn't been able to find a successful route to Gary. He was asking me now for drinking water. I could only imagine how much dust from the debris he had probably ingested. Myself and my team tried to figure out a way as to how the hell we were gonna get water down to our comrade. He was under two floors of absolute shit. One of the guys went back to the main rescue area and soon came back with a long strand of metal piping. We decided to try and weave it through the layers of debris via the various cracks and crevices. Gary shouted up that he could hear us getting closer with the pipe.

It took us two hours to negotiate the pipe down to Gary. He was desperate for water. With the pipe in place I thought of an idea. I grabbed one of the bottles of water from my pack and told Gary to put his mouth up to his end of the pipe. Then I opened the bottle and poured the contents down the pipe.

'Ahhhh, water is so good! Thank you!! Thank you!!'

We laughed quietly up top as we heard him celebrate over the radio. All of my guys were happy that we could get him water. It was a small victory even though he was still trapped.

I looked around as more and more people were being found and rescued by other colleagues. I went down to our car where we had set up a makeshift center of operations. We had the idea to use the Close Protection satellite phone because most of the mobile phones were not working. I guessed that the antennas fell down and only the mobiles from the Digicel company were still working even though the signal bars were very low. We took turns to call each of our families. I told my family that I was still alive and everything was okay. My wife and mother were comforted to hear my voice. They were crying while talking to me. My wife said that when she heard the news of an earthquake in Haiti, she had thought the worst. She had been desperate to know if I was still alive. I couldn't stay too long on the phone. I was just happy to be able to talk to my wide. Her love for me gave me strength I would need to keep going. It was sad that not everybody would get the privilege to talk with their families again. I was one of the lucky ones and I knew it.

Gary was told that we were talking with our families on the satellite phone. He asked if somebody would call his wife. We did. He was able to talk to her from his walkie-talkie as I held mine to the phone. I explained for his wife to say 'over' every time she finished saying something. It was a bitter sweet moment. I could feel the love they had for one another as they spoke in the most bizarre situation. She knew he was alive now but she also knew that he was trapped. My heart broke for the both of them. I imagined if I had been talking to my wife in this situation, how would I have felt. Though she could hear Gary, she did not know if she would ever see him again.

When they said goodbye to one another, I was called over by my Chief. She asked if I could gather a small team and call to her residence about ten kilometers away to escort her family back to the Christopher Hotel. She happened to be pregnant and her young son and husband were somewhere out in the city in their residence. My Chief told me that she didn't know if they were alive or not and that she wanted to get to us as soon as possible. I put my gear on, grabbed my semi-automatic machine gun and slung it over my chest. This was my tool to protect them and myself should we come into any kind of trouble. My Chief decided that she would come with us. We took our two car convoy through the decimated streets, all the while dodging barricades, abandoned cars and debris. A unit from the Brazilian Army Engineer Corps and other forces from other countries were working with their green tractors and heavy machinery to open the roads. During the journey we saw many dead bodies along the streets. People were crying because of their lost loved ones and begging for help. My heart was truly broken for them and for what I witnessed. But I had to keep focused on the mission at hand. Eventually we ran out of accessible road so we parked up our vehicles and pushed forward on foot. Though we had torches, the streets were completely blackened out and awash with rubble. It took us about forty minutes before we arrived at the neighborhood where my Chief lived with her family. We found her husband and child safe and sound. She could not stop crying and kissing her beloved family the second she saw them. The Chief was one of the bravest people I knew. I was happy to see her family safe.

We needed to go so they got any necessary belongings and we soon departed their residence. We had to move quickly through the darkness as a group and get back to our vehicles as fast as possible. Port au Prince was in a state of turmoil and we were in an unknown zone where anything could happen. My strategy was to lead the group from about five meters out in front. I studied the ground carefully. My senses were hyped up. I could have heard a pin drop. It took us an hour to get back to the car. We got in and my chief drove while I rode shotgun. Eventually we made it back to the Hotel Christopher. I remember feeling happy that I had helped get my Chief's family to safety. But all throughout I couldn't take my mind off of Gary who was still trapped down below us.

When I arrived back at the Christopher, the sun was already rising. According to the Brazilian Army, almost the entire route from the Hotel Christopher to the UN Logistics Base down at the airport had been cleared. They had sent us a search team from the base to help in our efforts. They arrived with more equipment that was capable of busting through concrete. It couldn't go too deep, but enough to save those who were easier to extract. While they were working, a few buses arrived from the Logistics Base. We lined up those who had been rescued and boarded them onto the buses. Many of them were badly injured and needed to be evacuated to hospital immediately. I was again given a mission. This time I would drive the lead vehicle to ensure that the buses made it to the Log Base safely. I ran this mission twice.

As another night closed in, Gary was still trapped under the masses of concrete. At least we had kept him hydrated throughout the day. That night I realized how tired I was. I hadn't slept for quite some time. We had been working rigorously all day with the Brazilian Army Engineers. We were still finding people. Many were dead but some were alive.

Eventually I was told by one of my supervisors to go and get some rest. I found a spot where I could safely lay my head and slumber. I closed my eyes and slipped into a deep sleep from sheer exhaustion.

Later that night I was tasked to work in the center of operations with my supervisor to run the communications. I was really tired, hungry, dirty, and just wanted to close my eyes. But I could not as I was on duty. I fought to keep my eyes open. Messages kept coming in on the radios and this kept me focused to relay the messages in a timely fashion.

The day time came in again and the day duty team arrived. I left to go to the Christopher to see those rescued, but did not stay long as I was exhausted. I returned to my apartment at the Apollo Market in Petion Ville. I remember taking a nice long shower and having some food before I finally slept.

The United States, Brazil and dozens of other countries sent many rescue teams with the proper tools to break through the fallen concrete. The Americans were the first ones to arrive. One of their teams was sent to the Hotel Christopher. Finally our trapped colleague, Gary was rescued. I did not see this happen as I was sleeping, but I heard the story later in the afternoon when I got back to the Christopher. I had tried to sleep that day but it was practically impossible. With every aftershock I would immediately wake and run from my apartment building. My mind had no time to catch up with my body until I was out on the road. Some of my teammates were kipping in my apartment. They would run out from fear of dying just like me. It was a really scary experience to feel everything shaking right beneath my feet. Nothing felt safe. By the afternoon I had begun to think that it was a bad idea to stay in my apartment building in case it fell down. My team and I packed up our bags with fresh clothes and whatever supplies we could find. We decided to head for the Logistics Base down at the airport.

The next day I went to see some colleagues that were waiting to be evacuated to the US. I met the wife of a Brazilian friend of mine. She had her two year old son in her arms, but said she did not want to go because her husband, my Brazilian friend, was still trapped in the Christopher hotel under the debris. She desperately wanted to know if he was alive or not. We were all praying for him. I took her son in my arms as I saw she was a little tired from holding him for so long. I looked at him sleeping so soundly with his head resting on my shoulder. I thought about how I could have been the man trapped below amidst the rubble. I could be dead and my son would never know me. Nor would I ever get to see him go to school, make his Holy Communion, go to college or even fall in love. How terrible that would be for my family. Soon it was time for the evacuees to go so I handed the little boy back to his mom.

Today is January 13th, 2013. Three years and one day after the tragic earthquake in Haiti and I am still working here. Many of my colleagues left for psychological treatment and never came back. Others never came back because they were afraid of another big earthquake hitting the country. Other kinds of tragedies have hit Haiti since, such as the hurricanes that hit the island of Hispaniola almost every year. Many people thought God had given them a second chance to be with their families. I thank God for giving me the strength to deal with all that had happened and still be here to do my work and do my best for the UN Peacekeeping Mission in Haiti.

The day before yesterday there was a Memorial Ceremony at the UN Log Base to pay respect and remember all of our colleagues who died on January 12th, 2010. It was sad to see all the faces of those people who gave their lives to work for the mission on the video slide show. These were great people. Even more difficult was just outside at the memorial plaque. The names are there for all of the fallen. I watched as their families laid flowers and wreaths and cried at the loss of their loved ones, now taken from this world. I could not hold back my tears.

January 12th 2010 will remain in my memory forever.

Bryan Gonzales (HR Director, Digicel)

It was my first day back in the office after vacationing with family in Puerto Rico. It was a busy day. Today I was being appointed as not only the Director of HR but also Facilities. In the morning, I was welcoming a new employee, Suyen Fombrum, who was starting in corporate sales. I had a couple of key meetings set up for the afternoon. One of them was with our CEO, to discuss the handover of the Facilities Department from Jean Marc Le Hir to me.

I was finishing up a meeting with Jean Marc, preparing a list of recommendations for our meeting with the commercial team. The meeting was running late so we went down to the parking lot to have a smoke and left a message with the CEO's personal assistant to have to call us when he was free.

We were talking about trivial things and our families. Jean Marc was looking forward to travelling that Friday to Martinique for some time to see his own, especially his son. Awe met a couple of other people who were already in the parking lot. Everybody was playing catch up after Christmas.

I then received a phone call from Martinique which I had been expecting throughout the day. I stepped away from the group to take it. While on the phone, the call dropped. I tried calling the number back but couldn't get through. I thought it was the connection. I headed back to the group. The phone rang again but I couldn't hear anyone on the other end.

Then I heard a rumbling sound and the ground began to shake. We all realized what it was.

We immediately started running. Jean Marc was the first to run. We were all looking for an exit. I remembered to stay close to a wall. I was running between the back ends of cars and the wall. I was going towards the exit of the underground parking lot. One of the bigger waves hit and a Nissan Patrol flew up and pinned me against the wall. I thought I was going to die being pinned against a wall.

I managed to escape from behind the cars to the middle of the lot. I ran from underneath the building and into the open. I had cleared the building and soon reached safety and open air. Just behind, there was a security driver working in the building. He was running just about 5 or 6 feet behind me. I heard a loud crack from over my shoulder. By then, the earthquake was in full swing. I turned around and saw the top of the parking wall give way and saw the wall crushing the driver. It was horrendous to witness such a thing.

I reached open air but things were falling all around me. I decided to run and stay underneath the network antenna in the back part of the building. This was a 30 meter tall antenna with large heavy radios on top. I looked up because I knew the danger was coming from up there and I went there because I thought it would act like a cage, protecting us should anything happen to fall. As I looked up I saw how badly the building was shaking. There was a lot of dust in the air. The shaking ended while I was under the antenna.

When it stopped I headed towards the back gate. I saw that by now people had started to evacuate the building. They were heading to the back gate going down Impasse Duverger because the wall of buildings had fallen. There were telephone poles collapsed and houses across the street that had crumbled. The only clear path was down the street of Impasse Duverger. I told people to go out to the right. Then I heard an explosion at the gas station. It was the propane tanks.

"My God! I escaped from under a building. Now, I am going to die of suffocation."

I could barely breathe. The dust was so thick. I saw different senior management people come out. It was very clear that the damage had been colossal. There was no going back in and people needed to get home. After the propane tank explosion, I was worried that the gas station itself would go next. Jean Marc and I had already discussed concerns regarding the proximity of our building by the gas station a few weeks earlier. If those fuel tanks should ever blow, we would have a disaster for about a one kilometer radius. After the propane tank blew, I started instructing people to go towards the street, instructing them not to walk by walls or buildings but rather stay on the middle of the street.

Then, I met a friend who came out of the building and ran across the street to find his wife who had just opened a restaurant in a nearby building. I'd actually had lunch there that day. The same building had fallen but miraculously my friend and her staff had escaped unscathed.

When the Digicel building was finally cleared (as far as we were aware at that time), there were a few guys left in the vicinity. Myself and some technical guys. There was also, the CEO, CFO, the security country manager and some security guys. We decided to try and contact Digicel in Jamaica or someone in the world to let them know what had just happened. The security guys went in to find people who may have been stuck in the elevators. We got back into the building and set up the satellite phones and tried to capture a signal. We started calling Jamaica or any other market we knew to call to let them know what was going on. All of this felt like it had transpired in a really short space of time.

I then began to worry about my kids and my wife. We had just returned from a trip and the fridge was still empty. Usually my kids would be heading home around this time from school. My wife had plans to go to the supermarket that day. I didn't know where the rest of my family was. As the network suffered from massive damage, it was difficult to make or receive calls. I tried calling different people. I used a security guard's Haitel phone and reached the caretaker of the yard on his Digicel phone. Our network was still up in some other areas. He said that my kids were at home. A few minutes later, I was able to get in touch with my wife. The signal didn't last long but long enough to know that she was okay. I was so relieved. Knowing that my wife and kids were safe and I was still alive was enough. I was very, very lucky.

We started to assemble an emergency team. We went looking for Jean Marc since he was Head of Facilities. I sent Jean Marc's housemate, a fellow colleague, to see if he was at home. By that time, we had moved the driver's body to a more secure area. When it was confirmed that Jean Marc was not at home, we knew something was wrong.

Meanwhile, the CEO asked the guys to work on an emergency plan because the network core was shut-down and it needed to be switched on. The switch had shut down just after the earthquake. There was an automatic sequence that happened. The technical team did a quick assessment of what the issues were. It seemed that there were broken cables that needed to bypass the regular routing to the antenna and that was when the team looking at the damages. It was there that Jean Marc's body was discovered. I had turned to the right to escape the earthquake. Jean Marc had gone left. He actually took the shorter route to daylight, but tragically never made it.

Some of the guys went back to the switch and the bypass to turn on the servers and equipment, having full knowledge that it would be short term because the alarms would eventually turn on. There was no air-conditioning and the systems were overheating. But people needed to communicate.

By this point, I realized I had not heard any sirens. No noise of police or the UN. Nothing.

There were other reports coming in that the UN building, supermarkets, and other buildings had collapsed. There was confirmation that the Caribbean supermarket had definitely collapsed. That was where my wife usually bought our groceries.

We couldn't get in contact with the outside world until the core switch was turned back on. When we finally got through to headquarters in Jamaica and explained the situation, they promised to get back to us by the morning.

I was finally getting reports from extended family that everyone was okay. However, I got a sad report from my best friend of a mutual friend of ours, that his son was trapped in their fallen home.

When I eventually left the office later that night, I knew I wasn't going to get back home. Myself and a few other managers went to the security house in Pacot to get some rest. We were a ragtag group of people. Two guys with suitcases who had business with Digicel, accompanied us by foot all the way up through the darkness of Pacot until we got to the house.

Along the way I happened to meet my friend Philip, who had been searching for his son. He had found him alive. However, he told me that his mother-in-law and niece had died. His son, on the other hand, had two crushed legs. Philip was on his way to the hospital with his him and I asked if he needed any help. He said he didn't. We parted ways and I continued on to the security house.

Earlier that day, the Head of Legal had just arrived from Canada. He had gone directly to the Hotel Villa Creole with his wife from the airport. Prior to his visit, Greg and I had a back and forth conversation about the hotel reservation. His hotel of choice was the Montana. When Greg finally got in touch with me, he was very glad that he had been placed at the Villa Creole instead of the Montana. The hotel Montana was the most prestigious hotel in the country and it had completely collapsed. Of the group of people who were on the same plane as him, only two made it out of the Montana alive.

My wife was upset that I wasn't coming home that night. I wasn't going to walk 21 km to my home at that hour of the night. I was exhausted. We were all okay and that was the most important thing.

When we finally got to the security house, we found one area with a phone signal in the courtyard. I had several conversations with my wife. I told her to make sure that the kids slept in the car. As for me, the security team living room furniture was outside. I was lucky to find a couch in the front yard to sleep on.

There were a lot of aftershocks throughout the night and people remained cautious of surrounding buildings. I remember looking out over the city. I said to one of the bodyguards, 'No red or blue lights.' For me this was amazing. I knew that the UN Headquarters had gone down. However, it wasn't their main base. What we didn't know was that the entire senior cabinet had died. There was no UN leadership in the country at that point. The only thing to be seen out on the streets was the movement of heavy machinery attempting to move rubble.

The next morning I woke up very early and went back to the Digicel building. The elevators weren't working and the lights were still out. We basically had to walk up 10 flights of stairs and did another sweep of the building securing people's belongings. We went down to the back part of the building to continue with restoring power and service and by then, Digicel Jamaica had sent in its first plane with support staff.

I had to go home too to see my family. Luigi, Roy, Gino and I walked from Digicel to Luigi's in-law's house which was about 4 to 5 kms away. We helped them move two pieces of luggage to go and stay with their son-in-law up in Canape Vert. We passed a lot of rubble along the way. A friend of ours came half way down the mountain and gave us a ride up to another friend's house and then I got a ride on a back on a 4-wheeler all the way home.

I was happy to find my wife and kids safe and sound. It was so good to see them. Our home was fine from what I could see. Everyone, along with my neighbors were camped out in the yard.

I was rooting through some boxes in my garage when my wife called to me.

'Do you need anything? Are you hungry?' she said.

'No thanks honey. I'm fine. I just need to take a shower.'

I felt as though I was covered in death. It was on my skin, in my nose and matted into my hair. It was everywhere. As I stood in the shower, the water felt incredible as it hit my skin. Each bead of water was cleansing, in more ways than one.

After I put on a fresh set of clothes, I hugged my kids. When I first got there they wanted to hug me but I told them no. Then I had breakfast and used the internet to send messages.

After what I had seen and the little knowledge I had about earthquakes at the time, I told my wife we were sleeping inside our home.

'What if it happens again?' she asked.

'Look at our house. It's fine. We are not sleeping outside,' I said.

Having left my car at Digicel due to the debris, I took my wife's car to find fuel, medicine and promised her that I would be back.

Not long after, I got a call from management that I was to go and locate fuel for the generators. I called a few friends who had fuel factories. Normally they would have big reserves. I found people who were willing to sell us what they had in their tanks. Meanwhile, Evelyn Theard coordinated water trucks.

When I came to the office I found a huge group of people already set up on the ground floor. Supplies were coming in from Jamaica and from some of the larger food distributors. Many of our employees came back to see how they could help. We started a long process of bringing stuff from the upper floors and moving equipment into areas where we could set up a base of operations.

There were people I was meeting for the very first time to come and help in any way they could. There were people from everywhere, even people who were no longer working with Digicel who came back to help. I met some really amazing individuals who volunteered and asked us what we needed.

We were divided into different response teams. We created care packages for employees, providing water purification tablets, vitamins, and energy bars. We weren't sure how safe the water was so the tablets were really important. The energy bars were a comfort because we didn't know how much food there was available either. I expected things to be problematic for another day or two.

Starting the following day, we were working on getting the network up and running. I was staying away with work for hours and my wife was getting upset with me. However, I would go home at one o'clock to have lunch so I wouldn't be a burden on the food situation at work. That afternoon, I asked her to come down with me to help get the car. When we got to Digicel I went inside. I assumed that she had left not knowing that she decided to wait for me. That afternoon, there were six major aftershocks. That was also the first time she had seen the dead bodies and was overwhelmed by the smell of rotting flesh.

When I got out of the building that night it was almost 7pm. My wife told me that she did not want to stay in Haiti any longer and that she wanted to leave. The next day I took my wife and kids to the airport. I gave her a phone to keep in contact with me. There were planes coming from dozens of countries all over the globe.

As we were sitting there, a pilot came up to us and helped our next door neighbors onto an airplane because their daughter had suffered massive brain damage from a three-hour epilepsy seizure months before the earthquake. She was now being tube-fed. With healthcare facilities being severely destroyed in Haiti, they had to leave and find adequate medical attention elsewhere.

The pilot came back and said, 'I have room for three more.'

I wasn't sure at the time if the previous arrangements I had made would follow through. So, I said to my wife, 'Go.'

I asked the pilot, 'Where are you going?'

'I am going to try and land at Fort Lauderdale.'

I turned to my wife and said, 'Just try to get to wherever you are going and then get to my sister's place.'

It was hard to say goodbye to my family but I was relieved that they were going to be safe. As my wife and kids were boarding the plane, I got a call from work.

'Bryan, where are you? We need you now!'

We started to get medicines to vaccinate our employees from typhoid, tetanus, etc. The next day we started on the food and water distribution for our employees.

There was unity amongst us and the way we all worked together was impressive. Haiti has a reputation of being one of the most dangerous places in the world. What was so amazing was that people were walking to go home for 5 to 6 hours. On their way, strangers would help others, helping people get out of the rubble. There were many acts of humanity. Basically, people were helping other people to live. But at night you could hear the screams of thousands pleading for help.

Quickly, the company was able to mobilize and get people on the ground. We asked for water and 1000s of liter bottles started coming in. We worked with local restaurants and ensured people had food. People were working together towards basic but important goals.

The most senior individuals from Digicel flew in and asked us how they could help our employees. More work was being done in contacting employees to see who lost family members. We also asked to see if everyone was okay and find out what they needed the most—finding places for employees to sleep, medical care, water, and helping families of other employees. We brought in tents and all employees received a tent no matter if you lost a house or not. This was also extended to the families of the employees. Placing the interest of the employees first was very powerful to me. I was proud to be part of such a group of people.

Frantzy (Care Assistant)

Let me tell you a little bit about myself. My name is Frantzy. I am 37 years old and I live in the capital city of my country. I work as a care assistant. My job involves taking care of an elderly couple called Henry and Anna. In the morning time, I usually take them for a ride around the city in my car. It is good for them to leave the house and visit some of their friends. That January 12th, I remember that I had to take Henry for his medical check-up at Canape Vert hospital. But first, we went for our drive as normal. We stopped to buy fresh vegetables and fruits from the early morning street sellers and then we drove up Montagne Noir to the home of Henry and Anna's friends. I always liked to sit and listen to these wonderful people share stories of old adventures over lots of cups of tea and coffee.

At about 3pm, we headed back down into Petion Ville and on to Canape Vert hospital for Henry's appointment. I remember the afternoon being very hot and very sunny. The nurses took Henry in and told me to come back to pick him up in about two hours. I decided to head back up to Petion Ville to see my mom and dad. I had been there for more than an hour and a half when we were sitting down to eat our dinner. That's when I first felt the ground shaking. My parents tried to run off but fell down three or four times. All I can remember is the terror in her face. I heard people in the neighbourhood cursing loudly. I also heard people shouting that it was the end of the world. We didn't know what an earthquake was like and I think we all believed that it was the end of the world. Some people shouted for Jesus to help them. Everybody was so afraid.

From the distance we could see a dark cloud of smoke mixed with dust, lots and lots of dust. Dogs were barking on every street. Terrified children were crying so loudly. That's when we started to get some of our senses back. We started running to those who needed help. In my mind, I thought that the next day, the news would report up to three hundred dead. We started to spread out and help those in the neighbourhood who needed help. Suddenly, I thought of Henry. I had to find him. I told my parents that I was going to Canape Vert to look for my old friend. So I started the engine of my car and tried to make my way from Petion Ville down to Canape Vert. As a boy, I walked these streets. As a man, I drove them. But today was like no other time before. Everything was upside down. All I could hear outside my car was people and babies crying. So much crying. I could see people trapped under the rubble. All the roads were blocked with abandoned cars. Rubble, dead bodies, people looking for relatives. There were so many wounded but they couldn't find medical help. It was like one of those movies about the end of the world. I had to leave my car and start walking down to the hospital. I was so worried about Henry all alone. But as I walked down through Delmas I began to think about my sister who was working in a restaurant in the area. I took my phone from my pocket but then I realised that there was no network coverage. I really wanted to get down the road Henry, but my sister began to occupy my thoughts more and more. I felt that she needed me.

I can still remember the houses and buildings on the hills of Canape Vert. They had all collapsed that it looked like a giant pile of thrash, but instead of rubbish, it was people's homes. I could see people buried in the rubble.

Legs, heads, arms. Age or class didn't matter. There just was no difference. People from all backgrounds were no longer alive.

When I arrived at the hospital, I could see Henry sitting in the front car park. He was amongst so many other people. The staff had evacuated them outside. I was so happy to see Henry and I wanted to get him to someplace safe, but he wouldn't be able to walk very far at his age. I lifted Henry's fragile body and placed him on my back, like you would a child. I began to walk back uphill to where I had left my car many miles before. I now only had one question in my mind. I had to find my sister.

When I arrived back at my car, I saw that the road was completely blocked with more and more cars. It was a difficult decision, but I had to leave Henry in my car. He would be safe there. The scenes just remained the same everywhere I went. More and more bodies and more people injured. I wanted to help but I had my own search mission to do. As I walked and walked and walked, I feared the very worst for her. I felt that she was not with us anymore. When I finally arrived at the restaurant, nobody was there. I was exhausted from everything that had happened, but I felt hope when I didn't see her there. All of a sudden, an aftershock hit. I watched as houses in the neighbourhood collapsed. It happened before my eyes as if it was in slow motion. I felt my little bit of hope disappear from my heart. What if she had been killed by such a collapsing building. I searched for her all around, but no luck. It was time for me to go back to Henry. He was still by himself. I felt confused by my decisions, but I had to make them.

When I got back to my car, my old friend was still there. I could read the fear on his face as he could read mine. When Henry asked about my sister, I told him she was fine. I drove my car back to my parent's house. When I got out of the car in the yard, I saw my sister standing there with my mom. It was one of the happiest moments I can ever remember. I loved her so much. To have lost my sister would have been to lose my heart.

With my sister, father, mother and two other sisters, we sang prayers to Jesus and to God, thanking him for keeping our family alive in this time. We did not know the future of our country and this made me very concerned. But for now, I was just so grateful for all my family to be alive.

Sophia Stransky (Sales Director)

It was just an ordinary day. I was attending my weekly meeting with the CEO, along with some of my colleagues. Today we were discussing the new campaigns to be launched and reviewing the strategic aspects of products, marketing and sales. The meeting was taking longer than expected.

Tatiana was presenting a new soccer campaign with Haitian schools. That's when the earthquake hit. Tatiana and I both ducked under the conference table. Things started to fall all around us and onto the ground. There was stuff breaking everywhere. I had no idea it was an earthquake. Then I heard an explosion at the gas station next door. I could see dust in the air outside and I saw what I thought was smoke.

"Is this a bomb?" I said to myself. "We don't have any enemies? Do we? Who would want to bomb us?"

The shaking kept continuing and I realized that it was an earthquake. I thought this would be my last moment on earth. There, I started praying and said 'God make this painless.' I was looking at everyone's face. The CEO's face was so pale. My colleague David was standing underneath the doorway. Then, after what felt like an eternity, the shaking stopped.

We got up and just started to walk out of the building. Everyone started to flood the stairwell. I had no purse, just my notebook. When I got outside, I said to myself "I made it. I'm still alive." We all grouped in front of the building across from the hospital. The hospital had collapsed. There were patients in their robes standing in the streets. It was just a mess. The tremors continued so I started to look for poles and other things from above to stand clear of.

After a certain amount of time standing in the middle of the street, it was clear that no one could return inside the building. Tatiana and I left. We were heading pretty much in the same direction towards Pacot. Tatiana was going to her cousin's house and I needed to get to my mom's house, which was close by.

We were walking along quite quickly. I was having trouble breathing like I was having a minor asthma attack. We got up the mountain and met a friend of mine. He was sitting outside on the street smoking a cigarette. I had just quit smoking.

Suddenly, Tatiana said, 'Give me a cigarette!'

'Give me one too!' I said following Tatiana's lead. Mind you, she didn't even smoke.

I smoked half of the cigarette thinking "well, I didn't die in the earthquake. I might as well enjoy smoking one cigarette." When I was finished, I stubbed it out and we continued walking. We got to the point where we had to split directions and head our separate ways. I was now walking up the street to my parents' house by myself. I could see some of the houses in the area were very badly affected. At that point, I was just walking faster and faster to get home. My mind was racing.

The gate was locked when I arrived. It was a pretty high wall so I climbed over the gate. I couldn't believe my eyes when I looked over. The house had fallen down. I started screaming and screaming. I was hoping somebody would come but nobody did. I went around behind the house and found my niece's nanny with my niece and the lady who works at my mom's house with my daughter. They told me my mother was stuck in the house and my father was trying to get her out.

I didn't really know what to do. A part of me wanted to go into the house but the tremors kept on coming. I had my two kids to think of, and if something happened to me and I was to die, they would be orphans. I didn't go in. I stayed outside. It was one of the most difficult decisions I have ever had to make. Eventually, I found somebody to help and after 45 minutes, they got my mother out.

We couldn't stay there. The rubble blocked the driveway and there was no way to find the keys so we left the house. We passed the front gate and my mother said that she couldn't walk. I noticed that there were people in the house next door. It was a house belonging to the US embassy. I knocked on the gate and told them that our house had fallen and my mom was not able to move well. The guard opened the gate and let us in. There were quite a few people who were already there from the neighborhood. The Spanish Ambassador's house had fallen and he was there. My mom, dad, niece, and daughter as well as my niece's nanny who was also hurt stayed there. Everyone else who worked at the house decided to go home to find their families.

There were just a couple of chairs. I think my mom and I had a chair and the others sat on the floor. It was getting dark and the tremors kept on coming. I was so scared. A few calls came through with rumors about buildings falling. Someone said that the Caribbean Market had gone. Someone even called and said that the Digicel building went down. I kept on trying to call my sister and her family. If they were alive then they would be here by now. It seemed like the kids knew there was something wrong. My niece is not the easiest baby but she just went to sleep from exhaustion.

Throughout the night, there was a lot of noise at the gate with people coming and going. At some point, I was hoping it would be my sister or my brother-in-law. We were just sitting out in the dark. Suddenly, a pipe burst and there was water all over the floor. I had just put the kids to sleep on the floor and now the damn place was soaking wet. I felt that God was really pushing my patience and sanity to the limit.

Then, I heard this really loud noise of a truck approaching. It was my brother-in-law. He had one of those big, obnoxious oversized pick-ups. I got up and went to the gate. He got out of the truck and told me that Monica, my sister was okay and that she had gone to his mother's house. The place was fine and we could go there. By then, it was midnight when we left him and he dropped us at his mom's house. He had to leave because his sister, Francesca, was under the rubble at the Montana Hotel.

I met up with my sister and I was so happy. But I started to worry about my house and was quite worried that it might be gone. I had no idea and I was completely exhausted by now. I took a few pillows and went outside and fell asleep. I was so tired, I dozed off straight away.

By morning, the communications situation had improved. I was able to make a couple of phone calls and I was able to get in contact with my house. I left my brother-in-law's mother's house to walk up to my own home. That's when I started seeing so much of the damage, bodies covered in the street, pillage of food at a fallen supermarket, and so many destroyed homes.

I finally got to my house. There was damage but nothing catastrophic. Everyone who was there was pretty much okay. My home was part of a complex and the courtyard had been turned into temporary housing for the neighborhood. The dead bodies were placed on the tennis courts. I didn't want to stay too long so I took clothes for myself, my daughter and my mom.

Later I returned back to the other house. It was then we realized that both my mom and daughter were in need of medical attention. My mom was having difficulty doing routine activities. My daughter had not even told me about her injuries from the day before. My mother had back problems and broken fingers and my daughter was in need of stitches.

We went to find some medical care. All the clinics that we passed had so many people lined up in front of them. Most people were in far more need of care than us. We went to my daughter's paediatrician's house to see if he could stitch her and deal with my mother's injuries. He didn't have anything so we went to his clinic. When we got there it was just the craziest scene. The hospital had become completely full with so many injured people. Cars and tap-taps were all parked in front of the facility. It was a triage center by now and all the medical rooms were full, treating people. There were people screaming loudly every time the building would shake. The doctor stitched my daughter. Then other priorities came and they took the doctor away for another medical emergency. Afterwards, we made our way to my car and went home.

We went to the airport the next morning at 4am and waited for several hours by the tarmac for a plane to arrive. There were planes waiting for authorization to land and take off. Meanwhile, my daughter, Lorena was unable to keep her food down. It was just nerves. My mother, who always had an opinion about everything, had not spoken much in the days that followed. She was still in shock. The plane finally arrived and they left on a flight bound for Jamaica. They went to Digicel Jamaica, contacted the Embassy, and worked out some papers to travel to the US. Digicel also helped me get the children of my boyfriend to Turks and Caicos. Once that was done, I went to work.

During that time, Digicel helped to provide food baskets to each employee. They also provided cash because banks were closed. They provided a lot of psychological counselling also. There was compassion for employees who didn't come back right away. The company also tried to get a sense of who needed what, who lost houses and relatives while they provided tents and foam mattresses. Overall, I was never happier to be an employee of such a company. Digicel did an amazing job to support its people and its families.

In my own case, my sister was in the states and at the time, my niece was only five months old. My mom also met with doctors in the states who reviewed her x-rays and could not believe that my mother was still able to walk. She had to undergo immediate surgery. When I became aware of this, Digicel assisted me to get to them by putting me on a Canadian Air Force flight to Jamaica.

The next day I took a flight to Florida and went directly to the hospital where my mom was already in surgery. She was in ICU for a while and in the hospital for about two to three weeks after.

Once I organized arrangements for my mom and daughter for transport, food and general support, I then returned back to work. By then, more employees returned to work and activities were more structured.

Josefa Gauthier, Chief Executive Officer,

Digicel Foundation

It was time for me to go home. My son, Claus, had just called me to let me know that he was waiting for me in the parking garage and that we needed to move quickly and get home. I told him I would be right down as soon as I was finished up.

I started getting ready to leave. I gathered my belongings together and I was heading out from the Foundation office, which was located on the 9th floor. As I was walking away from my desk, I felt a tremor. I saw that trinkets and office supplies on my desk had fallen to the floor. I thought to myself, "What's going on? I don't think it's an attack." I didn't think it was an earthquake at the time. When I opened my office door I kept on feeling the shaking. I called out to Esther, my assistant.

I said, 'Esther, earthquake. Get under a doorway or a table.'

By the time I told her this, we began to experience the full tremors of the earthquake. The earthquake was so hard. My shoes and my glasses had flown away from me. By then, Esther was trying to reach me, but instead, we fell. All over the floor, we could see and hear people falling and screaming out loud, calling out to Jesus to save and protect them.

At one point, certain employees had received training on earthquake and disaster preparedness. Team leaders were to wear red hats and lead people to exits or have people follow them to safety. I looked all over the floor and found no one donning a red hat. I told Esther for us to just go and so we left.

I picked up my glasses that were now missing a lens. I am near-sited and cannot see well. I would rather see with one eye than to not see at all. I took my bag and we left. We tried to leave but the exit door would not open because of a security system. I couldn't push the door open.

'Oh, lord!'

People started to crowd behind me insisting me to open the door.

'Come on, we need to leave,' someone shouted.

I tried to push the door open but no luck. I saw a small switch at the top of the door and turned it. The door opened. We saw all the people walking down the stairs with women holding their shoes in their hands and the guys helping the women. Fortunately we had had some training the month prior on how to evacuate the building in event of a fire or any other problem. Everyone more or less remembered this and the evacuation went quite well.

I could never have imagined what I was about to see outside. I was feeling heavy and couldn't really run. When we arrived outside, there was white smoke. And then, I asked myself, "Where is my son?"

I first tried to call him on the phone but I couldn't get through. I started going in the direction of the parking garage. That's when I noticed all of the injured people being escorted from the garage. They were walking in my direction. I started praying to God. He had given me this boy, now he couldn't just take him away from me! When I was young, I had lost a child and God had blessed me later with Claus. Someone said to me that I had to stay with them and it wasn't a good time to look for him. I didn't care. I started to look for him. I tried calling him several times again but there was no signal on my phone. While walking around trying to find him, another aftershock hit. I started thinking to myself, "what the hell is going on?" Then the explosion from the gas station happened.

'Fire is coming. We're gonna burn!' someone said in the crowd.

I asked a guy if he knew of anything that happened in the parking lot. I knew my son was not trained on the protocol, so I could only imagine. The man informed that two young men had just died in the garage.

'Was this a heavy young man with my complexion,' I said hastily.

'Madame, I don't know. This was the only news I heard,' he replied back.

Right there, I felt my knees giving away from under me. I didn't know how I could leave. However, I said to myself that I wasn't going to let tears fall from my eyes. I wasn't going to cry. God was with me. I kept on walking closer to the garage entrance. When I got closer, security told me that I could not go any further on so I went back up to the main avenue. There, in the middle of the street, who did I see but my son with his arms open.

He said, 'Mama, Mama!'

We embraced each other with hugs and kisses.

'I thought I would never see you again,' he said.

I started to cry right there and then.

'Do you have any news of anyone at the house?' he asked.

'No I don't Claus.'

'We need to go home. Grandma and grandpa are in the house,' he said.

'Maybe the earthquake was only here? Maybe it didn't affect the other areas?' I said.

'Mom, we need to start walking.'

'Where's the driver?' I asked.

'I don't know. The second I felt the first shake, I ran out through a door. I knew it was an earthquake from the first tremor. When the earthquake had stopped, I started looking for you and tried to go inside, but they wouldn't let me. And then I found you here.'

My son and I joined a small group of Digicel people. When we got to Canape Vert, we saw people hanging through windows, people on the ground, blood. A lot of blood.

My son said, 'Don't look to the sides mom. Keep focused on the road ahead of you.'

I asked him if we could do something for these folks.

'Let's go home first and we will come back and see if we can help these people,' he replied.

We walked and walked. At one point, we split from the group. We took a break at the gas station on John Brown Ave. The guys in our group suggested that we continued because it was getting dark. People were coming from all over the place and coming out screaming out to Jesus. Mothers were screaming for their children, asking God for them to wake up. There were people bathed in blood and no one had a real notion of anything. People were just in shock and the tremors simply would not end. Nobody really had an understanding of what had happened. While we were sitting on the ground, another aftershock came. There, one of the guys in our group said we would go to his house to get a car and he would drive us home because we were tired. We all started trying to reach our loved ones. I started losing it because I didn't have any way of reaching my parents at the house.

My son said, 'Don't cry mom. In life, you have to stay strong.'

I thanked God in my heart for my son who was being so supportive and encouraging. He could see that I was tired.

'I know its hard mom but you have to push yourself to continue to walk with the group. If not, we will have to stay behind and walk on our own.'

We arrived in Musseau. One of the gentlemen said that he lived nearby the Montana and he was going to go to his house there. There were two or three people who happened to be where we were who said that the Montana was gone. Apparently it had collapsed and most of the people inside were now dead. The man said that he would have to leave us to go deal with this matter. My son told him that it was fine and he would take care of his mother. The other ladies went on their way to Delmas and we kept on going up Bourdon.

As we kept on walking along, my son would tell me where to put my feet. There was a landslide of houses either side of the road with people everywhere, so we had to walk over the bodies and the rubble. It was horrendous. When we walked by the Christian Brother school in Juvenat, we saw two abandoned cars on the road. Claus told me to stay where I was and he would go up to the house on his own and would come back and get me. I told him no and that I would not stay there alone. Instead, we just kept on walking, together. We had never seen so many Haitians dead before. People from the shanty towns on the hills were placing dead bodies wrapped in flour bags or any type of cover that they could find. People were being carried to hospitals. Family members were crying for their dead children, and asking why this terrible event had happened. Someone there said Haitian hearts were so hard to one another we didn't help each other. The end of the world had arrived. We were all going to die because we never cared for one another and we never repented?

When we arrived by the El Racnho Hotel road, we saw a pickup pass us by. The pickup had my house driver, my gardener and several other people in the back. We were in front of the 'Nos Petits Freres et Soeurs' hospital. The entire building was destroyed. Parents were trying to find their children and hope for news. Meanwhile, I found my entire family sitting across the street at the gas station. I told everyone that the gas station was unsafe and we had to get away from the station in case of an explosion. My chauffeur saw me with my family and called out my name.

'Madame Josefa!! Madame Josefa!!'

'I went down to Digicel and they told me that you weren't there and that Digicel had fallen,' he said.

People were saying that Digicel had fallen but what they meant to say was that the network was down. However, in the confusion, my family thought that the building had fallen. While driving to find me, they found a few people who were from Digicel on the road telling them that they saw me leave the building. I asked the driver how he got my parents out of the house. He said the minute the earthquake began, the neighbors went inside the house and wrapped them in blankets and got them out of the house. When we arrived at my house, we invited all of my neighbors to meet at the parking lot across the street. There were no trees and I felt this area was secure. We agreed to sleep outside because everyone was afraid to go inside. My son said that we needed to get food so that everyone could eat. Each person there told stories of how they had witnessed schools or buildings that had fallen and of people and children who were dying. At the time, nobody knew how many children they had lost. That night, no one slept as the aftershocks continued.

During the night, I also got calls from Digicel saying that I needed to give interviews and share information on the radio of what had happened. I didn't understand how the phones were working and calls were getting through. Maria Mulcahy called me and said she heard that something terrible had happened in Haiti. That's when I told her about everything. She said that I should do interviews to let people know what was happening. That night, I rounded up volunteers to go back down to Digicel with me.

After giving people food, at around one or two in the morning, the volunteers and I left the parking lot. We went back down to Digicel and on the way we took a few injured people with us to give them a ride to the nearest hospital we could find. We soon arrived at Canape Vert Hospital, but there was no one there to meet us, no doctors, nothing. There were too many people who were critically injured flooding the car park and the hospital corridors. We continued on, but we reached a point where we could not go any further. The streets were blocked with abandoned cars in the Bois Verna area. The volunteers carried the injured on doors and corrugated tin all the way to CDTI Hospital by foot. When the volunteers dropped them off at the hospital, we returned back to my house.

By then, it was about four in the morning when we got home. At seven o'clock, my son came to me saying that he couldn't stay, there were two people from the neighborhood that had not returned. We need to go down and find them. The family members are pleading for me to find their loved ones. I said that the aftershocks were just as dangerous and you may not be able to find the person in the building. "What if the building falls on you?" So, my son and I escorted a neighbor's wife to find her husband at his workplace. When we got there we found that the building was gone.

The next morning, I came back to Digicel at eight with Eddy and Claus. I worked with other staff members to figure out how to help and support those who came to the building. That's when we started to distribute blankets, water and other materials. During the meeting, I didn't feel like I was there. We kept receiving bad news of someone dying here and another person dying elsewhere. Each person was suffering a personal ordeal. It felt surreal. For those who didn't have family in Haiti, or weren't directly affected by the earthquake, they may have been able to perform better. Whereas, many of us were dealing with our personal issues and could not concentrate on our work completely. But we did all that we could.

Three days later, Denis O'Brien arrived. We met with the government crisis response team at the airport. The government had shared with us their plan and Denis wanted to see how he could work with them and support the response. He had met with President Preval, the Minister of Education, Ministry of Foreign Affairs, and several others. Once we finished the meeting with the government, I advised Denis to focus our resources on Leogane, given the amount of support already being provided to Port-au-Prince from other international organizations.

A day or two later my driver and I went to Leogane to determine the damages and the needs. Once we saw that there was a need, I convinced Denis to have the Foundation help with the needs in that area. Firstly, the Foundation ordered one thousand drums of food items from USHA to give one thousand families. This happened one week later. All the Digicel Foundation members helped out and we did a chain of distribution for over three days with the help of the scouts. Two weeks after, we went to Petit-Goave and distributed food kits to 200 families.

In Leogane, all the schools were either severely damaged or destroyed. In partnership with USAID and

IDEGEN, we constructed a modular school using containers. The first school we selected was Ecole St. Gerard because 35 children had died there. The construction started once parents retrieved the bodies of their children.

Digicel searched for all of the Irish people also. Maria contacted Gena Heraty to see what the Digicel Foundation could do. I have to say that Digicel saved 600 employees because of the efforts they had made in ensuring that the new Digicel building was built to withstand earthquakes.

Digicel's preparedness and its value for people really showed during this crisis. I will never forget the experience and the way that Digicel impacted on my own life and my own country, Haiti.

Dominique Francinque   (Teacher)

My name is Dominique Francinque. I teach 5th and 6th grade classes at the École Municipale de Portail Leogane. It is a primary school that runs the morning and afternoon lessons.

January 12th was the first week back from the long Christmas vacation. That day, I was teaching social sciences and French. Usually after teaching the afternoon session, I would head to the teachers college, École Bernard. They offered courses until 7pm in the evenings. At the time, I was also enrolled as a student. However, I had not returned to classes that semester because I couldn't afford to pay the fees.

I remained at the primary school and was supervising the courtyard. My mind was really occupied that day. I was worrying about how I was going to pay for my classes. Especially the math class I wanted to take. Meanwhile, I had an instinct to tell the students to go home and not stay at the school late. I recall the kids looking at me strangely for a second or two. They were happy to obey my unusual request. They collected their things and headed out the classroom door. I still wonder how I made this decision.

At 4:53pm, the land began to move and shake. The last earthquake was in 1948 and most of my disaster training was only for hurricanes. So, I didn't know what precautions to take or what was going on. I thought it was some brawl of gangs fighting on the street. Then, as I was standing I felt the shaking. I fell to the ground. Another strong wave came again. I looked at the fruit tree in the yard and went underneath it for safety. I called out to Jesus and then I didn't see anything.

I looked up and saw white dust all around. I closed my eyes for a moment. I was really afraid of what was happening and was almost too petrified to believe what my eyes were seeing. I opened them again. I looked up and saw that the school had been completely destroyed. It had collapsed like a house of cards. I walked out of the school yard and saw that houses and other buildings around had also fallen. I saw the local hospital also destroyed. There were so many people all over the streets. There were people screaming and that was when I realized that it was an earthquake.

I was traumatized. Each time I stood up I felt like the earth was still shaking beneath my feet. I felt like I had problems. I started to ask myself after the earthquake, how could life continue? I was wondering if we would see tomorrow. Would life go back to normal? Seeing all the houses destroyed and the bodies on the ground, I didn't know what to think. I was wondering what was going to happen to all of the bodies. My mind was simply racing. I know now that it was shock.

After, I went to the football stadium. That was the closest open area to the school. Everybody at the stadium was trying to locate family members. Nobody knew where their loved ones were. Also, my own family didn't know where I was. While I was there, I tried to make phone calls, but the calls were not going through. Since I couldn't reach my family, (my mother was in Jacmel and my sister was in Petion Ville) it was very possible that they had perished in the quake. It would turn out that my family also thought that I had perished too, because the teaching school I was enrolled in had also been destroyed. It wasn't for another two days when I went to look for my sister in Petion Ville that I would have been able to get in contact with my family and let them know that I was fine.

That first night after the earthquake, I stayed at the stadium. I saw so many wounded people suffering beside me. Many were in complete shock. That night, I didn't sleep a wink. There were a number of people I recognized; colleagues, parents and children from the school. I spent around three days total at the stadium. During those three days, we started discussing what to do, offering the children activities and offering counseling to those who were finding it very difficult to deal with it all. Many of the parents and the students were asking if there would be school. We said to them that despite the fact the school was destroyed, we would see what we could do to teach them.

I went back to teaching the students in the 6th grade. Despite the challenges and the issues the students faced, 75 of 85 students passed their sixth grade exams later in the year.

The school was rebuilt by the Digicel Foundation in May 2011 and inaugurated in November 2011.

I am a teacher by calling. The earthquake was where and when I truly realized that this was my vocation while I am alive. But I can never forget the loss and tragedy that we all suffered on that day.

Dear Reader,

I'd just like to take this opportunity to thank you for spending your hard earned cash on a copy of my book. Whether you are reading from your kindle or have a paperback in your hands, all I can hope for is that you walk away knowing a little bit more about Haiti and that fateful day in 2010.

My story is merely a snippet from millions more. I'm proud to say that my experiences were turned into words, which found a way into your hands.

Perhaps if it's not too much trouble, I might ask you to click a 'like' on Facebook or follow Broken Ground on twitter. The more 'likes' and followings I receive, the better chance this book can do some good. Please see the links on the next page. Also, the website is regularly updated with some interesting stuff. It's worth taking a look.

Best Wishes,

Website: www.brokenground.ie

 @brokenground_ie

 facebook.com/brokenground.ie

 info@brokenground.ie

37081615R00226

Made in the USA
Charleston, SC
24 December 2014